THE AUTOBIOGRAPHY

David Gower was born in Tunbridge Wells in 1957. He started
playing cricket as a child in Tanganyika, before moving back to
England, where he was educated at King's School, Canterbury. He
joined Leicestershire County Cricket Club in 1975, moved to
Hampshire CCC in 1990 and retired from first class cricket at the
end of the 1993 season. He lives in Hampshire.

Martin Johnson, with whom David Gower has collaborated on
this book, is the cricket correspondent of the *Independent*. He started
his journalistic career on the *South Wales Argus* in 1970 before
moving to the *Leicester Mercury* in 1973. During his twelve years as
cricket correspondent for that paper, he was able to follow David
Gower's career at Leicestershire at first hand: indeed no other
journalist can claim to know him better. Married with two children,
Martin Johnson still lives in Leicester. This is his first book.

GOWER
THE AUTOBIOGRAPHY

DAVID GOWER

with
MARTIN JOHNSON

CollinsWillow
An Imprint of HarperCollinsPublishers

First published in hardback by
CollinsWillow 1992

Published in paperback by Fontana 1993

Revised edition published by
CollinsWillow 1995

ISBN 0 00 218719 1

Tabular statistics supplied by Bill Frindall and Wendy Wimbush

Photographs supplied by Patrick Eagar, David Gower,
Graham Morris, Allsport (including cover)
and Syndication International

Set in Plantin Light

Printed in Great Britain by
The Bath Press, Avon

Contents

Preface

*T*HIS book was conceived in the autumn of 1991, following a somewhat disappointing season of below par achievement, and with the problems of the 1990-91 tour of Australia still very much in mind. It was a time when the fortunes of my personal career were at a low ebb, and I was not at the peak of my form either in terms of performance or mental outlook.

There were several questions in my mind, which no doubt were also being asked elsewhere, largely along the lines of how I was going to approach the rest of my career, and whether or not I was going to be able to regain the sort of form that would allow me the chance to pass Geoff Boycott's all-time England run scoring record, a target that had been there for the taking in Australia.

My subsequent omission from the Test side and ensuing poor form, with my perfectly logical further exclusion from that winter's touring party, meant I had already begun to accept that number two in the list might be as far as I would ever get. This in itself was no problem as I could quite easily convince myself that what I had already achieved was not an overall disaster – and besides there are always other challenges in life.

However, a positive attitude was what I needed to begin the 1992 season in good shape, especially in view of the other potential problem lurking in the back of my mind. I knew that if this season did not bring success, I would be thinking very seriously about retiring from the game. My spirits were definitely at a low ebb!

Happily, I returned to Hampshire in April in the right frame of mind, and started the season in good enough form to realize those targets. My most important task was to try and convince people that my intention to play cricket for England for some years to come was entirely genuine. There were those, even in positions of power, who suspected that the Boycott record was my only motivation, a suspicion that I resented and strongly wished to dispel. Whenever a potential milestone has loomed on the horizon, I have always regarded it as incidental to the main course of events and taken the stance that if the job is done properly in the first place and often enough, then milestones will come and go automatically.

On the other hand, there is no point in denying that this particular milestone did mean a lot to me. When I did finally pass the magic figure it was a very proud moment. As it happens it was not a record I was to hold for any great length of time, and I suppose I have to admit that it does irk me gently that the man who passed me was largely instrumental in not allowing me to be able to make the target harder for him!

Still, one of my guiding principles has always been to look forward and not waste time pondering what might have been, an attitude probably fostered the first time I made a first innings duck and found that the prettiest girl at that night's party went off with someone else. Find that story in the book if you can, but please don't complain if the publishers seem to have left it out!

When I did retire at the end of a frustrating but nonetheless productive summer in 1993, I did so content that I had done what I could to succeed in and enjoy my career as a professional cricketer, and happy that I chosen the right time to do so.

Watching the game for a living will never be as exciting as playing it, but by embarking on a career as a broadcaster and journalist, occupations equally and deceptively demanding in their own way, I hope to remain involved in the game for a long time yet.

Thus with cheerful countenance I proffer what follows as a mixture of fond memories and tales of woe, all of which are an integral part of any sportsman's life, safe in the expectation that, as time goes on, inevitably the highlights will outlive the disappointments.

David Gower
Deepest Hampshire, April 1995

CHAPTER ONE

Fun, style and excellence

I HAVE, during the course of a career stretching back to 1975, won a good many medals and trophies in all parts of the cricketing world, mostly for performances on the field. However, pride of place on my mantelpiece at home is reserved for an award from a national newspaper that does not, on the face of it, mean anything much at all. And yet it means as much, if not more than any cup final medal, or the International Cricketer of the Year trophy I won in Australia in 1982-83. It is a plaque, inscribed with the words: 'For Fun, Style, and Excellence.' If I had the choice of words to be chiselled on my tombstone (actually, I suppose I do ... where's the will?) it would be those. In many ways I am happy to forget the mere statistics of a career in cricket, and to remember the fun of it as well as feeling that I have given spectators a little pleasure too. It is a philosophy I carried with me throughout my cricketing career, and despite the fact that it torpedoed me in the end, it is not one I would have changed even with the benefit of hindsight. Fun, style and excellence is a nice way of summing up what I tried to do. I started playing the game because it was fun. I acquired a certain style while I was doing it (unfortunately, 'laid-back' was the way it was described most often), and if I have touched excellence at various points along the way (and as I played 114 Test matches I must have got quite close once or twice) then you could not ask for a great deal more.

When young players have asked me for a philosophy of the game, or something to bear in mind when they are embarking on their cricketing careers, I have invariably said: 'Enjoy it. You started playing the game for enjoyment, and whatever helps you retain that outlook, go ahead and do it.' If you are not enjoying it for any reason, you cannot bring out the best in yourself. There are times, of course, when you have to push yourself beyond fun, so that you can achieve the results that will give you the satisfaction to make it fun. There may, on the other hand, be a few lessons to be absorbed from this book that may prevent our star of the future from having his head lopped off like I did. Graham Gooch, whose fingerprints – among others – can be found on the lever that operated the guillotine, has accused me, ironically, on more than one occasion, of not having fun – or at least not enjoying the lifestyle on the field as much as I did off it. To a certain extent he was right, and if I am accused of not always sporting a mile-wide grin during a dull game in a howling gale, while cursing to myself for not putting on two pairs of long johns instead of one, then I apologize to him for this major character weakness. This book, I hope, is not a whitewash. I admit to not taking either cricket or life seriously enough at times, but while this has occasionally found me out, I would like to think that my warts are mostly friendly ones.

I do get bored easily and hard graft has never come naturally, but nothing annoys me more than hearing that I fell short of some people's expectations because I appeared to find the game too easy. I have never found cricket easy. My external appearance has not always been deceptive, and when I once turned up for play one morning wearing one black shoe and one brown one, this was a fairly accurate indication of what I am like first thing in the morning. On the other hand, wearing a smile on your face, or making the occasional facetious comment, is not evidence that you are an idle dilettante either. There is no one way of playing the game that is right or wrong, and cricket is a sport that lays your character bare like almost no other. I was latterly perceived, wrongly in my opinion, to have had a lack of commitment to the England cause, that somehow I rocked the boat with an indifferent attitude. I scored nearly 500 runs in my last series in Australia with this lack of commitment. I did however commit the unpardonable sin of looking more cheerful after a flight in a Tiger Moth than during some of the management's interminable training routines, on a tour when runs around the block counted for rather more than runs in the middle. There was an atmosphere in Australia in which fun and cricket had no place together which was alien to my interpretation of how to bring out the best of international cricketers, leaving me often at odds with the likes of team manager, Micky Stewart.

Character differences are part and parcel of all team sports, and a diversity of opinion can of course be used constructively. Unfortunately, my relationship with Micky Stewart was not enhanced on this tour, which worried me less than the fact that I was finding it so difficult to communicate with Graham Gooch, who I had known and liked over a much longer period. It seemed to annoy both of them that I could succeed without conforming to the methods they laid down. The attitude that came across was that I did not deserve to succeed. The argument that often came out was that I was not setting the right example to younger players, that I was somehow inhibiting or retarding their development. I didn't accept this, nor did I find anything remotely like this impression among the other players. I was no different at thirty-three than I had been at twenty-one. The idea, so it appeared to me, was to fit in with whatever the system was at the time, but yet to do what you needed to do yourself to be happy and confident about playing when required.

The fact that our relationship suffered the terminal fracture in Australia was not without its irony or significance. Micky in particular had taken note of Australia's change in selection policy after we beat them on Mike Gatting's 1986-87 tour. Bobby Simpson and Allan Border decided that a certain type of character was required to play for Australia, hence the more flamboyant and slightly rebellious people like Greg Ritchie, Tim Zoehrer, Craig McDermott and Greg Matthews all got thrown out. Looking at their subsequent results, you have to say that their decision worked, but at least two of those players got back into the side eventually, proving that no system need necessarily be rigid to the point of inflexibility. If it had happened to me ten years earlier, it would have been easier to shrug off, but not only had I been given a label, I was also approaching that period in my career – if not my sell-by date – when a slightly rebellious older hand could more easily be cut adrift.

When I was left out of the West Indies series in the summer of 1991, I had not been in form for Hampshire, but I did feel they could at least have given me the chance to prove that I still had it in me, or otherwise as the case may be, for one or two of the early Tests. I'm told that Stewart's report on the tour to Australia suggested that the only reason I wanted to play on was to get the thirty-four runs I needed to beat Boycott's record. This not only shows a complete lack of understanding as to my own character, but also sums up the peculiar way in which Stewart's mind operates. True, I would dearly love to have broken Boycott's record while still in Australia and I continue to rue missed opportunities to do so, but I would say that my primary aim is to still be playing Test cricket for the satisfaction of succeeding again at that level, not just for the sake of thirty-odd runs but for a lot more beyond. Gooch intimated to me early in the summer that it would be easier for the proverbial camel to pass through the eye of a needle than for me to get back into the England side, which did not correlate with his simple message at the end of the Australia tour to go out and get runs. Whereas I was looking for a bit of a lift, a smidgeon of encouragement from the top, this left me dispirited and with an overriding sense of futility. I knew it had more to do with scoring runs, whatever Graham had said after Australia. Stewart did not seem to want me back at any price. Unfortunately, the way he went about things irritated me and I was not always very good at concealing my feelings. Come to think of it, I do not believe I was, or am, the only player to think this way.

His was a difficult job in many respects and one certainly cannot accuse him of not working hard at it. But despite his efforts and good intentions, I still found him unconvincing and uninspiring. As for Graham, I had – and still have – great admiration for the way he transformed his own game from the late eighties, putting in a huge amount of effort in order to prolong his own career, but it ultimately came close to an obsession for him. He then looked at me in a different light because of it, wondering no doubt why I was not more like him, and it caused us to grow apart. He set off with a method in Australia, and it didn't work on that occasion. This is not unusual, and it has certainly happened to me. Indeed, every system will have its flaws in this unpredictable arena called international cricket. Yet when I tried to get him to involve more people, to give them a greater sense of their own importance, and above all not to talk at people rather than with them, it merely seemed to bring my motives under suspicion.

It was a bad sign. Senior players should carry some weight. Junior players are mostly going to conform come what may, although there are exceptions that prove every rule, and Philip Tufnell was one of them. However, the inference that Tufnell would pick up bad habits from me was hard to swallow. Tuffers might take a certain interest in the attitudes and opinions of players like myself, but Tuffers is the way he is because he is Tuffers. Like the case of Phillip DeFreitas in 1986-87, he had to work out how to mix in international company, and, like many before and since, did not perhaps reach the right note first up. Nor did I hit the right note when I took the aeroplane trip, so it is not a failing exclusively attributable to younger players. Having said that, I think it was getting out last ball before lunch in Adelaide – in the way that I did – that later became more significant in the management's assessment of my future.

Graham has said that he didn't feel he ever really got to know me, not deep down anyway, and I can take some of the blame for that in that I have usually presented a flip and light-hearted view of events instead of getting terribly serious. It is, of course, a form of defence that people like myself present to the world to cover up any insecurity or worries that they may have in the same way that many comedians have deeper, darker sides to their natures. Where it told against me was that I gave a false – or not entirely true – picture of how dedicated I was to the game. For instance, I did not much care for Stewart's training routines, but when I thought I needed hard work I usually went out and did it. Before the Sydney Test I went out and had a private net with Cardigan Connor, who was playing in Australia that winter, along with a couple of local bowlers, and when Stewart later brought this up as evidence of preparation equalling results (I got a century in the Sydney Test), I didn't have the heart to tell him that I benefitted a lot more from not having him hovering over me while I was practising.

The way things went for me on that tour always gave me the impression that Perth had every chance of being my last Test match. I had been dropped before by England, three or four times in fact, but the coming English summer seemed more than just uncertain. What I found dispiriting and depressing about it all was that with my place under threat, I had dug deep to get 150 against India in the final innings of the previous summer when my place on the tour had been uncertain, and battled hard for my runs in Australia. Now I was cast as a wayward spirit, who sometimes got runs by accident, and it hurt. As a subscriber, however, to the no smoke without fire theory, I do plead guilty to a certain amount of underachievement, and the one thing I would like to have been is just a bit hungrier in the pursuit of runs. I'd hate to guess at a figure, but in about 95 per cent of all my innings I can look back and think: 'You could have done a bit more there.'

The Boycott record frustrated me in that I could and should have got past it. The compensation, from what I've read and heard any way, is that more people enjoyed watching me bat than Boycott. Who knows why we are the way we are? Why do some cricketers have more single-mindedness than others? Why can't some people give up smoking? I don't know why I got caught in the gully off wide deliveries more than Boycott did – probably because it was more in my nature and probably because the two previous wide ones had been pinged through extra cover and I enjoyed the feeling enough to try it again. Looking back, there has been a lot of enjoyment, but a lot of frustration as well. Most disappointing of all was the way that it finished. Having watched Hadlee and Richards bow out at the time of their own choosing, you think to yourself, 'Well I wasn't too far behind these guys, it would have been a lovely way to go out.' Instead, the rug was whipped away from under me, and I was left on my arse. It seems to me that you should ultimately be judged by results. If the Stewart-Gooch regime decided that regimentation was the way to get results, and it worked, then fine. I'm not sure, though, that they ultimately applied the same test to me.

The irony is that it sounds as if they modified their rules slightly by the following winter's tour of New Zealand and for the World Cup. The idea that breaks in a training and practice session could also be beneficial has crept back in, giving the players a little extra respite from the rigorous demands that international cricket makes upon the minds and bodies of its participants. Work and practice must be done – and I fully acknowledge their benefits – but as cricket, in essence, is time consuming, I will always maintain that time off, judged and used wisely, is almost as valuable as another practice session.

CHAPTER TWO

Laid back – and think of England

*I*F fun, style and excellence are three words that I think of most fondly, then the two that have irritated me most (with the possible exception of 'caught Dujon') are 'laid back'. I don't know why they should annoy me so much, but the mere fact that they do should be evidence in itself that I am not as laid back, whatever that actually means, as people might think. I do, in fact, have a pretty short fuse. I have been known to explode in both dressing room and on the field, and you ought to see me on the motorway, although I do have the happy capacity to hose those flames fairly swiftly. I suppose, though, that I do have this ability to suggest that I am more interested in the *Telegraph* crossword than the state of play, and that my mid-pitch conversations with batting partners occasionally have less to do with the fact that Ambrose has just replaced Marshall than whether the evening's repast should involve fish and chardonnay or steak and claret. Mostly, those impressions are spot on – but cricket has always been the sort of game to switch on to and off in my opinion. Spectators nip into the members' bar between overs, so why can't players take a mental break at times? In any case, when Ambrose is pawing the ground and there is an outside chance of ending the day with your jaw wired up, chatting about eating a nice steak can have the effect of concentrating the mind wonderfully well.

Much of the image is created by your own peers, and how they perceive you. I remember picking up the soubriquet of 'Fender' on the 1986-87 tour. The TV drama, although drama is used here in the loosest sense, *Bodyline* was showing on Australian TV when we were out there, and to give you a clue as to its absolute devotion to

13

historical accuracy, there was one memorable scene of Les Ames completing a stumping off Larwood. As for poor old Percy Fender, he was portrayed as a party-loving, champagne-swilling, ukelele-playing, monocled buffoon – a strokemaker, both on and off the field. As I was well in with the Bollinger man in Sydney, a wonderful man named Rob Hirst, and as the lads curiously felt that I fitted the bill in other respects as well, 'Fender' is the nickname I acquired.

The image was further enhanced at a Sunday League match at Cheltenham during my first period as Leicestershire captain, when both Leicestershire and Gloucestershire were so utterly convinced that there could be no possibility of play – it had started raining hard at tea-time on Saturday and was still stair-rodding down at 2 p.m. on Sunday – that the players readily accepted the offer of lunch and hospitality in a sponsors' tent. We had already left four or five players back in the bar at the hotel, where a Sunday lunchtime jazz band was in full cry, and they eventually staggered into the tent to join the party. While we were getting stuck into the Pimms and sundry other concoctions, the elements outside had transformed themselves into sunshine and wind, and the College Ground's legendary draining properties were coming into play. In short, while the ground got drier, the players got wetter.

It was round about half past four when one of the officials, Mervyn Kitchen, popped his head around the tent flap, and I confidently expected him to deliver a message like: 'Don't bother turning up tomorrow either.' However, what he actually said was: 'We think we can start a ten-over slog at ten past five, at which point I said: 'Nice one, Merv. What are you having?' His reply was: 'Captain, I'm afraid we're serious,' at which point I spilled most of the contents of my glass and led a concerted weave from tent to pavilion. David Graveney, canny captain that he is, and armed with a certain local knowledge, had remained reasonably sober, but the captain of Leicestershire – and most of his troops – were in no condition to make contact with a medicine ball. I attempted a knock-up on the outfield without much success, declared myself unfit to toss, or in any event to be able to recognize a head from a tail, and entrusted the operation to Nigel Briers. We decided to bat first, largely on the grounds that nine of us at least could get down to some serious coffee drinking, but we were forced to make a late team

14

change when Ian Butcher popped his head around the home dressing room door. His timing was bad, in that Paul Romaines had been busy practising his golf swing with a three-pound cricket bat and Ian's nose had taken the full brunt. Paul, whose exertions and embarrassment had sent the Pimms rushing to his head, also retired from the contest.

I went in No 4, gave Graveney the charge first ball, and although I never saw it I somehow hit it over long on. I then played several air shots, before deciding to unveil the reverse sweep, and actually made contact with one of them. By some miracle we managed to get 70 or 80, which turned out to be ample. They were something like 20 for no wicket after 6 overs, and every time one of their openers took a swish, a large divot flew out of the ground. It was slightly ironic, I thought, when I brought Gordon Parsons on to bowl – one of the few who had not touched a drop – because his first ball ended up on top of the press tent. I would like to think that our successful defence owed something to my inspirational leadership, but in point of fact they only got as many as they did because I kept diving the wrong way at cover. Mind you, Bill Athey picked up the fielding award for circling underneath an interminable skier to eventually hear it plop to earth about ten yards away. Anyway we won, and in honour of our triumph, I duly led the troops straight back into the tent. There were many questions asked in the Gloucestershire committee room, but the near-total absence of spectators, and the generosity of the press in putting it down as on off-day all round, somehow allowed both sides to get away with it.

There was another, less shameful, incident involving a tent at Grace Road. The visitors were Essex, whose ground at Chelmsford is festooned with hospitality boxes. Their end-of-day drink when they came to Leicester consisted of one crate of bottled lager (warm) bunged underneath the dressing room table. They once protested by taking all the tops off and leaving them there, and on one occasion John Lever had wound me up so much about the lack of conviviality at close of play that I rummaged around in the attic for a miniature one-man tent that I used to play with as a child. I erected it just over the boundary rope at fine leg in a pathetic attempt to imitate the throng of sponsors' tents Essex would have expected to find at home, took half a dozen bottles of the aforementioned lager down into the tent, and at the end of the day we had a fairly silly ten-minute party in this particular sponsor's tent.

I suppose it all added to the general image, although 'laid back' was largely an invention of the press. The words press and invention have not been entirely separable throughout much of my career, even though I have had some highly complimentary things said about me as well, and the TCCB's concern about the altered concept of modern cricket reporting led them to appoint a media relations manager in 1988. They were also considering at one stage organizing some sort of press awareness course for England players – pitfalls for the unwary, so to speak. In point of fact, there are also pitfalls for the wary these days. Your first exposure to the press is normally a pleasant one, in which the callow youth picks up his weekly copy of the *Loughborough Echo* and finds his score faithfully reported somewhere near the back page. As time goes on you save the clippings: as time goes further on, you screw them up and hurl them towards the wastepaper basket. When I first started playing, the dunce's cap superimposed on a player's head – so beloved of the tabloids when we were getting hammered by Australia in 1989 – was not even an idea. I can recall in my early England days being asked to pose topless and sit on top of a circus horse, although I can't imagine Hobbs or Hammond ever having accepted this sort of request.

I have tried not to get too carried away by some of the things that have been written about me, or indeed too upset, but there are times when you just cannot believe what a complete stranger has just written about you. One of my regular tormentors has been a reporter for *The Sun*, who has poured out some amazing vitriol about me. We sat in the same press box in Jamaica when I was hired by *The Times* for the 1989-90 West Indies tour, and I thought about introducing myself, but really could not think of what to say to the guy. In most respects, though, it hurts more if you are lambasted by comments in the 'serious' papers, such as when I was advised after the first Test against Australia at Headingley in1989 to book in for a lobotomy at the same time as my shoulder operation. I shan't mention his name, but suffice to say that, in terms of this book, he is a ghost writer of his former self.

Pure human instinct dictates that if you are criticized by the media, you don't really like it. Cricketers do not care much for criticism from former players, and players are incredibly defensive nowadays. Most of the bad language in a Test match dressing room comes from players reading the morning papers, or listening to some former player giving you stick on TV. Having said that, I still believe that players and the press have to work together, and for my own part, I would like to maintain my own interest in the game through the pen or the microphone. Reading rubbish about yourself in a newspaper is not the most difficult part for a player, unpleasant though it might be; it is the thought that someone might pick it up and believe it. Interpretation is another problem, in that you can sometimes say something perfectly innocuous and see it blown up, taken out of context, or both. If you go through a press conference with an unsmiling face you run the risk of being called angry, and if you crack the odd joke you become flippant. Sometimes you can see the question that comes attached to a limpet mine, and sometimes you can't, but you certainly have to be on your toes.

There are other times when you find yourself abroad, and being ripped to shreds by people who have not even left the country. It happened on the 1985-86 tour to the West Indies, where there were also many unfamiliar reporters – tennis correspondents, you name it – specifically sent to dredge up the dirt, that it was a sheer relief to talk to a cricket reporter. I remember seeing a copy of the *Daily Mirror* in Barbados that devoted an entire centre spread to rip into our off-the-field activities, including one piece from a woman fashion correspondent who was there on holiday and had spotted someone daring to have a bottle of wine with his evening meal. None of them had a clue about cricket, and even the bloke who covered the tour for the *Mirror* was a stand-in seconded from some other sport. Years ago, a cricketer's private life used to be respected by newspapers, but that ethos has long since passed away.

With regard to the genuine cricket press, England players these days regard it almost as an obligation to fume and rant, but it frequently becomes counterproductive. It is too easy to moan about what is being said or written. In some ways it is cathartic – it allows you to let off steam – but it is not necessarily useful in terms of producing the right mood and spirit that you need to play the game. If you can talk yourself into ignoring the media most of the time, take the view that they are getting on with their job and we are getting on with ours, then that is the ideal approach. We have to coexist, however uneasily. It is very hard at times, but each time a player gets involved, he is wasting his energy on a conflict that is always fruitless.

Although there have been one or two disasters along the way, and my Test career ended in a way that left a slightly sour taste in the mouth, it is nice to be able to reflect that the good times far outweighed the bad. I cannot, in all honesty, claim a memory of elephantine proportions, but certain moments stay with you quite vividly. My first Test century against New Zealand at the Oval in 1978, my first century overseas against Australia at Perth later that year, my double century against India, and involvement – either as captain or player – in a good many Test series triumphs.

I had the experience of playing with or against any number of famous players, and if I had a mentor in the professional game, it would have to be Ray Illingworth. As someone who had done little more than give it a swish at King's School, Canterbury, it was a good education to learn the serious aspect of the game from a man with one of the harder noses in professional cricket. There was a good atmosphere at Grace Road under Illy's captaincy, and it was also a benefit for me to launch my career in one of the better county sides around at that time. He had his foibles, and the amount of mickey-taking he took from the other players without it in any way undermining his authority reflected a happy dressing room. In some ways, the club never recovered from his return to Yorkshire in 1978, and the way things turned out, I wonder whether Illy regretted leaving. However, he was never one for power sharing, and as Mike Turner was very much in charge at Grace Road, the chance to become player-manager at Yorkshire rather than remain answerable to Mike at Leicester was the more attractive option.

It's ironic to think back now that Mike actually gave me £5 a week more than I was asking for when I signed my first contract in 1975, because in all my time at Leicester, the prime topic of conversation was how little we were paid in contrast to other counties. Mike, who more or less ran the club, was impossible to crack on wages – on almost anything come to that – and he was the sort of man who commanded either love or hate in his business dealings. He was known as the Ayatollah, because he had to have a finger in every pie that came out of the oven at Grace Road. Whether it was picking the side, or some piffling request from a gateman, Mike had a say in it, and he took such a work load on himself that he only really slowed down (and then only minimally) when he had a heart attack. As an administrator he was second to none, knew his cricket, and as far as I was concerned he was very supportive. If you were on the wrong side of Mike he was a hard opponent, but if you were on the right side he was a good friend and ally. Much of the good work he did for the players, myself included, was done quietly behind the scenes and with no great drama.

The player I was closest to at Leicester, both in cricketing outlook and as a kindred spirit, was Brian Davison. Davo was a larger than life character, and no-one could possibly have guessed from his early wild man days at Grace Road that he would end up as a member of parliament in Hobart, Tasmania, which is where he and his family emigrated after a long career at Leicestershire. I assume his canvassing methods are slightly different to those he employed in the Rhodesian army, when the members of the opposition were dangled from helicopters to help them in conversation. He was a destroyer of a cricket ball, and a phenomenally strong man – nor would you aim to get on the wrong side of him. When his nostrils flared, it was time to make yourself scarce. He liked a drink, smoked like a chimney, but there was a highly cultured side to him as well, and he became, among other things, quite an expert in antiques. He was appointed captain of the club in 1980, a short engagement that ended with too many adverse umpires' reports, but I loved batting with him for the confidence he exuded at the crease. I loved driving with him rather less, as he tended to solve traffic problems with 90 m.p.h. excursions on the wrong side of the road. On his day, he would murder any bowler, and although he now lives in Tasmania, we still keep in touch.

I also learned a lot from Roger Tolchard, not least in refusing to play him at golf for money. His will to win at everything manifested itself in a self-appointed handicap of about 18 when he was closer to scratch. Tolly, who was my landlord in those early days at Leicester, was a fabulous one-day batsman, who was perhaps never quite the same player after having his cheekbone caved at Newcastle on the 1978-79 tour to Australia. He was not the most popular player on the circuit, as he consistently got up people's noses, and as a teetotaller never gave himself the chance to undo the damage in the bar afterwards. However, he was a marvellous influence in our own dressing room, and was always at you about your cricket. I took over from him as captain in 1983 when the club fired him, a decision that he certainly did not expect at the time, and which closed the door on his career with an emphatic thud.

My closest mate in the England team has been Allan Lamb who made his debut about four years after mine. He is the only man I know who has been collared by a policeman on the beat for using a mobile hand-held telephone: he was in a traffic jam on the King's Road in London and doing about 1 m.p.h. Lamby is a remarkable straight-up-and-down guy, with as large a capacity for having a good time as anyone I've met, is an extraordinary good host – dangerously so – and has this huge energy and vitality that rubs off on any dressing room he is in. He has, down the years, been the wheeler-dealer of the England team, having as good an eye for business as he has for a cricket ball. On his day, he is as ruthless a destroyer of good bowling as anyone. Like most South Africans he is fond of the outdoors, and has now become something of the English country squire, always out hunting, fishing and shooting, and it was Lamby who was with me when I first went down the Cresta Run, another little part-time diversion that we will come back to later.

Lamby and Ian Botham are similar characters in many respects, and there is a common denominator in my relationship with them in that I can't keep up with either after dark. He has never shirked a challenge, and the fact that this applies off the field as well as on it has dropped him into the fertilizer once or twice. 'Both' is quite a vulnerable character, who tends to overreact if people set out to rub him up the wrong way in a bar, as many have, but he can also be as good as gold. He's much brighter than people give him credit for, and because he has done so many things, there is a lot of depth to him. Again, contrary to public opinion, he does not down the nearest bottle of Beaujolais nouveau in one gulp (although I dare say he could) but is actually quite a discerning wine buff. He's exceptionally loyal to his friends, and can be equally hard on people he has no time for. It is perfectly possible, also, for people to change categories with him, and one example was Leicestershire's Les

Taylor. Botham had no time for him at all until the 1985-86 West Indies tour, but when he found out what a character Les was, they became bosom buddies. It was said that I had problems captaining him, but rarely ever did, and I always enjoyed playing with him.

I enjoyed playing with Graham Gooch until that last tour to Australia in 1990-91, but we have been good mates down the years, and I have nothing but admiration for what he has achieved for himself. He is, as most people are aware, an intensely private man, extremely shy with people he doesn't know, and has become more and more dedicated over the years. He was a good bit wilder in his younger days, which might surprise some people, but as time has gone on he has become immersed in the game, and in making money out of it. He is still a social animal, with a dry sense of humour, but can be horribly intransigent at times. He always resented the punishment that was dished out to him for going to South Africa in 1981, and it is either an irony or a triumph for his character, depending on your point of view, that a cricketer who was banned for three years by his country has now become a national figurehead. Whether, when we drifted apart in Australia, he thought I had become a subversive influence I don't know, but it cooled our relationship and this has left me a little sad.

Whenever I have come in for criticism during my career, I have invariably been compared, unfavourably, with Geoff Boycott. Why could I not have been as single minded as he was? The answer is I don't really know, but as I said before, I might possibly have entertained a few more people than he did. He always liked being the centre of attention (when he's on TV he always speaks louder than anyone else) and would like to be loved more than perhaps he is. He has always been an enigma. He can be very rational, he has an immense knowledge of the game, he's a very fine analyst of techniques and of situations within a game, and he is, potentially, one of the world's great commentators. He certainly has the knowledge and understanding, but unfortunately you have to temper that with a very one-eyed view of the rest of the world, which largely centres around himself. I've never managed to finish one of his books (although in fairness this applies to most books I pick up) but the gist always seems to be: 'I'd have done this, I'd have done that,' and all the rest of it. Everything is based on G. Boycott. There are the archetypal Boycott stories, such as the time he reckoned he had cracked John Gleeson's googly but refused to tell anyone else in the dressing room how he had done it.

The only time I ever heard him admit to feeling vulnerable was in India, at a cocktail party in the grounds of the Maharajah of Baroda's palace, when he sought me out for a heart-to-heart and said that he didn't think people understood him properly. Well, following a conversation in his hotel room during a previous trip to India, I certainly knew someone who did not understand him. Me. We had arrived in Bombay for the Jubilee Test after the 1979-80 tour of Australia, a match I remember for three distinct reasons. Firstly, Both did his 'Wilson of the Wizard' bit and more or less won the game single-handed, then there were two strange incidents on the field. John Lever turned a ball off his legs for two, dislodging a bail as he did so. When he got back to the striker's end he realized that no-one had noticed, surreptitiously put the bail back on, and got away with it. The other, even odder event, concerned Boycs, who had got a thin tickle down the legside to the wicketkeeper and was given out. However, at no stage did he look up at the umpire, and simply carried on marking out his guard and doing a spot of gardening. Eventually, the umpire put his finger down, the Indians appealed again and this time Boycs was given not out. It was extraordinary. I did not get any runs in that game, and had also had a poor tour to Australia. (I did get 98 not out in Sydney, having enjoyed a lot of luck in getting to 40, then ran out of partners when Willis lost his wicket. It was a barren period for me.) During the Bombay Test, I had some autograph sheets that needed signing, and I popped in to Boycs' room at the hotel to get a few signatures. He looked up at me and said: 'I can tell thee what tha doing wrong, tha knows.' Pause. 'But I'm not going to.' I thought to myself: 'Thanks very much' and walked out.

On the tour of India in 1981-82 Boycott had the world record for Test runs in his sights, and he passed it with a century at Delhi. Our next game was in Calcutta, and although he got a couple of rough decisions, it was as if the whole mental effort of getting past the target had drained him of motivation. After the second dismissal he went straight to bed, stayed in his room through the rest day and reports came back through his lady friend that he was very ill. The doctors were called in, and we didn't see him again until round about lunchtime on the final day. With the game heading for a draw, we were still in the field, and as we went out again after lunch, Boycs turned to the boys left in the dressing room and said: 'Anyone fancy a game of golf? I need some fresh air.' It was widely believed that if he really required fresh air (always assuming you can find any in Calcutta) then perhaps he should have been inhaling it out on the field. Anyway, he took himself off to the Tollygunge Club for nine holes, and the overwhelming feeling that Boycs' personal ambitions were coming a long way before the team's general well-being, and the suspicion that his continued presence would be divisive on a tour already proving difficult in terms of morale, earned him an early ticket home. He left us a farewell note, pinned with a corkscrew to the side of a very pleasant redwood cabinet in the team room of the Oberoi Grand Hotel. Some of his unscheduled time off, of course, was spent organizing the Breweries tour to South Africa.

He's certainly different. He takes his ginseng tea with him everywhere, and he even had it written into his contract with Sky TV in England that he had to have a 'proper' cup or mug – no plastic. There are times when you can get on with him, and he has a lot to offer – although he got up Lamby's nose during coaching before the last tour to the West Indies when he did everything except sing *My Way* to us. Technically and mentally he was a very strong player, although his first philosophy was always not to get out. We dropped him from the one-day side in Australia once, and when we brought him back he suddenly discovered a few shots. He had a lot of guts, and the number of runs he scored points to him being a more than useful player.

Boycs always made me concentrate harder when I was batting with him, although this was largely to avoid getting run out. He did me once in Jamaica, and during a Test at Edgbaston I erred on the side of safety when he glided one down behind square, declining his call for a single. Not long after, he returned the compliment after I'd knocked one into a space, and at the end of the over he said: 'If you're not going to run mine, I'm not going to run yours.' He has the ability to be extremely charming, and an equal ability to be a complete sod. He has said many times that a combination of my ability and his brain would make quite a player, and I would admit that had I had more of his application and dedication to the game I might have scored a lot more Test runs than he did. I might not, however, have had quite so many chums.

I would count Mike Gatting among them, and we go back a long way. I have always admired his fighting qualities, and I thought it was typical of him to have scored so many runs in the summer of 1991 when he came back from South Africa. People who thought he would not have sufficient motivation without the incentive of a Test place, did not know the man. He murders bad bowling, and his eyes come out like organ stops when a spinner comes on. His eating habits are legendary, and the biggest shock I had all last summer was reading a report of a Middlesex game in the morning paper in which the captains, Gatt being one, had agreed to waive the tea interval. He has acquired a little dangerous knowledge about wine and crosswords, and although he invariably finishes the *Daily Telegraph* puzzle, he is not averse to putting a word in that fits the space rather than the clue. I like Gatt, although we are not that similar, and we don't often seek out each other's company after hours. I have never spoken to him on the subject, but it is rumoured that Micky Stewart told Gatt that he was about to be reappointed England captain ahead of me in 1989 when Ossie Wheatley applied his veto. What with getting sacked in 1988, his mother-in-law dying soon after, getting fined by the TCCB for an unauthorized chapter on the Shakoor Rana business in his book, and then getting knocked back by Wheatley, it was perhaps not surprising that he took the South Africans' money later that summer.

Mike remains a very committed cricketer and loves his role as Middlesex captain, following in the footsteps, if not the style, of Mike Brearley and the likes, and continues to bat with complete assurance and disdain for most opposition bowling. He has a down-to-earth approach to both the game and the people who play it which endears him to most of those who play under him, who in turn are prepared to excuse his foibles in exchange for his support and leadership.

CHAPTER THREE

A millionaire? That's rich

I WAS never tempted to play cricket, unauthorized cricket that is, in South Africa. It was nothing to do with any great moral stance, but I was strongly recommended against it by my advisers when the Breweries tour was being organized for the winter of 1981-82, and no approach was made in 1989 when I was England captain. The only time I have played there was in the mid-seventies, as a member of the Crocodiles touring team selected from seven southern England schools and captained by Chris Cowdrey. We were there for three and a half weeks over the Christmas holidays, visiting Cape Town, Port Elizabeth, Durban, Bloemfontein and Johannesburg, and it was a fabulous trip. The cricket was good and the hospitality even better.

The rebel tour that Boycott organized in 1982, and which Gooch eventually captained, had sprouted its initial roots the previous winter during the England tour to the West Indies. There were a series of clandestine meetings, with shadowy figures emerging from hotel rooms, and various players were asked if they would be interested in a trip to South Africa should one be arranged. Most people kept their options open, waiting to see what sort of money was being offered, and it was all very hush-hush. It did not really gather momentum, however, until the tour to India the following winter. South African intermediaries would fly in, meetings were arranged in hotel rooms, and money was placed on the table. The standard plea, of course, was: 'If you don't want to come, fine, but please don't blow the whistle on us.'

My agent, Jon Holmes, had told me that I would be risking too much from the commercial angle by going, and 'Both', whose solicitor had flown out to discuss the matter with him, received much the same advice. Simply as a cricketer I would love to have played there, but in practical terms it did not seem a good idea. There was no set punishment – as there was to be when Gatt skippered the 1989 side – but the players knew that repercussions were likely, among them a possible ban on playing for England. You don't get paid that sort of money and go around behaving like an MI5 agent without suspecting that there might be a penalty clause. The code word, which still makes me giggle when I think back, was 'chess'. So when someone wanted to talk to you about South Africa, he would sidle up to you and say: 'Do you know how Karpov and Spassky are getting on?' or 'It's a cool (k)night, but do you fancy a trip up to the Maharajah's castle?' However, once I had made the decision not to go, I never attended another meeting. Keith Fletcher, the captain, was another who turned it down, but Boycott, Gooch and John Emburey were strongly in favour. Graham's tack was that 'England never offer any guarantees', and poor old Fletch quickly found out how true that was when he was sacked the following summer. Graham felt that money in the bank was worth more than any potential earning power he might or might not have by turning it down, and it is not always appreciated that he was a lot less confident of his own ability than he is now. He had been dropped before and his career had not blossomed to the extent that perhaps it ought to have done. When they came back from South Africa, and were fighting for their right to play for England, there was a certain naivety about their actions. When you are being offered figures that do not tally with normal cricketing rates, then you have got to assume that there is a price to pay. So although a three-year ban might have seemed harsh, it was nothing more severe than I had expected, and I cannot believe that those who went could have thought otherwise. I make no bones about my own reasons for not going. I was advised that it was likely to be commercially unfavourable for me. As for the 1989 tour, I was literally the last person in the dressing room to know, although South Africa had been a recurring theme almost every year. I had been out there on holiday many times between the two tours, and on one occasion in 1988 had been a guest of the South African Board at a couple of matches. The way I was pumped for information during those games left me in little doubt that another tour was on the cards. Even so, when the news broke during the Australian series in 1989, I had no real inkling before reading about it – like most people – in the morning papers. I can honestly say that had the organizers of the tour offered me a place, my answer would have been 'No'.

Because my main ambitions all centred on playing cricket for England and for as long as possible, with or without the captaincy to worry about, resisting the kruggerand did, I think, turn out to be a sound commercial decision. And there is no doubt that I have earned a tidy living from professional cricket. It is not a well-paid sport, however, and while I will not have to spend my retirement years playing the harmonica at the bottom of tube station escalators, nor am I wealthy. I have a lovely house in leafy Hampshire, but when guests come to stay, I am not able to send the Rolls to meet them or offer them the choice of accommodation in east or west wing. Comfortable would be the right word, I think. I would be more comfortable but for a financial settlement after splitting with my former fiancée, and a property deal that singed the fingers, but by and large I have done reasonably well out of the game. I am not in the same league as another of my agent's stablemates, Gary Lineker, and I certainly can't afford to do nothing after cricket. Life after cricket, in fact, might require a change of lifestyle, and indeed a change of attitude. Like growing up.

Fortunately, I have been talented enough to earn wages at the higher end of the cricketing scale, but more importantly from the bank manager's point of view, I have also had the good luck to be personally marketable. It is not quite true to say that I have sponsored cars to kitchens to lounge suits to underpants, but the spin-offs have augmented a fairly ordinary salary into one that has allowed me to pursue my various pleasures with a certain amount of style. A county cricketer's wages, on the other hand, are not brilliant. It varies from club to club, and with sponsors playing a bigger and bigger role, certain players can command a useful basic wage. Sponsors helped Hampshire put together a very good deal for Kevin Curran when he was leaving Gloucestershire, comfortably above my own, but Northants in fact were able to top this by similar means. Yorkshire TV's cash was also instrumental for Yorkshire to secure

27

the services of Sachin Tendulkar, but the lesser players still have to scratch around for work every winter to make ends meet. A senior capped player's basic last summer was between £12,000-£15,000, which is not a fortune. When I was captain of Leicestershire I was on £15,000 and although it was not the money that made me leave, I got a £10,000 rise by joining Hampshire. Had I taken Kent's offer instead, I would have doubled what I was on at Leicester.

Clubs will often point out that a player is only required to do six months work, and he has the potential to augment this over the other six, but it very much depends on what qualifications or abilities he has. Some go on the dole, some drive milk floats. Some are driven out of the game because employers eventually decide they cannot afford to give them summers off, as happened to the Leicestershire fast bowler Peter Booth. There were players at Grace Road last winter coaching in the indoor school for about three pounds an hour.

Missing last winter's tour to New Zealand and the World Cup might have cost me something in the region of £30,000, about half of which I would have recouped doing other things, such as contributing to the media and one or two other promotional ventures. My agent, Jon Holmes, has been my greatest ally, and I would be worth a lot less without his advice down the years. I have never signed a contract with him, or ever felt the need to. I had a good benefit year at Leicester, and when my earning power was at its maximum we shrewdly tied up a lot of my money in investments, some of which I have since had to sell in order to buy my current house. I do have the odd indulgence, such as a special edition Jaguar XJR-S of which I am very fond, buying paintings, and I have a lot of claret and port laid down in various warehouses so that if I ever do go broke I can either sell it or drink myself to death. I don't spend my money on anything in particular, apart from music, and I gave up the flying lessons when I got Peter Lush's bill for twenty minutes in the air in Australia.

If I leave cricket with no regrets at all, it is probably in the knowledge that I will never have to play another one-day game. Around the world it now attracts more spectators than Test cricket, but from a personal point of view, it was in the 'watching paint dry' category of enervation and excitement. I enjoyed it when I first started, probably because it allowed me to play bad shots with some sort of excuse. After a while, though, the repetition of the thing began to wear me down, and the fact that everything was geared – for the fielding side anyway – to the negative side of things. By and large, if a spectator turns up for the last fifteen overs he won't have missed anything. It is purely about the result, otherwise you wouldn't be standing there at extra cover wondering why the crowd was going bananas over a leg-bye. I enjoyed the day-nighters in Australia more, for the different atmosphere and theatre they generated, but they don't stir my adrenalin quite like Test cricket. Latterly, of course, with fielding such an important part of the one-day game, I enjoyed it even less because my shoulder injury would not let me contribute properly. To be unable to do something you actually used to do reasonably well – in my case, throw the ball with slightly more grace than a shot-putter – was frankly depressing. Sunday League games were the worst, and I got to the stage where I almost got resentful about playing in them. The formula is numbing and unless the team is close to the top of the table, the game becomes the chore it shouldn't be.

If there is a bonus to Sunday League cricket it is perhaps because you see fewer batsmen wearing helmets, owing to the restriction on bowlers' run-ups. Ironically, the only time I have ever been badly 'pinned' was on a Sunday afternoon in 1977, during a rain-affected ten-over slog, when I top-edged a pull into my face. I first wore a helmet on my first tour to Australia in 1978-79. The idea had been around for a long time, and it was probably only tradition that prevented helmets from coming into general use many years before they did. The more macho characters resisted at first, some of them holding out for years, but very few players have never worn one at all. Viv Richards and Richie Richardson, in fact, are the only two who come to mind. It may have taken some of the romance out of batting, particularly for the spectators, but when you have just collected one on the cranium from the likes of Richard Hadlee, you tend not to dwell too much on the loss of some precious heritage: preservation of your head seems somehow more important. I've tried batting without one against quick bowlers, and I remember leaving it behind in the dressing room after tea during a Test against New Zealand at the Oval. I was feeling pretty confident – en route to a hundred – when Hadlee (hackles raised by my impertinence no doubt) let me have one, and it zipped off the side of my head for four leg-byes. He gave me a look that suggested I'd be better off going back to the dressing room to fetch it, but on the 'lightning not striking twice' principle, I carried on. Happily without further damage. It's not a hardship, nowadays. It does get hot wearing one, but they are now quite lightweight and a long way removed from the old motor cycle crash hat. I'm sure that no-one who thinks properly about it would suggest that players should run the risk of serious injury when there is equipment on hand capable of preventing it. I have no truck at all with anyone who suggests banning helmets for either batsmen or fielders. There is the old argument that they make you less aware of danger, a bit like cycling through the rush-hour traffic plugged into a Walkman, but when you are twenty-two yards away from an object that could easily kill you, it really doesn't cut much ice. I thought about not wearing one in Antigua in 1981, because I was in such good form, and was rather glad that I resisted the urge when Colin Croft crusted me with one that I had lost in the crowd. A lot of great batsmen have got by without one, but the history of the game is also studded with people who would have been a lot better off with one on. Nari Contractor, for example, required several blood transfusions and ended up with a fractured skull and a plate in his head after being hit by Charlie Griffith in the West Indies. I'm pretty sure Larwood and Tyson were something above slow-medium, but there have been some rapid bowlers around since I started playing, not all of whom appear to regard the bouncer as an occasional weapon.

'Who was the fastest you ever faced?' is a standard question, and although one or two m.p.h. here or there hardly matters when you are talking in the nineties, I think Sylvester Clarke might receive my vote on the strength of several deliveries at the Oval one day. He ripped the top of my glove off, and he would also bowl you the occasional delivery you simply never saw. He also had a genuine streak of meanness that made it additionally unpleasant to face him. Everyone gets worn down by fast bowling in the end, and I was certainly less keen to face it at thirty than I was at twenty. Barry Dudleston, who was a fine player for Leicestershire, told me that when he first came into the game that if anyone bounced him he said,

My parents, Richard and Sylvia, were both responsible for my early cricketing development in the back garden. The garden on the right was in Kent, but the cap was that of the Twigas (Swahili for giraffe) in Dar es Salaam.

An early (legal) overseas tour to South Africa with the Crocodiles, a schools team from the south-east.

Receiving my county cap in 1975 from Ray Illingworth, eyes still black from a mishap the week before.

Three key figures from my early days at Leicestershire: Brian Davison (above), a merciless destroyer of any bowling attack; Roger Tolchard (above right), seen here catching M.J. Smith of Middlesex in the B & H final of 1975; and Ray Illingworth (right), a very shrewd captain and particularly miserly – as a bowler!

Peter Willey was never a bad man to have on your side in any sort of battle whether against the West Indies or here as man of the match in our victory over Essex in the 1985 B & H final.

'Thanks very much.' However, when he was starting to get on a bit, he wasn't so much thinking of four runs as staying out of hospital.

The game is nastier now, no doubt about it – verbally as well as physically. When you've got the two combined, someone bowling very fast at you and also being rather unpleasant, it can be highly disconcerting. If the world sledging championships were held tomorrow, you would have to install the Australians as 1/2 favourites, and they invented the term of course. On the other hand, some of those who have complained about them have thrown their stones from exceptionally large greenhouses. The West Indies, Pakistan and India are not too far behind them I'd say. It's a hard old game today, not always edifying, and you can even find some high-class sledging in county cricket. It might be more acceptable if it was more witty, but most of it is very basic stuff.

Another perceived problem with the modern game is over-rates, although the authorities are convinced it is one of the major evils and the only cure is to impose harsher and harsher fines. It's one of the few jobs in the world whereby the longer you work at it the less you get paid. Personally, I think the powers-that-be have become a bit paranoid about this question, although when play was still going on at twenty to eight against the West Indies at Lord's in 1988 I might have had a different view on the matter. I would guess that the game has become a touch more professional now (maybe more cynical as well) in that the Don would never score 300 in a day 50 years on. The fielding captain would have put his men back, and ordered his bowlers to snap a bootlace twice an over. It's sad for the spectators if this run feast dries up, but the modern professional will see it as a legitimate tactic. I did it in Lahore in 1984, when we set Pakistan a target on the last day, and Mohsin Khan and Shoaib Mohammad smashed the thing all round the ground. I had to slow it down, and we eventually frustrated them into giving away wickets. Fines may be the answer, and the spectators may deserve more for their money, but I'm pretty sure that if I had walked into that press conference in Lahore and said, 'Sorry, lads, I could have saved the match, but it would have cost us five hundred quid apiece,' then anyone picking this quote out of the morning papers would not, understandably, have been very impressed.

The respect in which I count myself most fortunate was to be

31

born a batsman. There is a lot more glamour in scoring a century than taking wickets, and from a marketing point of view, it is also more lucrative than being a bowler. Endorsing bowling boots is not the sort of sideline calculated to make you rich, and players such as myself, Gooch and Robin Smith have made more money out of spin-offs than the likes of Dilley, Foster and Willis. The one source of income open to all, provided he puts in the required amount of service, is the benefit, and I picked up £105,000 tax free from my own in 1987. People will say that the benefit system was not really devised for the likes of people like me, more for the honest-to-goodness county pro who has not really had the chance to earn bigger money, and I would have a certain amount of sympathy with that. However, the common denominator is the reward for long service, to which all players – Test or county – are entitled, and if potential benefactors do not want to give to a player because they consider he is already earning enough money, then that is his or her privilege. Benefits are much more commercialized than they used to be, and in coming ever closer to the technical limits that are imposed upon them, may well attract the interest of the taxman at some stage in the future. In my year we did something like twenty theatre shows the length and breadth of the country, which were too close to being a commercial venture not to declare it to the Revenue as such. No player wants to queer the pitch for others who are following.

There have been any number of more successful benefits than my own, including some of the county stalwarts who deserve them most. Paul Pridgeon, for example, managed to raise £150,000 at Worcester, which came about through a combination of his own popularity and having very efficient people running the benefit for him. Others have not done so well, and when Graham Roope was awarded one with Surrey, it went so badly wrong that he almost ended up losing money. One or two Test players, myself included, have raised eyebrows by staging events outside the county they have been playing for, but when you perform on a higher stage your supporters are not all confined to one county. There is a publican near Worcester – inappropriately named David Drinkwater – who has been a supporter of cricket and cricketers for a very long time, and has been a great friend to players from all parts of the country. I had three lunches there during my year, and Worcestershire queried it with him. Quite rightly, however, he told them that it was entirely his business who he chose to help in this way, whether it be Worcestershire players or not. The only other point to make is that if you compare the modern benefit in real terms to benefits of twenty or thirty years ago, you will find that there has not been a vast increase in the rewards. If you costed W.G.'s benefit out on today's retail price index he would have to be the wealthiest man who has ever played cricket. And he was an amateur.

Overseas players have been a bone of contention over the years, but I think they are good for our game. One argument against them has been that we have helped many become better players through county cricket, and then suffered because of it when they turn round and beat us in Test matches. Border would have taken home a lot of useful information from playing with Essex, likewise Hadlee, Marshall, Waqar Younis, Wasim Akram – the list is endless. However, I still think that it works both ways. Unless our own cricketers play with the likes of these people, they will become too insular. Where our system falls down is in having so many cricketers playing for so many different clubs. In Australia, for example, with only half-a-dozen state sides, the real talent is more concentrated, and this is why they have perhaps more player movement than we do in this country. If someone can't get into the New South Wales team, but is wanted by Queensland, he will just up and move from Sydney to Brisbane. The fact that we have more players to pick from does not necessarily give us a stronger international team, and rather than taking on new counties like Durham, we should ideally be creating a smaller pool of top players. A smaller number of stronger sides, playing less but more intense cricket, would serve us far better at Test level.

Four-day cricket is also, I feel, the right way forward. It can, of course, be a tedious game at times, but it does have the enormous advantage of giving the stronger sides a better opportunity to win. There is certainly more scope for batsmen to occupy the crease (Hick, for example, might never have had the time to make 400 in a three-day match) and it also makes bowlers work harder for their wickets. More importantly, it is so closely related to Test cricket. Whatever system is employed, they have certainly got two things right after years of brainlessness. The extra day's preparation for

Test matches is so obviously a benefit that it boggles the mind to think that it has taken so long to be introduced, as indeed is the fact that Friday is no longer an automatic travelling day. Asking players to perform on a Saturday morning after spending ten hours on the road staring at the back of a caravan, was something that only recently occurred to the TCCB as unreasonable. All this legislation defining what professional cricketers do is passed by the chairmen of county cricket clubs, some of whom appear to have no better grasp of the mechanics of the game than I have of Serbo-Croat. The number of times that I attended county captains' meetings and saw recommendations passed on that were cither totally ignored or chopped to pieces, would make another book. You would make a proposal in September, disappear overseas for the winter, and come back to another captains' meeting in April to find that the thoughts of what are supposed to be the seventeen or eighteen people closer to the game than anyone, had been deposited in the nearest wastepaper basket. The fact that the Professional Cricketers' Association has never had anything like the influence at Lord's as the county committees, has got to be slightly mad.

County committees are generally comprised of people who have the game at heart, but who are attracted to a club for any number of reasons, and to have them responsible for running the game is sheer folly. The captains, by contrast, are treated like schoolboys by the people at Lord's. They pompously issue 'we know best' edicts from those offices next to the museum, when half of them should be in the museum themselves. It is very hard to monitor the game if you are not in the dressing room, and even though players can be selfish, short sighted and need monitoring by a higher authority, there is no excuse for their voice being as feeble as it is. You get people like Ossie Wheatley vetoing the appointment of an England captain. Why did he have that sort of power? Who on earth is he? There could have been very few county cricketers at that time who either knew who he was or what he had done in the game, and what is the purpose of appointing an England committee only for its decisions to be over-ruled by a face-less official deep behind the scenes?

Lord's have only recently cottoned on to the idea of consulting umpires about players. They are closer to the action than anyone, and almost without exception, have played the game at a high level

34

themselves. Our umpires are consistently better than they are anywhere else in the world, because of the experience that cannot be bought or acquired from an examination paper. They are familiar with players and their attitudes, and the fact that they have played the game automatically invests them with a cloak of authority. In places where this is not the case, such as Australia, the players find it almost obligatory to abuse their umpires from the moment they get onto the field to the moment they leave it – and that is probably one reason why so few ex-players don't take it up. Someone like Tom Brooks, who was a pretty good umpire, more or less gave it up in 1979 when he gave Graeme Wood out caught behind off John Lever. It was a poor decision, but the flak he copped was unbelievable. How Tony Crafter, who is a lovely man and a fine umpire, has kept going all these years I don't know.

I am more in favour of an international panel of umpires than so called 'neutral' officials. It doesn't do Australia or England any good if they are saddled with a substandard Pakistani umpire, or indeed India or Pakistan any good if they get a poor one from us. The pressure on umpires these days is horrendous, with all the trials by TV and newspapers, and mistakes are highlighted and exaggerated more than ever. As for the idea of electronic aids, a kind of replay booth of the sort they have in American Football, I tend to think it would be a benefit. I love the theory and tradition of the umpire being the sole judge, and his word being law, but if there are technical aids that can help, then there has got to be a move towards using them. There are so many things for them to do nowadays, that to be infallible is more impossible than it ever was. The days when all they had to do was check the coat pocket for six marbles are long gone. As always with the game of cricket, traditional thinking such as 'the umpire's word is law', remains at the heart of all discussions on the subject. At the moment, the technology that exists can only help with run-outs or stumpings. We will have to wait until there are foolproof methods for clarifying catches behind and lbw decisions, so that those dismissed erroneously in these ways no longer feel aggrieved by colleagues who have been reprieved by cameras ideally sited to deal with a contentious run-out.

CHAPTER FOUR

On the piste and on safari

FROM early childhood through to adulthood (some might say semi-adulthood) cricket has been the dominant feature of my life, and most of the things I've done have stemmed directly from the game. However, I have always tried to ensure that cricket does not take over my life completely, and there have been times when I have had to get right away from it to preserve a degree of sanity. Getting right away from it by taking to the air in the middle of a match was perhaps an extreme example, and in terms of career advancement, not a very wise one. I bumped into my old cricket master from King's School, Canterbury, during a county game last summer, a lovely chap by the name of Colin Fairservice who would be well into his eighties by now. He brought up the Tiger Moth business and said, 'The trouble with you, David, is that you've never grown up.' I don't think this is entirely true, but I guess this is how most people perceive me, and I would have to own up for supplying a certain amount of evidence to this school of thought.

I have developed many outside interests, enjoying them both for what they are and as a partial antidote to cricket. You cannot get much further away from a cricketing environment than snow, and winter sports have figured prominently in my more energetic leisure pursuits. I first went skiing at the age of ten, when my parents took me to Switzerland, but it was another twenty years before I had my first serious go at it. I had become very close friends with a keen social skier and bobsledder by the name of Simon Strong, having met him through Allan Lamb, and one year the three of us and our respective ladies took ourselves off to the resort of Verbier. It was a

36

somewhat painful introduction to the sport, largely because our hosts had booked lunch at a place situated at the bottom of one of the more demanding slopes at the resort. It was certainly not for novices, and having made most of the trip on arse and elbow, the wine was consumed less as an aid to digestion than as an anaesthetic.

I later took a ride in a bobsleigh at the Italian resort of Cervinia, behind the then British No 1, Nick Phipps. It was exciting – a little like being on a trapeze without the safety net – and just before the West Indies tour of 1985-86, Strong decided that it was about time Lamb and myself had a go at the Cresta Run. Essentially, you lie on a one-man toboggan – two runners with a frame and sliding seat – and we were simply plonked at the start and shoved off. I have been back many times since, acquiring membership of the St Moritz Tobogganing Club, and I have certainly caught the bug for it. There is a corner on the Run called Shuttlecock, which is designed (for both experts and beginners) as a safety valve: if you are going too fast, it ejects you like a cork out of a bottle, bringing you back to earth – hopefully unharmed – in thick snow and hay. It qualifies you for the Shuttlecock tie, not an exclusive club by any means, and if I had one for every time I've been catapulted off the toboggan, I would have an awful lot of ties in the rack. Like all of these things, it is a combination of fear and exhilaration that gives you the buzz. The first time we went down, Lamby and myself thought that if we could pull off something like the Cresta Run, then facing the West Indies' attack would be a piece of cake by comparison. We were not exactly proved right, I must confess. Put it this way, the Cresta went a lot better than the West Indies tour, during which, in all five Tests, the team went the same way as a Shuttlecock tie-holder.

I went to the winter Olympics at Calgary in 1988, which was fabulous, and one of my most enjoyable experiences was watching the USA versus Czechoslovakia ice-hockey match. The Saddledome Stadium was packed to the rafters, and I have scarcely enjoyed watching a game of anything more than that. It is a sport that does not come over that well on TV, largely because it is so difficult to pick up the puck, but I would recommend a live match between two good teams to anyone.

I have developed a reputation as something of a bon viveur, although it is a general misconception that I always am, as it were,

37

out on the piste. In this country, I am quite a homebird, but it is very easy to be out most nights on a tour. You live out of suitcases by and large, and as there is a certain depressive aspect about room service, I do like to go out and eat. The occasional cork has been heard to pop close to my table, I admit, but the eyes are not bloodshot every morning. I have acquired a taste for champagne, and one of my closer friends, Simon Leschallas, by happy chance works for Bollinger. They always have a tent at Lord's, and our friendship developed through the frequency of my visits, and the fact that he is a very amusing and amenable host. He introduced me to Rob Hirst, who is Bollinger's Australian agent, and on Mike Gatting's tour in 1986-87, Rob not only had a bottle waiting in the room when we arrived in Queensland, but also ensured that supplies were more than adequate (not to mention agreeably priced) over the next four months. On that tour I spent as much time packing Bollinger cases (scribbling 'medical supplies' all over the wrapping paper) than my kit bag.

Having acquired some fame, there is a mixture of good and bad in terms of invitations that come your way, and whenever one accepts an invitation to some sort of function it is a question of keeping the fingers crossed that all will be well. The good news is that more often than not people are very pleased to see me, and are accordingly very generous and helpful. There are some especially attractive invitations along the way, including film premières and the like, but it would be wrong to suggest that we all live in a constant social whirl. And often it is the smaller local functions with Rotary Clubs and the like that are the most enjoyable and satisfying.

You have to balance out the number of requests with the time available, and one of my bigger chores is getting through the mail. Our postman does not quite qualify for the lead role in *The Hunchback of Notre Dame*, but the paperknife does get a little warm most mornings. On the other hand, during the occasional crises in my career, the tone of the letters has mostly been very supportive, and I do feel I owe it to these people to reply as often as I can. I try and meet requests for autographs and photographs, and there is a never-ending stream of mail asking for items for charity auctions. So many, in fact, that you could end up with an empty house if you're not very careful. Not everyone gets what they want, of course, but then few do.

When the clerical bit gets a mite wearing and I need a bit of a blow out, I tend to head for the tennis court. I also play a bit of golf, and the interesting thing for me is that my temperament for both games tends to be a lot more fragile than it is for cricket. My brain wants me to be an Edberg or a Ballesteros, but the body tends to be irritatingly disobedient. I've done a bit of McEnroe-ing with the racket, and I have to say that he's always been one of my favourites. I can sympathize with the mental pain he appears to go through. Like his, my language on the tennis court (and the golf course) does have scope for improvement.

I also play a bit of squash now and then, but my most passionate off-duty pursuit has always been for Africa and wildlife. Having spent my early life in Tanganyika, there has always been a lingering affinity for that part of the world, and the umbilical cord became unbreakable after a private safari to Kenya. We went with a guy called Tor Allan, on a recommendation from Tim Rice's wife, Jane, and his knowledge of where to find the wildlife – the game, the birds, and all the rest of it – made it a fabulous nine days. To be almost on your own in the middle of these unspoiled places, surrounded by the sights and sounds of the wild, is an unbelievable feeling. But I have to say that what suited my nature just as well was not rubbing two sticks of wood together, and trying to catch supper with a primitive rod and line. Tor's African boys all donned waistcoats and bowties to serve us four-course dinners, and we kept the Bollinger chilled in an old kerosene fridge. Sitting out there at night in the middle of nowhere was paradise.

Southern Africa is just as rich a venue for wildlife, and on Allan Lamb's recommendation I went one year to a place called Londolozi, a private game reserve on the western Kruger in Eastern Transvaal, run by two brothers, John and Dave Varty. John, who had played a little bit of first-class cricket for Transvaal before falling out with the management (so we had something in common) makes docu-dramas about wildlife all over the world. He specializes in leopards, and one of the first films he made – *Silent Hunter* – was devoted exclusively to these particular cats. I also have a wonderful book at home entitled *The Leopards of Londolozi*. The brothers inherited the park, and turned it round from nothing into one of the best in the Transvaal. They try to leave the habitat to nature as much as they possibly can, although a certain amount of management is required for the animals' own welfare. It is a wonderful spot. The basic form there is to go out in an open topped Landrover with six to eight people, although I have got to know the brothers well enough now for them to entrust me with a warden or a tracker and allow me to take a landrover out myself. It is so much more exhilarating, because you are not tied to the routine of the organized outing. If you want to stay in one particular spot for hours then you can. I have been back four or five times since that first visit, and will continue to do so just as long as I can continue to find the air fare.

Complementing my general love of wildlife is a keen interest in the art side of it. Several years ago, I was in Lincoln to watch another mate, Robin Askwith, in pantomime, and was walking back to the hotel when I passed a shop displaying a framed print of cheetahs by the wildlife artist David Shepherd. I liked it so much that I forked out £250 on the spot, and that was the start of my collection of wildlife prints, paintings and artifacts. I have also got to know the artist himself, who lives in a fabulous renovated farmhouse near Godalming. David is one of the world's great enthusiasts, not only about wildlife, which has made his reputation as an artist, but also about trains – he even has his own steam railway line in Somerset.

He is passionate about the preservation of the world's heritage, and several years ago he started the David Shepherd Conservation Foundation – my own involvement extending to a seat on the Board of Trustees. There are the obvious species generating concern for conservationists, such as elephants and rhinos, but David also raises money for any number of different projects worldwide. He is a lovely man, very kind hearted, and if I thought I was busy at times, I didn't really know what busy meant until I met David. I got myself sponsored for so much a run in the summer of 1991 on behalf of the foundation, and as my form was slightly better than one of the cricket reporters made out (who dryly observed that I was on course to save half a tusk), I managed to raise around £16,000 for the cause. It could have been better, but the irony was that my highest score of the season – eighty-odd not out against Middlesex – came at Lord's when David was there to watch the game as a guest of Joe Hardstaff. I saw him before going into bat, and responded accordingly. I later suggested, not surprisingly, that he come and watch me more often.

I am also involved in SAVE, a charity that raises money to buy equipment for use in places like Zambia and Zimbabwe. Its headquarters are in New York, but a friend of mine by the name of Nicholas Duncan, who I first met while playing club cricket in Perth in 1977-78, has now started an Australian branch. On England's last tour to Australia he organized a fund raising dinner, which I spoke at, and I accompanied a party of tourists on a cash gathering mission to Zimbabwe after the tour. The major target for SAVE in Africa, and especially in Zimbabwe, is the black rhino, which is now being poached out of existence. Another integral part of my involvement with wildlife is my interest in photography, but not everyone shoots animals with a Canon. Sadly, the poacher's rifle is more common. The only rhinos we saw in Zimbabwe on that trip were on a private farm at Imire, an hour-and-a-half's drive from Harare, where the collection extended to seven orphans. We did not see any in the wild, and their plight is frankly desperate.

There was a mixture of English and Australians in our party out there, and, inevitably, we had a game of cricket for the 'Ashes'. We played on an airstrip near one of the tourist camps using a tennis ball, a piece of wood, and a deckchair for the stumps. Yet again, the Australians made off with the Ashes – and guess who was out to a careless shot? Actually, it was an unplayable ball that swung and seamed both ways. That's my story anyway. The overall story, I suppose, is that I, like the rhino, also wanted to roam a little more freely than people with metaphorical rifles cared to allow. I only hope that the modern game will continue to cater for the occasional free spirit, and that we do not end up with a clone factory for marathon runners and net addicts. Cricket is too rich a sport not to accommodate different types of character – and it would be a shame if players like myself were to become, like the black rhino, an endangered species.

CHAPTER FIVE

Out of Africa

I WAS born in Tunbridge Wells in 1957 on April Fool's Day (which some people might say explains a great deal) although there is a good deal of evidence to suggest that I was actually conceived in Africa. Sadly, neither parent is available for comment on that one. I lost my father in 1973, and Mum died in what was to be a particularly awful year for me, 1986. My father was in the Colonial Service, having worked his way up through the ranks to become a District Commissioner and then on to a more senior administrative position in Dar es Salaam, Tanganyika – which is now Tanzania – and had been there since the end of the War. We lived there until I was about six (at which time the country's independence brought us home) and my earliest memories are of living in a bungalow down by the beach just outside Dar es Salaam. Our next house adjoined the golf course and was built on stilts, partly to lessen the prospect of finding some of the less edifying wildlife at the bottom of your bed. I can recall the occasional passing snake, which the garden boy would obligingly hammer to death with a rake. He would have been a decent player – middled it every time. I've still got a photo of him, actually, posing with the rake and a dead snake. We lived in true colonial fashion with a small retinue of servants, who lived with their families at the back of the property. With no brothers or sisters, I used to spend a lot of my time with them during the day, running around outside their huts, which were a long way from being palaces I can tell you, and accepting the occasional chunk of bread and a cup of hot sweet tea, which appeared to be part of their diet. It made no difference to me whether I was filled up by that or with whatever my mother came up with back in the main house. Basically, it was a very happy and carefree childhood.

My father was an accomplished all-round sportsman. The social life revolved around the Gymkhana Club, where he played cricket, hockey, golf and tennis to a fairly high standard. He also played fives and rugby, and certainly had a greater all-round talent than I ever had. He won a hockey blue at Cambridge, and also had the potential to win one at cricket as well, and perhaps had the talent to become a sportsman if had he not gone to Africa to launch a proper career. Maybe if he'd been alive when I was at university studying law it might have persuaded me not to do precisely the opposite of what he did. It was my father who first put a bat in my hand, although my mother spent as much time lobbing a tennis ball in my direction as he did because he was away at work quite a bit of the time. If it had not been for my mother, I would probably have been a right-hander, because while my father tried to get me to hold the bat the normal way round, it was she who persuaded him to allow natural instincts to prevail. So now you know who to blame for all those lazy nicks to gully. The only other thing I've ever done consistently left-handed, in fact, is dealing cards.

The last thing I remember doing in Tanganyika, which has a lot to do, I imagine, with my passion for wildlife now, is going on safari with my parents to some of the northern game parks. There was one close call with a fairly truculent elephant, thanks to the driver of our Land Rover panicking and stalling the engine, but it was a lovely way to say goodbye to Africa, as a child anyway. We finished up by taking the boat down to Cape Town, and from there it was onto the *Union Castle* and back to England. We settled in Kent, and for my father, now commuting to Victoria every day, it was a different climate, in all senses, after twenty-odd years in Africa. We were there for a year or two before he applied for a job as registrar at the Loughborough College of Education – the idea being that he could still use his admin skill while being close to sporting activity. It was also good news for my own sporting education, in that my holidays from prep school coincided with student holidays at Loughborough and I got the run of all the facilities there. We also had a snooker table at our disposal, although you would hardly think so to see to me play now.

Before long, though, having done a year or so at primary school in Quorn, my parents packed me off to prep school at Marlborough House in Kent, which was a bit of a wrench at the time. It was fairly intimidating at first, and I did the customary bit of bursting into tears when the parental car disappeared down the drive. I remember thinking when my mother sent me my first cake through the post that I wished it had a file in it, but you soon adapt and I spent five happy years there until the age of thirteen. It was a smallish school, about one hundred boys or so, and without exactly being Wilson of the Wizard, I stood out at most sports. I enjoyed rugby as much as anything and was the all-action-fly-half-cum-goal-kicker, and was a big fan of Wales in those days, when, as I recall, Welsh rugby supporters actually had something to cheer about. As the family name suggests there is some Welsh ancestry – not so much on the Gower around Swansea as further west towards Cardigan – although by the time it got to me the blood was becoming severely diluted. I don't recall supporting Glamorgan at cricket (there is a limit), although cricket was becoming more and more my best sport.

I scored my first century against a school who were one of our main rivals. I was thirteen then, which caused a bit of excitement as centuries were not that common. I had some very good coaching, and the cricket master, Derek Whittome, was a big influence on me at an important stage of my development. I caught up with him again during my benefit year in 1987 at a cricket talk-in evening in Hastings, and he brought along a party of boys from the school. It wasn't all sport, mind you, and hard to believe though it is I actually paid a bit of attention to my school work in those days. Going back to my early upbringing, I harboured more ambitions towards becoming a game-warden than a cricketer. Dreams, shall we say, of fishing on a game reserve as opposed to outside the off stump. Anyway, I did well enough in the classroom to win a scholarship to King's School, Canterbury. I was going to sit for one at Repton as well, the idea being to get closer to home, but King's delivered a take-it-or-leave-it ultimatum, and family finances at the time were not quite up to taking the gamble. My father had been to King's, and not only won most of the supporting trophies going, but also rose to the dizzy heights of head boy. A hard act to follow, and needless to say I didn't. I started pretty well, getting into the rugby, cricket and hockey teams, knuckling down to my piano and clarinet lessons, and actually studying quite hard. On the cricketing side, the First XI used to play about seven or eight other schools during the course of a summer but also a number of club sides – mostly from Kent, but including the likes of the Stragglers of Asia and the MCC. Now when we played against the clubs, the visiting captain was allowed to invite the boys into The Beverley, which was the pub just around the corner from the cricket field, for the odd half of shandy. Like most people, I suppose, my first taste of beer was pretty foul, but after a few net sessions, so to speak, I began to see the attraction. So much so, that óne or two of us decided not to wait for the next club match for our next visit and try a spot of freelancing instead. Inevitably, having cycled with a classmate early one evening and ordered a couple of pints of foaming best bitter, we had hardly started an illicit glass of Kent's finest hop when in walked a couple of adults we were more accustomed to seeing in gowns and mortars chalking Latin verbs up on the blackboard. I attempted some weak joke, along the lines of 'What are you having, sir?' which for some reason failed to reduce the two masters to helpless laughter, and we were duly ordered to leave and await further developments. Fortunately enough, it was a fairly enlightened establishment – no Flashman to roast you over an open fire and not much use of the cane. But although we avoided physical retribution, the next few weeks were not terribly pleasant: confined to barracks, report cards, jankers – that sort of thing.

So that was an early blot, head of school prospects out of the window, but the cricket was going well. I had made the First XI at the age of fourteen, which was by no means a school record, but it did mean that I grew up fairly quickly in cricketing terms. The difference between fourteen and eighteen-year-olds is quite a large one, and, like all sports, if you are stretching yourself against better and more experienced opposition then you learn a good bit faster than you would against boys of your own age. On top of this I was playing club cricket in Leicestershire during the summer holidays, which also broadened my social horizons, as a boarding school is somewhat cloistered, and in my last year at Canterbury I had gone on to captain the side. I made a few cock-ups, of course, but it was all part of the learning process, as indeed was the earlier business of getting caught in the pub. Entering a hostelry so closely connected to the school was not a great idea, particularly when Canterbury has one of the highest densities of pubs per square mile in the country. Ergo, if you are a schoolboy in Canterbury you can find a pub that is unfrequented by authority and have a fairly good chance of avoiding detection – as most of us proceeded to prove.

Anyhow, it seemed like a good idea to get the hang of beer drinking in preparation for a rugby career, having at that time established a nice, undemanding little number as Fourth XV fly-half. We had a choice between rugby and athletics, which involved tedious things like jumping into sandpits, over hurdles, and cross country runs. The only time I did a cross-country run I cannily missed off a third of the course, and still only came about 80th. My big mistake on the rugger field, however, was to play well enough to get into the Second XV where, with King's having a strong tradition in the sport, they took the game fairly seriously.

The school rugby coach was a Welshman by the name of Ian Gollop, a man dedicated to mathematics and rugby, and who possessed an overwhelming desire to win that was conspicuously absent on the Fourth XV pitch. We even had training sessions, which was not quite what I had in mind when I gleefully kicked athletics into touch. The Second XV backs did an awful lot of running around without the ball – as a foil to our first-team counterparts – and I raised this point with Mr Gollop. 'Do you really need us for this?' I inquired, whereupon he told me that if I didn't like it, I could get on my bike and clear off. So I did. However, this actually turned out to have much the same effect of saying 'sod 'em' to the England selectors fifteen years later, as I then found myself in the First XV. I didn't quite make it until the end of the season, though. Dropped for 'lack of effort'.

Even in those early days I realized I was a touch closer to the Baron de Coubertin's philosophy than Ian Gollop's. Critics have since earmarked it as a failing, a character defect, and maybe they're right, but I've always liked to win. Life's much easier when you win – it's just that I sussed out from a fairly early age that you don't always. I actually had to learn and develop a stronger competitive spirit at school, where I made the discovery that losing in itself is not something to tear your hair out over, but not performing as well as you can certainly is. I remember playing in the school squash competition against a lad I should have beaten. I'd won the first game, and was so far ahead in the second that I almost felt sorry for him and relented. Then, of course, I started to play very badly, and to cut a long story short, got stuffed. That annoyed me so much that I actually felt ashamed of myself. So it's not so much the winning or losing – it's more that if I feel as though I've played as well as I can, I feel okay. Translated in to cricket, if you've done well, scored a century maybe, but the side has lost, there's definitely a feeling of disappointment but you're not personally depressed.

I used to play a fair amount of tennis with a good friend of mine from Leicester, Tim Ayling, and to be perfectly frank he can beat me anytime he wants to. As I recall, the only time I've ever won a set off him was when we had not prepared in the regulation manner, and he was slightly more pissed than I was. But as long as I've felt I've played hard and competed against him, I've enjoyed the game. It might sound a bit futile, but I'd sooner play out of my skin and lose than beat an inferior player. But as for the so-called lack of a competitive streak, I once played tennis with Robin Askwith when he came up to stay with me in Leicester a few years back, and for all Askwith's charms and abilities, he happens to be deformed. He's actually got one leg shorter than the other, which he's hidden quite well in most walks of life, but it doesn't do much for his agility on a tennis court. He'd also done something to his ankle, so he could barely move at all to his left, which is where I kept hitting the ball. By the end of the game, he was barely able to crawl into the shower, and he said: 'If anyone says you haven't got a competitive streak in you, I am living proof to the contrary.'

I don't think you can get through sixteen years of first-class cricket, with a reasonable amount of success, without some kind of competitive edge. It's all about maintaining a balance in many ways. For instance I play golf, or a strange version of it, not too often and not too well a lot of the time. But if I can make a contribution, make the odd par here and there, then I'm happy, but if I go round like a total novice, and spend half my time hacking out of bushes or failing to drive past the ladies' tee, then frankly, I get bloody irritable. Going back to the rugby, and the 'lack of effort', I scored plenty of points with the boot, and also popped over for a few tries – but apparently there was something wrong with my work-rate. Even in those days,

47

it seems, skill took second place to sweat. Micky Stewart would have loved Ian Gollop. Generally, I think my philosophy has stood me in good stead. I've never been one to mope around looking miserable after losing, which in some ways is a good thing, and in others bad. Putting on appearances to suit other people is not really me, but I now know, for example, that had I looked a touch more suicidal after losing a Test match to India in 1986, I might not have been relieved of the England captaincy. I felt bad about it, but to the man that mattered – Peter May – not bad enough.

King's has a fabulous setting, well worth a walk round if you are ever in Canterbury, and most of the school is within the Cathedral Close. To get to breakfast in the morning there was a walk of about 250 yards past one of the great cathedrals of the world, and a passage through a dark alley reputed to have been haunted by Nell Gwynne. You are surrounded by architecture dating back to the eleventh century, and wherever you go you are surrounded by history. I can perhaps appreciate it better now than I did then, because as you became older as a schoolboy boarder, your main thought is not so much 'Look how beautiful this all is' as 'How do I get out of here?' You are well aware of one or two social attractions outside, and basically you are walled in. The gates are shut, wander lust strikes (or just lust), you get a bit thirsty and your mind is not so much on Latin or cricket as mountaineering. A young man's thoughts lightly turn to spring, or to be more accurate, springing out.

There was a light on top of one of the walls we used to climb, and you had to move pretty quickly to get over without being spotted. It was a bit like Colditz really, although the penalties for a break-out were perhaps not quite so serious, although the penalty for failing to negotiate one of the spiked railings was fairly severe. I remember one lad losing his footing one night, and instead of the planned evening out he ended up with the school matron applying several layers of sticking plaster to his posterior. Mostly we made it though, and the prime job then was to get around town without detection.

Two of my better friends at King's were one Andrew Newell, the headmaster's son, and Stephen White-Thompson, the Dean of Canterbury's son. Andrew was similar to Alec Stewart in as much as he did not let his background prevent him from being one of the boys. The point, however, is that between the two of them it was not very hard to acquire a key that gave one access to the postern gate, and thus an easy exit to the town and beyond. It was relatively easy to take away a key for long enough to get a copy cut, which of course ruled out the need for crampons, pitons, and the possibility of reporting to matron with a punctured posterior. I nearly got rumbled once when one of the masters found this strange key in my possession and gave the relevant gates a try. Fortunately it had been cut badly, and only worked if you waggled it around in the lock, so I got away with that one.

I was doing well with the work and sport, but the blots on the copybook were beginning to add up, and discovering girls was next on the agenda. On one particular occasion the school had been granted a day off for some reason or other, though this was due to finish with a roll-call at round about six o'clock in the evening. I had made it as high up as a house monitor, which in terms of high office would hardly give you vertigo – roughly equivalent to lance-corporal I suppose – but I thought at the time that it might be enough not to qualify me for roll-call. Wrong. I'd actually disappeared off to Ashford, which was about a twenty-minute train ride away, to meet a girl I had met at one of the dances that the school occasionally organized, and after a couple of drinks we decided to see a James Bond film at the local cinema. By this time, apparently, we had both been reported AWOL, and as we came out of the movie the search party that had been put out for her came upon us strolling down Ashford High Street. She was dragged off, not quite in chains, and off I went to catch the train back to Canterbury. Unfortunately, the events of the day – in particular the sojourn in the pub – had left me drained, and I woke up at the end of the line in Ramsgate. I did manage to hitch a lift back to Canterbury, where a vast tub of hot water awaited, and it was back to the ranks – an unfamiliar feeling then, if not now.

In most respects, school had gone reasonably well. I'd enjoyed my sport, and if I had also enjoyed one or two extra curricular activities too well for an unblemished record, I'd studied hard enough to end up with eight O levels, three A levels, and one S grade in history. I sat the history exam for Oxford, and although I wrote quite competently on half the questions, I found myself rambling on at one stage about King Arthur, a man whose career I had never actually studied. I was, much to my surprise, invited up for an interview. So I spent the next few weeks swotting up on Arthur, before driving up in the family Anglia (the car which we had brought back with us on the boat from Africa) for the interview. Unfortunately, Sod's Law struck, and most of the interview consisted of questions about what Richelieu and his mates were doing at the Court of Louis XIV, all of which I'd just about forgotten. Needless to say, it did not go well. Another piece of misfortune was that I had applied to St Edmund Hall, which had quite a sporting reputation, but apparently at precisely the time they were starting to think about their academic reputation. Bye, bye Oxford.

I already had a place at University College, London, but between my mother and the headmaster at King's it was deemed to be a good idea to stay on at school and try for two more A levels. This is where I lost enthusiasm. In the summer of 1974 I had played a few games for Leicestershire 2nds and their under-25 team in the previous school holidays, and had rubbed shoulders with the likes of Micky Norman, Maurice Hallam, and Terry Spencer, scored a few runs, and had an offer to join the county the following season. This also had an extra bearing on a distinct lack of application concerning these two extra A's. So I went to the headmaster, told him I'd had enough, and he more or less agreed that I was wasting my time. My mother was upset, of course, but off I went to Leicestershire and said, 'Here I am, I'm yours for the summer.' Mike Turner said, 'How much do you want?' I replied, 'How about £20 a week?' He said, 'I'll give you £25,' and we shook hands on it. This to me was bliss, though the wages and my attitude to the game have both changed somewhat since.

I'd enjoyed my previous summer's cricket, and Leicestershire represented the next beginning in my life. I'd arrived at Marlborough House at the age of eight which was a bit intimidating, starting again at King's was much the same, and believe it or not, so was turning up at Lutterworth for Leicestershire 2nds versus Middlesex 2nds. Even though a certain amount of natural eye and ability got me through okay, the one thing I remember most from those first senior games was how much I struggled against the turning ball. Good spinners take a long time to develop, and I had hardly any previous experience against this type of quality bowling. Still, here I was back for a full summer, living at home with no overheads and no commitments, and getting paid what for me at the time was a handsome amount of pocket money. I knew I would be taking up my university place in London come October (Mike Turner was the first to advise me not to abandon the academic option), and although to a certain extent I was playing as the carefree amateur, deep down I think I was already two thirds of the way towards full time cricket. The summer of 1975 did nothing to alter that view. Leicestershire won the championship for the first time in their history, in which I featured in about three games, and I also played in half a dozen Sunday League matches.

I was never that committed to university, where the only thing we really had in common was the fact that the place was situated in Gower Street. I was supposed to be studying law, but in the six months I was there I learned a good bit more about kebab houses in Charlotte Street. The best way to put it is that we parted company by mutual consent the following summer, and almost before I knew it I was playing in a Benson and Hedges quarter-final at Worcester. I forget who was missing from our side, but I opened the innings and got thirty-odd, which was satisfying enough at the time, even if we did lose a high-scoring match.

CHAPTER SIX

'Bloody hell, Gower.
Have you just come in?'

THE first game I played for Leicestershire was a Sunday League match. I'd been in The Hague for an under-19 youth tournament, playing for England North against sides from Holland, Belgium and Canada. I got a stack of runs there, and won a bat as batsman of the tournament, so I was in a pretty good frame of mind when the team caught the ferry back across the channel to Harwich. I got a train to Liverpool Street Station, tube to St Pancras, train up to Leicester, and phoned my mother from the station to tell her that I was just about to get the connection to Loughborough and would she be so kind as to come and collect me? She said, 'Oh no, darling, I think you had better stay in Leicester and get a taxi to Grace Road. They want you to play this afternoon.' She was right. John Steele was injured and I opened the innings with Barry Dudleston. It was very sudden and I was too tired to be nervous, but I do remember thinking that the Surrey attack was a little more tricky than Belgium under-19's. Caught Skinner bowled Intikhab 11. 'Gower played one or two pleasant shots before falling to a careless stroke,' according to the *Leicester Mercury*. Doesn't sound like me, does it? He must have been mixing me up with someone else.

My next match was also in the Sunday League at Grace Road, against Sussex, and I appear to have made 21 before getting out to another spinner, John Barclay. The *Mercury* man must have spotted something, though, as he wrote: 'Gower, slung in at the deep end at 28 for 2 from nine overs, showed a great temperament and is clearly a man with a big future.' I got a couple of fifties later on, and I made my championship debut that year against Lancashire at Blackpool.

The match was drawn, and I made 32, batting at No 7, before being caught Reidy bowled Shuttleworth. I don't remember how, but the one thing I do recall from that match was dear old Raymond Illingworth, 'Illy', blowing a gasket in bizarre circumstances. During the course of an unmemorable century from David Lloyd, our wicketkeeper, Roger Tolchard, had missed stumping him off Illy because he was standing too far back. Tolly then got injured, Barry Dudleston took the gloves, and soon afterwards he whipped off the bails with Lloyd about a yard out. Unfortunately, the bails fell back into the grooves on top of the stumps, at which point Raymond exploded. He booted his chewing gum up in the air, and frothed: 'Well, bugger me. One useless (expletive deleted) can't reach t'bloody stumps, and t'other useless (expletive deleted) hasn't got strength to knock t'bloody bails off.'

I didn't play the next game – possibly because of Illy's tantrum at Blackpool, we played two wicketkeepers, or at least David Humphries made his debut as wicketkeeper and Tolly played as a batsman. I then played against Northamptonshire (0 and 21) and my only other championship match that summer came in fairly unusual circumstances against Kent at Tunbridge Wells. I was actually 12th man, but Brian Davison went home to Leicester when news came through that his father-in-law had died. The game had already started, but Mike Denness gave permission for me to step in, and although I didn't contribute much (1 and 11) it was a vital match in the championship, and we sneaked home by 18 runs. It was an average start to put it mildly, but it was marvellous just to be involved that year. We not only won the championship for the first time, but also the Benson and Hedges Cup.

I was a bit wet behind the ears to begin with, and had turned up for pre-season training in a suit. I had no idea of how I should be dressed for my first day at the office, as it were, but it appeared to cause a fair amount of mirth. I was very shy and retiring to begin with, but the atmosphere at the club under Illy was so good that the little boy lost feeling didn't last very long. All in all, this was to be a good summer and a turning point in my life. The attractions of a career playing cricket meant that from now on the idea of poring over books in the law library was never likely to be a serious rival.

I might never have gone on to become a full time professional cricketer had it not been for the death of my father in 1973. When the various crises came at school, only my mother was around to deal with them, and knowing my father's determination for me to pursue an academic career, things might have turned out very differently had he still been alive. I was 16 when he died. He had been ill for two years – a combination of Hodgkin's disease and Motor Neurone disease, which by and large comes under the umbrella of Multiple Sclerosis. He had not been working, and was gradually fading away. The brain remains very sharp, but the body just gives up. Eventually he got too weak to do anything at all, and went into hospital and died. It left a big gap.

Because I was away at school so much it probably helped me cope better than I otherwise might have done, and it was harder for my mother than it was for me despite her own independent and strong character. I'm sure he would have tried to be a bit sterner on school matters, but he was very supportive of my sporting pursuits and maybe things would have turned out much the same way. That's something we'll never know. Sadly, he only had one chance to see me play representative cricket before he died, and that was at Rugby School playing for Public Schools against the English Schools at under-16 level: the likes of the Cowdreys against the likes of the Gattings. I remember hitting a six which he greeted by tooting the car horn. It was a cold and windy day, typical cricket weather, and what with his illness he had sensibly confined himself to the car with the heater turned on. He loved watching me do well that afternoon, and I'm sure he would have enjoyed most of what has happened since. My father's encouragement on the cricket front had also extended to rigging up an old net in the back garden, although my mother probably ended up bowling more overs in it.

He was an intelligent, well-organized man, which just goes to show that not everything is inherited in the genes, but he also had a keen sense of humour that I like to think was handed down. He also loved his sport. He would quite often take me to soccer matches on a Saturday afternoon, Nottingham Forest one week, Leicester City the next, and occasionally to Leicester Tigers or Loughborough Colleges for a rugby match. Things were okay financially when he died, in that while we were never what you could call genuinely wealthy, one of my father's talents was that he was quite clever with the financial side of life and made all the right sort of provisions. He dabbled in the stock market, leaving my mother with a reasonable amount of collateral in stocks and shares, which she in turn passed on to me. He was a good bit shrewder than me in this sort of area, and definitely less extravagant.

My father's death obviously left a void, but we were both able to cope fairly well. Nevertheless, as my cricket career began to develop, there was always this feeling of how much he would have enjoyed being around to see it. I felt it most acutely in the summer of 1976, when I scored my maiden first-class century. We were playing Middlesex at Lord's, and I had a fairly undistinguished first innings, bowled by Selvey for 0. However, in the second I had played pretty well to be not out at lunch on the second day, and came out after the interval to complete what one or two observers imagined to be a thoroughly relaxed and nerveless hundred. On this occasion they would have been confusing relaxed with half asleep (I spent the lunch break fully asleep) because, I have to admit, I had not spent the previous evening preparing in a wholly professional manner.

I'd been out on the town somewhere, and while I think I managed to beat the milkman to the hotel door the next morning, it would not have been by much. The apparently laid-back Gower at the crease the next day was in fact trying desperately hard to stay awake, an exercise only achieved by repeated stabs between overs from the business end of Brian Davison's bat. It was probably the least he could have done for me as Davo had become something of a soul mate of mine – and when it came to burning candles at both ends he was close to being world champion. If, after the likes of Roger Tolchard and Jack Birkenshaw had scuttled off to bed in mid-evening, anyone felt like giving it a bit of a late thrash Davo was definitely the man. What I took rather too long to discover was that he was better at it than me – better than most if it comes to that. Anyway, Davo was smashing it to all parts as we were looking to set up a declaration, while I was groping around in a fog attempting to make contact. I think Illy went on longer than he had wanted to so that I could make the hundred, so there was less glory attached to that innings than I might have liked. Lest anyone, by the way, get the idea that Raymond was a sentimental old fool on these occasions, I would like to point out that earlier in the season he had declared on me in the match against the West Indies at Grace Road when I was 89 not out. The Lord's innings more than made up for that disappointment, although it was probably the first time I had gone out to bat in what could be described as less than pristine condition. If the century suggested that it was possible to spend all night on the tiles and still deliver the goods next day, there have been one or two cases along the way since that have provided strong evidence to the contrary.

Shortly after that I spent six weeks in the West Indies with a Young England side that included the likes of Mike Gatting, Chris Cowdrey, Paul Downton and Paul Allott, and that autumn, immediately after the English season ended, there was a Derrick Robins' invitation trip to Canada. It only lasted three weeks or so, and when I came home, I went out to work for the first and (as it turned out) last time. Mike Turner fixed me up with a job with one of Leicestershire's bigger sponsors, Bostik, and, if you will pardon the fairly awful pun, being glued to a desk all winter did not quite fit my romantic image of the professional cricketer.

The next season was another enjoyable (and reasonably successful) one, and life at this stage seemed wonderful. I had climbed onto the rollercoaster and was going along for the ride. On the other hand, my cricket had become significantly more serious. I was earning a bit more than £25 a week by now, was sharing a flat near the ground with Roger Tolchard, and was being tutored by Illy in the art of becoming professional. 'These pretty twenties and thirties are all very nice, Gower, but if you could possibly manage the occasional hundred we'd be obliged.' Raymond was inclined towards the belief that cricket was a fairly serious business, and cricketers who smiled a lot were to be regarded with a certain amount of suspicion. Needless to say, I caused him the odd moment of aggravation, not least on one occasion while he was bowling during a Sunday League match against Derbyshire. We'd been down to Westcliff to play Essex the week before, put down every catch imaginable, and I'd dropped Kenny McEwan – who got a hundred – at least once if not twice. The result was that we'd spent most of the following week doing extra catching practice. Anyway, Ashley Harvey-Walker was batting well when Raymond came on, and I was despatched to patrol the leg-side boundary (these were the days when I had a decent throwing arm). Sure enough, he slogged one straight up in the air, and after swallowing hard at the thought of Illy's reaction should I happen to drop it, managed to cling on. Elation then took over, and as I was tossing the ball up several times and bowing to the crowd, I suddenly heard this apoplectic Pudsey voice bellowing, 'Get t'bloody thing back, Gower. It's a bloody no-ball!' Having already allowed them to run two instead of one, I then hurled the ball in, and it ricocheted away off the stumps for another single. Raymond was now giving a passable imitation of Vesuvius, and Graham Cross has collapsed with laughter at short mid-wicket. I thought about inquiring as to how the captain of England and Leicestershire, not to mention one of the most miserly purveyors of off-spin bowling in cricket history happened to be bowling no-balls, but thought better of it.

If I had mentioned it to him, he would more than likely have claimed that the groundsman had painted the line in the wrong place, because if anyone were to hold a world excuses champion-ship, Raymond would have won it with something to spare. Brian Davison used to keep a list of them, and believe me there were some absolute jewels. Illy once got caught at slip shortly after lunch to a ball that he claimed had seamed away on what was basically a flat pitch. He came steaming through the dressing room door claiming that a plantain had sprung up on a length during the interval. 'T'umpire must have given me t'wrong guard,' was another classic, and in one match when we were supposed to be defending, he was bowled having a wild slog at Allan Jones, whose trademark was a Jimmy Connors' style grunt (only louder) when he let go of the ball. It was such a horrid shot that none of us in the dressing room thought he could possibly explain that one away, but sure enough, Raymond was more than up to the task. He came through the door, lobbed his bat in the direction of his chair and sat down. The tension was unbelievable, when he spluttered, 'Would you credit it? That bloody Jonah and his grunting … I thought t'umpire had called no-ball.' At which point the dressing room fell apart.

Raymond was, nevertheless, a fabulous captain to play under, and while he came in for his fair share of the inevitable dressing-room micky-taking, he had this amazing knack of being able to switch us all on to serious business at a moment's notice. We'd be having a laugh and a joke, sometimes at his expense, and then the five minute bell would go. Illy would clap his hands, the place would fall silent and he would unveil some masterly tactical plan for the next session. Unfortunately, not every member of his team possessed his attention to detail, and there was one occasion at Taunton when one of Raymond's brainwaves did not quite go according to the script. Viv Richards was in his pomp at that time, and having faced just one delivery before the lunch break, inevitably walked off 4 not out. He looked, we thought, ominously in the mood. However, Illy had worked out that he was not entirely in control of the hook shot early in an innings, and that the ball occasionally went in the air to what would roughly be just backward of square. Raymond sat plotting over his lunch, and decided that Paddy Clift should field at fine leg, but move surreptitiously to backward square for Les Taylor's fourth ball after lunch. This, of course, would be a bouncer. Unfortunately, Les slipped in a no-ball, Paddy's mathematics got a bit confused, and when Viv did precisely what Illy had thought he might, there was no Paddy Clift. And Viv went on to get his hundred.

Illy was also a highly canny bowler. For instance, if Jack Birkenshaw was bowling you knew it was a totally flat wicket, whereas if Illy was on you knew it was either turning square or it was the last over before lunch. The latter case backfired on him quite badly in a match against Sussex, when he duly appeared for his ritual 1-1-0-0 but came off the field, wearing a slightly bewildered expression, with something closer to 1-0-22-0. The batsman in question was Javed Miandad with whom, it later transpired, Raymond had had an altercation a year or so previously, and called him something fairly unpleasant. Raymond had long since forgotten this, but Javed had not, so we spent a rib-clutching five minutes before lunch watching Javed charging down the pitch, and Illy peering – with a completely bemused expression – at one ball after another vanishing over the sightscreen. Getting hit for six did not amuse Illy at the best of times, and whenever teams came to Leicester in those days, they generally required a pair of binoculars to make out the boundary rope – except, that is, for the bigger games, when the sponsors (this is pre-executive box era) would pitch tents on the outfield, hence, shorter boundaries. Raymond used to play hell about this, and in one Sunday League match the sight of two consecutive deliveries dropping into the coleslaw in the Bostik guests' tent proved too much for him. For the next couple of minutes spectators were treated to the fairly unusual sight of the Leicestershire captain waving his fist at the committee balcony and giving them a fearful haranguing. Even so, I think he managed to drag himself into the tent for a sponsored Pimms or two afterwards.

I think it's fair to say that when misfortune struck, Raymond was not so quick to see the funny side of it, but the old boy was not without a sharp turn of repartee on occasions. Leicestershire did not have a strict dress code for players in those days, but they worked roughly on the basis of smart casuals. No tie and jacket required, but a reasonable appearance was demanded. I slightly tarnished my record one day at Trent Bridge when I woke up in my customary bleary-eyed state in the flat at Leicester and groped around in semi-darkness for a pair of shoes. What I had put on was one black shoe, and one brown. This didn't go un-noticed by the captain, and there then followed a longish lecture on the standards of dress expected from young professionals. I can't remember the exact words, but 'smarten up you scruffy sod' was the basic message.

I fancied there might be some mileage in this lecture, so, having recently acquired a dark blue dinner suit, I took it with me to our next match in Taunton. In the relaxed atmosphere of breakfast before a Sunday League game I strode into the dining room. Suit, bow-tie, polished shoes (both black), the works. Raymond glanced up from his plate, gave me the once over, and said: 'Bloody hell, Gower . Have you just come in?' Whether he meant this as a joke, or whether he was being serious, I'm not totally sure. You rarely could tell with Raymond. We got on very well, and he did try to nurture me through, as did most of the senior players, the likes of Davison, Dudleston, Tolchard, Steele and Micky Norman. They were a good crew to be with, and we also happened to be a very good side, and all this worked in my favour in those early days.

Those first three or four years under Illy were as good a grounding as a young player could have, and I made the transition from an averagely talented player to a slightly better than average player with a decent idea of what professional cricket is all about. It was certainly different from what I had imagined it would be like, and there were one or two instances of the talented but wet-behind-the-ears-public-schoolboy running into a bit of hostility from the hardened pro trying to make a living on a demanding circuit. I remember opening the innings in a championship game against Surrey at the Oval and timing a few cover drives early on against the new ball, which appeared to draw a fair amount of steam from Robin Jackman's ears. He has always been a bit volatile, and the sight of this angelic looking youngster creaming him around the Oval with no apparent effort did not do a lot for his sense of humour. He wanted to know, in fairly blunt terms, whether I was interested in playing the game properly. This did enough to unsettle me and I was lbw not long afterwards. It's the sort of thing a batsman eventually comes to terms with, and occasionally learns to enjoy, but it was all rather new to me at that time and I didn't quite know how to keep my concentration in the face of it. In a nutshell, I was beginning to learn that county cricket was a job as opposed to a recreation.

There were also, contrary to popular opinion, one or two recorded cases of nerves. Before scoring that 89 not out against the West Indies, I remember downing a scotch in the pub next to the ground in the company of the landlady – Roberts and Daniel were sharing the new ball, so it seemed appropriate to try and settle the stomach. Hazel was her name, loved by all, and the place was never quite the same when the brewery moved her on. I did a certain amount of hopping around during that knock. The old duck-hook came out several times – the sort you play when you start going for the hook and end up having to bail out in a hurry when you realize that the ball is homing in on the eyebrows rather more rapidly than anticipated. Chris Balderstone got 125 and 98, which got him into the Test side. As for myself, I was starting to get a few honourable mentions in more influential organs than the *Loughborough Echo* (proud though I was of earlier cuttings snipped from that paper), although mention of me in connection with the England side did not really begin to build up until the following year, 1977.

I overheard Illy voicing his opinion around the dressing room that I would be playing for England within the next couple of years, and coming from him I thought that was as good a recommendation as you could get. In subsequent years, when he appeared to be recommending sons-in-law and prospective sons-in-law for the captaincy of Yorkshire, England, and the Universe, I would have questioned his judgement a touch more than I did then, but at the time it was a pretty impressive reference. By the end of that summer, there had been enough speculation from other quarters to make me wonder, even anxious, about that winter's tour to Pakistan and New Zealand. Ian Botham was now in the side and it seemed to be a question of whether someone like Mike Gatting or myself might make the squad as a young batsman, taken along to gain some experience. As it turned out, Gatt made it and I didn't. I was disappointed because I had actually become quite excited about the speculation, but it soon wore off and I was happy to make yet another Derrick Robins' tour, this time to the Far East. I developed my friendship with Chris Cowdrey out there, behaved pretty poorly, but also got in some decent cricket in Malaysia, Hong Kong, Singapore and Sri Lanka. From there it was a short hop to Perth where I played club cricket for the remainder of the winter, with a fair amount of success, and did well enough in the early summer of 1978 (one of the few years I've started off a season in good form) to get myself into the England side for the one-dayers against Pakistan. I scored a century in the second of the two matches, and was then selected for the first Test at Birmingham. So I had already had the settling effect of having played at international level when I made my Test debut, and although hitting your first ball for four would have to rank as a reasonable way to launch a career, the Pakistani attack at that time could hardly be equated with that of the West Indies when G. Hick arrived at the wicket in 1991.

Imran wasn't playing, barred through Kerry Packer, and had he delivered the same ball on the same length as dear old Liaquat Ali, or Liquid as we came to know him, they might have been picking bits of me out of the fence as opposed to the ball. Mind you, I might not have been quite so keen to unveil the pull shot first ball against an Imran or an Andy Roberts. I might have been young, but I had learned a few of the facts of life by now. I did actually wonder to myself at the time whether I should have played the shot, even against Liquid. First ball, first Test, probably not the done thing, and if it had gone straight up in the air it might have caused a bit of a stir – Brian Johnston choking to death on his chocolate cake I shouldn't wonder. But as I remember, it was just an instinctive shot to a bad

61

ball. Eventually I did hit one straight up in the air, having made fifty-odd, relaxed a little and did something silly when a century was there for the taking. Some might say 'So what's new?'

Whenever I have made fifty in my career, I've invariably said to myself, 'Okay, head down, let's get fifty more.' The trouble is, I've always had to work to say it. It's a failing, simple as that. I have to fight to stave off the feeling of: 'Oh yes, I've hit a few good shots today, that'll keep me happy,' as opposed to having the blinding determination to plough remorselessly on. Sometimes when I get a little bit too relaxed, a bad shot that I get away with might snap me back into it, but contrary to a certain amount of public opinion I am always fighting a battle with the little man up there in my head. I believe that it is all part of the character: some parts may be good, others not so good. Some people have the capacity to put a padlock on the brain and throw away the key – mine likes to go for a wander. More often than not, I don't like it any more than an exasperated spectator, or selector, but no-one is entirely free of weaknesses, and this happens to be one of mine.

The philosophy I've tried to live by is to retain a sense of enjoyment in what is a sport as well as my livelihood. If you can be successful by asserting your own character rather than someone else's, that to me is the ultimate in personal satisfaction. Sure, I've fouled up many times, but it would be a tedious old game if we all came out of a factory would it not? At the same time, there is a lot of satisfaction in succeeding almost against your own character – such as grinding it out when you are itching to give it a go – but it's not something I have managed all that often. I was annoyed with myself for getting out in that first Test innings because I realized that I had missed out on the chance for a really big one. But, character failing or not, I wasn't going to sit around all day moping about it.

What I envy any new Test player is the feeling you get before your first game. It's an event just to walk into the dressing room for the first time, where there might be one or two players you have never even met before. Just looking at the team sheet gives you a buzz – Brearley, Wood, Radley, Gower ... it's a big thrill just to see it pinned up there. There is a special feeling about a Test match dressing room for the first time, a sense of anticipation and excitement that is beyond anything I'd had before, and corny though it sounds, the blood does start pumping a little harder through the system. And then, once you have played for your country, it gives you a billing to live up to when you return for a county match, and maybe puts a bit more pressure on you as well. As a young up and coming potential England player you are allowed to make the odd mistake, but as an actual England player you've got less leeway in terms of how other people see you. A lot more, for instance, was expected of someone like Mark Ramprakash after he had played relatively well in his first Test series against the West Indies.

Cricketers, by and large, are a very supportive lot, but some pros look at their colleagues and opponents with fairly critical and sometimes jaundiced eyes. This is especially true if it concerns the solid county cricketer who is never going to play for England casting his eye over the fresh-faced youngster who has just won his first cap. When Sachin Tendulkar, at seventeen, scored a century at Old Trafford to save India from defeat against England in the summer of 1990, one English player said, 'Let's see how he goes at the Oval when the ball will be up around his nostrils.' It's the traditional English reaction to someone doing well.

I averaged 51 against Pakistan and 57 against the New Zealanders later that summer, but if a lot more was expected of myself at Leicestershire after I had made it into the Test side, the bare statistics of 1978 do not suggest that they were fulfilled to any great degree. Nine games, 15 innings, one not out, 347 runs, top score 61, average 24.78, and in the county game against Pakistan I was bowled by Liaquat for not very many. In a season like that, with six Tests and four one-day internationals, you end up by playing barely any cricket at all for your county, and given the poor scores I made when I did, it was probably fair to say that I batted for England and fielded for Leicestershire. My county average has always been significantly lower than my Test average, and as such it is hardly surprising that the odd grumble from the ranks of the county membership has come my way. The bigger the occasion the better I seem to perform. Yet overall, I was definitely on a high at that stage in my career, and my form for England at least was good enough to win me a place on my first overseas tour that winter. It was a memorable tour both for me – a century at Perth and a decent amount of runs overall – and for the team itself, although a 5-1 victory in the series had a lot to do with an Australian side seriously depleted by the absence of the rebels playing for Packer.

The 1978-79 tour to Australia was as one-sided as the final score suggests, but Australia felt the player-drain to Packer more acutely than we did. Both the Chappells, Dennis Lillee and Rod Marsh were signed up by World Series Cricket, and while they had some talented younger players to call upon – Kim Hughes and Rodney Hogg, for example – the key difference between the two sides was experience. To some extent, the Australian system allows their players to scale the jumps from grade to state to Test cricket a shade more easily than our own, but a good, inexperienced team will rarely beat a good experienced one and 5-1 was an accurate reflection of our dominance. Having said that, Hogg, in short spells, was as quick and mean a bowler as any I have faced, and he also had the temperament to match. When I was leaving the field with a century to my name in Perth, the fact that I had edged and missed a few against him early on had clearly been festering with him, and he came up and called me an 'effing imposter'. It didn't bother me though. As with most Australians it was nothing personal, merely business. Hogg was capable of some curious moods, and after bowling three or four lightening overs on a flattish track at Adelaide he suddenly ran off the field. His captain, Graham Yallop, was as confused as everyone else, and had to run off the field himself to find out what was going on. It turned out that Hogg was claiming he had been attacked by a bout of asthma, but no one really understood why he decided to vanish when he was bowling so well. His method was to bowl flat out for short spells, take a breather, then come back for another burst of the high velocity stuff. Hogg took a lot of wickets in that series, but in all other respects there was no contest. Even the captaincy – Brearley versus Yallop – was one-sided. Brears was baited by the Aussie crowds, who clearly thought he was as stuffy a Pom as Jardine, but as a skipper, he had a very hard core to him.

When we came back to Australia the following winter for a post-Packer three Test series, both Ian Botham and myself were more experienced, Alan Knott and Derek Underwood were back from their World Series spells, and all in all we thought we had a pretty good side. Perhaps Lord's thought otherwise, as they declined to put up the Ashes for a shortened series, and if so, they were right. We were absolutely hammered. Even though Australia had recovered some influential players from Packer – the two Chappells, Lillee and Marsh – I was not at all prepared for the stuffing they gave us. It was also a pretty average series for me with the bat, and the only time I got runs was in the second innings of the Sydney Test with 98 not out. Rain had delayed the start, and the cricked neck that Boycott had been complaining of did not get any better when he saw how damp the pitch was. In the end, we railroaded him into playing. It was not a good toss to lose (we were bowled out for 123) and with my 98 the only English innings over 50, we lost comprehensively. While I might have top-scored, Derek Underwood made the best individual innings – he was hit all over the body during the course of an heroic 43. The Aussies are not easily impressed by the opposition, but on this occasion they applauded 'Deadly' all the way off the field.

Lillee bowled exceptionally well in that series, and of all the great fast bowlers I have faced – Roberts, Holding, Hadlee, Marshall – I would have to place him as the best. He no longer had the blistering pace of his early years, but he was a better bowler. Given the combination of his natural talent and a ferociously competitive nature, he was as complete a fast bowler as there can ever have been. Dennis, like most Australian cricketers, was never short of the odd word, but what I particularly liked about the guys of that era – the Chappells, Marsh, Thomson, etc. – was that what happened on the field mattered not a jot off it. You could be smacked in the ribs at five minutes to six, and at five past the first two people into the dressing room to apply a cold beer to the bruise (plus a few more internally) would be Lillee and Marsh. In terms of the Test batsman versus Test bowler contest, Dennis and myself formed something of a mutual admiration society, and I'm very proud of that. It is always nice to have earned the professional respect of an opponent you yourself regard as one of the best to have ever played the game.

Rodney Marsh was a similar sort of character to Lillee, and was an integral part of the Australian brains trust on the field. Rodney always worked very closely in harness with his bowlers, and he was forever giving hand signals to them when he thought the time was ripe for a short one, a yorker, or whatever. Occasionally you would catch him at it with a sneaky glance behind, as I did one day at

Sydney. He was signalling for the next one to be up around the nostrils and when he realized that I had spotted him, we both broke into broad smiles. I don't think the bowler obliged on that occasion, but it scarcely mattered. The bouncer was never far away when you were facing those guys.

I suppose Marsh, Lillee and the Chappells formed something of a mafia, and if players fell out with them, life became very hard work. When Kim Hughes became captain they made it very clear that they thought he had come too far too soon, and Hughes never got their full support. Somehow he never commanded the respect he needed to be the Australian captain. I always quite liked him and found him easy to talk to, and could sympathize with his predicament. But he could be a pretty opinionated bloke and perhaps this is the reason why he seemed to rub so many people up the wrong way. Marsh and Lillee earned a certain amount of notoriety, of course, for betting against their team in the Headingley Test of 1981, although those two would have a punt on the Martians landing if they had got odds of 500/1. They've had a few bets on horses that barely answered to the description, although as the English team at the time bore more resemblance to a donkey than a racehorse, they could scarcely have imagined that they would collect.

Despite the supposedly deadly rivalry that characterizes England versus Australia games, it is still possible to respect your enemy and, believe it or not, make good friends in the process! One example of unexpected cooperation came during the 1980 season. I had been dropped from the England side against the West Indies and, thinking of my future welfare, Fred Rumsey contacted Greg Chappell while the Australians were playing their county games in preparation for the Lord's Centenary Test and arranged for him to have dinner with me. The resultant chat was full of good advice from an experienced and respected opponent, and both of us were able to judge its worth in as much as I returned to the England fold for that Lord's Test. Greg had a hard, abrasive edge on the field, as did his brother, although Ian was always more aggressive. I got on pretty well with Ian as well, and I recall also having a long chat with him over a few beers at the end of one day's play in the 1979 Sydney Test, so much so that we were the last two players to leave the ground. The Chappells were always good company and I liked them both.

The chat I had with Greg over the dinner table in 1980 did not mean that I had my greatest series ever against Australia the following year, although I did survive long enough to take part in that memorable Test at Headingley, the scene of one of Ian Botham's greater triumphs. As most people know, we had booked out of our hotel on the Monday morning, but what most may not know is that we had spent the Saturday night at Ian's house at Epworth attempting to forget a dreadful three days with an enormous barbecue and, as is usually the case when Ian is entertaining, enormous amounts to drink. When 'Both' went out to bat on Monday, the old cliché about going out there to enjoy it certainly applied. The shackles of captaincy had gone, and we were in such a hopeless position that he had nothing to lose. Brears issued him with instructions, which he would have totally ignored, and the rest we know about. He had a certain amount of good fortune, and in all honesty I believe his innings at Old Trafford was much better. However, it is still one of the most amazing Test innings that can have ever been played. That series has gone down as Botham's Ashes, and rightly so, as without him we would certainly have lost it.

Ian has this amazing belief in himself, which intimidates the opposition and allows him to get away with things that no one else possibly could. Even when he gets a wicket with a long-hop (and there have been quite a few of those) he almost convinces the batsman that he has been the victim of some masterly strategy. 'Both' is the sort of bloke who needs people around him (even on those tours when he avoided the media by locking himself in his room, there was a constant stream of friends and team-mates going in and out), and he is the kind of character who naturally attracts company. He enjoys the spotlight, and the glamour of being associated with famous names from other walks of life such as Elton John and Eric Clapton. But he has extreme mood-swings and tends to forget the more pleasant spin-offs of being well-known when he finds himself in company he doesn't like. He has an amazing amount of energy, and an equally amazing constitution, with methods of relaxation that have earned him almost as many column inches and headlines as cricket. He invariably sees things in black and white, never shades of grey, and has a tendency to speak his mind without giving too much thought to the immediate consequences. Even when he goes fishing, usually up in Scotland, he does not go in for the solitary routine of many anglers. He will try to make sure that he has a few mates with him – Allan Lamb is one of his frequent companions – and enough scotch to make sure that he has trouble saying piscatorial when he puts the rod away. When Ian is his normal, sociable mood, he is someone I like a lot.

Looking back on those days, there were some hard battles and it was one of the most testing periods of my career. Those names – the Chappells, Marsh, Lillee, Thomson, Botham – all give an indication to the high standard of world cricket then, for these are the great names. During that period from 1979 to 1982 I was going through a process of consolidation. There were some notable highlights, such as the 200 not out against India in 1979. My early season form that year had been dreadful, but the selectors kept faith in me after a good tour of Australia (which can't be said of more recent times) and I looked for a change by moving on to a new bat, new pads and new gloves. It seemed to work, and though I had never got close to scoring 200 before, by the end of that knock I started to wonder why I hadn't done so before – mind you, the fact that I have not done it too often since is a reminder that these things do not come easily.

Form comes and goes all too quickly and, after a good knock at Lord's of 82, I began a sequence of indifferent scores, so that the selectors eventually had to say take a break after the first Test against the West Indies in 1980. I came back for the Centenary Test against Australia at Lord's a lot more confident, and I revelled in the atmosphere. My first innings knock of 45 felt great and falls into the category of those that might and should have been more productive. For a while, taking successive boundaries off Dennis Lillee, I felt as though nothing could go wrong. I also became the first man in Test cricket to score five by hitting the fielder's helmet that had been placed behind Rod Marsh, who had been wrong-footed by an inside edge off Lillee.

On the subsequent tour of the West Indies, I felt I had played some of my best cricket, including a fifty in the second innings of the Barbados Test, but without making the substantial scores that might have been possible. I had a nasty tendency to get out whenever rain fell or was about to fall, until the last Test of the series in Jamaica when I got the hundred I had been looking for, and which I still remember as one of my proudest moments. These were interesting and educative years, and one thought that briefly crossed my mind then, and often later in my career, was that perhaps I would have been better off born an Australian and therefore playing a lot more of my cricket there. Quite apart from the fact that it is a country that suits my lifestyle (I think I could get tired of sun, surf and oyster beds given time, but I haven't yet), it has rarely let me down in cricketing terms either. The surfaces are generally truer, and their own domestic cricket is a long way removed from the commando assault course that ours has become. The system in England has much to commend it if you have a blood line back to the Marquis de Sade, and I am far from the only English professional who has said, at some point during a summer, 'Oh no, not other game of cricket.' It doesn't matter whether you are a batsman or a bowler, our cricket is so concentrated that it must strain your energy and enthusiasm. There are always exceptions of course, and Graham Gooch is undoubtedly one of them. If, having spent all of some biting windswept day shivering in the slips watching some bloke blocking for a draw on a dead pitch, you fail to turn half a dozen cartwheels at the end of it, he is genuinely puzzled – and it was the lack of enthusiasm he perceived, or thought he perceived, in me, that led to my exile after the Australian tour in 1990-91.

I can't deny that my own boredom threshold is not impressive, and I recall one day at Grace Road during my second spell of captaincy with Leicestershire when I aggravated a group of members. I got very annoyed with myself for getting out on a flat pitch – and anyone who thinks I do not have an explosive side should ask one or two colleagues in the dressing room well practiced in the art of diving out of the way of the flying Gray-Nicolls – and was smarting at the prospect of having only a balcony view of what was a dip-your-bread exercise against undemanding bowling. Sussex, for some reason, did not have a twelfth man, and when one was needed I nipped on to field for them myself. Some of the members, not unnaturally I suppose, wanted to know what their captain was doing standing in the slips and swapping a few jokes with the opposition wicketkeeper Ian Gould. It was a purely instinctive thing, as is so much of my cricket, and in actual fact was geared more towards staying keen and alert than an attempt to display any thought that county cricket really wasn't too important.

One of the things I have failed to master is how much store is set by outward appearance, and I often wonder whether people's views of my motivation, or lack of it, might have been different if I'd been able to look as wound up and fraught as I have often felt inside. Many cricketers are not good watchers. There are those you will see on the balcony scarcely taking their eyes off the cricket, but others you will rarely see unless they are padded up and getting acquainted with the light. They'll be inside, fast asleep, plugged into a Walkman, doing the crossword, signing autograph sheets, you name it. It doesn't follow that those who watch closest are any more committed to the team than those snoring gently in a darkened corner. Very few spectators stay glued rigidly to their seats all day, they like to pop into the bar for half an hour, or read a book if some blocker is boring the pants off them. The same applies, I've noticed (when the whims of the selectors have led me to pursue the game through the pen rather than the bat) inside the press box. Switching off from time-to-time is not only the norm, but considered more or less essential to the preservation of sanity.

What I find really irksome is the intimation, and I certainly got this impression from chatting to Gooch during the last tour to Australia, that I don't have that much love for the game. Sure there are days when a wave of ennui washes over me, but I've never lost the basic umbilical cord for cricket that has been with me from a very early age. Like most people, I had my boyhood heroes and not unnaturally they were largely left-handed batsmen: Sobers, Pollock, Edrich and the like. There are certain aspects of the game I may not like, as with us all, but cricket has been just about my only way of life, and a highly pleasurable one too.

The first rung on the ladder towards the England captaincy arrived in the summer of 1982, when I was appointed as Bob Willis's deputy for the tour to Australia after leading the side in one Test that year at Lord's against Pakistan, when Willis withdrew with a stiff neck. It was not, however, an auspicious start: Paul Allott and Ian Greig were making their debuts, but we did not have a lot of variety in the attack, and because Mohsin Khan was so strong off his legs, I thought it might be a good idea if our bowlers concentrated on a line just outside his off stump. This plan worked so well that Mohsin was tempted to go for one or two rash shots on the offside, and he kept smashing it through the covers for four, which was a trifle disappointing. Eventually Chris Tavaré came up to me and said, 'I think we've seen enough of his weakness, why don't we try bowling to his strength?' So we did, and got him out caught at square leg for a modest 200. We lost by ten wickets, but I didn't get much stick in the press – no Gower's Goons in those days – and in fact I think I got the sympathy vote for being slung in at the deep end.

What the reporters didn't know was that we probably lost the game on the fourth evening in a French restaurant in St John's Wood. Needing one run to avoid the follow-on, and the No 11 – Robin Jackman – at the crease on 0, Gower, Lamb and Jackman all trooped off for some French cuisine with their respective partners, and not being a superstitious sort of a trio, we all plumped for the breast of canard. Duck. Next morning, first ball – a big inswinging yorker from Imran, Jackman lbw 0. There then followed a stirring speech from the acting captain – Agincourt, the whole bit – and about an hour later we were 50 for 5. All five to Mudassar, including Lamb 0, Gower 0. I'm slightly more superstitious now than I was then.

CHAPTER SEVEN

The officers' mess

*A*s we saw very early on in Mike Atherton's Test career, and in the case of John Crawley while he was not even getting regular cricket in Lancashire's side, spot the future England captain becomes a popular game in the sporting press before the player has actually done anything very much. It was that sort of thing with me. I had previously skippered the Young England side, but up until then my only real experience of the job had been at King's, not in itself much of a reference. At school, they simply hand the captaincy to the best player, and tactical genius was not a basic requirement. As I could bat, and was able to differentiate between heads and tails, the job was mine. In a way there is a slight similarity, in that if you become an above-average player quickly, in other words start playing for England at twenty-one, you begin to be considered in terms of graduation to the officers' mess. I don't know exactly when it started, but I didn't take it too seriously, partly because superstition dictates that the minute you start to think about something it will never happen, and not least because I'd already taken on board the old maxim about never believing everything you read in the newspapers.

However, it was less of a surprise when I was eventually handed the L plates for Willis's tour, and it meant leading the side in a few of the state games in Australia while Bob was taking a breather. I had not received any official advice on the job, although I did have an informal chat about it with Robin Jackman in the bar of the hotel casino at Launceston. I can't remember quite why we were there, but it must have been either a rest day or one of those typical

Tasmanian days where a combination of wind, rain, hail and sleet has stopped play. Anyway, Jackman's advice was pretty straight-forward. Don't try to be Willis, or Brearley, or Fletcher – just be yourself.

I don't think he was worried that I might turn into a rampant disciplinarian, and rush around ordering extra nets and marathons before breakfast, but he may have thought it wise to check. Another piece of advice he gave me was to accept that you are bound to get things wrong from time to time – stick a side in on a flat one, choose to bat first on a green 'un, and bowl everyone from the wrong end. Jackers was nothing if not far-sighted. In the end, I didn't have too much to do on that tour. Willis was a fairly forthright sort of character who liked to take charge, and was a deeper and more committed thinker about the game than some have thought.

You would have thought that I would have picked up some of the arts of captaincy by playing under the likes of Illingworth and Brearley, but in all honesty I think I was more concerned with just playing in those early years. I wasn't taking notes on the nuances and finer points of the game, so in a sense some of the good work that might have been done was wasted. However, you do pick up a certain amount instinctively, and of course you do talk about things, both on the field and back in the dressing room.

I had always looked up to Brearley, my first international captain, and essentially I just assumed he would be doing the right thing, which most of the time he probably was. He always seemed to be aware of batsmen's weaknesses and would play to them accordingly. I can only assume that when we got hammered by Australia in 1979-80 their batsman must have been right out of weaknesses – or more accurately, I suppose, Greg Chappell found ours easier to spot. Someone like Ian Botham was an instinctive captain rather than a cunning one, with a healthy and admirable streak of optimism that all would be right on the day, and that if it wasn't he would personally rectify the situation on our behalf. Eventually, that wasn't good enough and Botham went back to solo feats of heroism with Brearley taking over the strings again. In a series like that of 1981, even Brearley must have thought his luck was in when 'Both' played so well – there is a limit to how inspirational a captain can be, and while Ian certainly respected Mike and worked well under him, it struck me that while 'Both' was in that sort of form anyone could have captained the side.

The likes of Fletcher and Gatting maintained a good understanding with their players. There is always a change in your attitude towards a captain as one gets more senior. For instance, I had great respect for Fletcher's abilities as a captain and appreciated his knowledge of the game. By the time Gatting took over, I had already had my own crack at the job, and so was naturally more critical of every little move. This is a long way from saying that Mike was doing things wrong, only differently, and he was becoming a very fine leader of England when disasters struck.

On the 1982-83 tour to Australia I was, however, not thinking of disaster and had, in fact, my most productive tour with personal success helping to make up for the team's failure to draw level in the Ashes series or to make the final of the World Series Cup. Although we went down 2-1, the side made a comeback at Melbourne, hanging on to win by three runs in one of the most nerve-racking Tests I have ever played in, Geoff Miller catching a rebound out of Chris Tavaré's hands to win the game. My batting on this tour for once achieved a reasonable consistency, which continued into the one-day games. My one Test hundred of the series, attempting to save the game at Adelaide, was followed by three hundreds against the Kiwis in these limited overs internationals, one of which took us to a record score in 50-overs cricket, a record which lasted all of four hours until the Kiwis won the game. My 158 at Brisbane was the only century large enough to help beat New Zealand, and it was one of those all too rare days when everything, but everything, went right and it seemed as though my bat only had a middle. At times like that you only wish that you could bottle the formula that leads you to such success, but human nature is such that you can only be grateful for the memories of the day. I cannot even begin to recreate the circumstances or mental preparation that led to that innings – perhaps even to remember what I had for breakfast might be a start, to see if there was a natural substance in Queensland fruit that aids batting.

Having failed to qualify for the finals, we took what can be described as a not very well earned but nevertheless welcome rest, and while most of the boys decided to stay and enjoy Sydney again,

I took myself off to Hayman Island to have a look at the Great Barrier Reef. This is what I call making the most of disappointment, because while I was up there I learned to scuba-dive and thus swim with the fish off the reef. I can almost say that I was glad we hadn't made it to the finals.

I had a good series against New Zealand the following summer after getting out cheaply to Hadlee both times in the opening Test, scoring back to back centuries at Headingley and Lord's and making 70-odd in the final match at Trent Bridge where we clinched the series 3-1. I was vice-captain again for the following winter's tours to New Zealand and Pakistan, which was almost exclusively under Warwickshire management – Willis, A.C. Smith, Norman Gifford, and Bernie Thomas, the physio. It is not generally recognized in this country perhaps, but New Zealand can be quite a testing tour. Partially in trying to stay awake – there's the old joke about arriving there and finding it closed – but also because there is a lot of travelling, and beautiful though the country is, it would be stretching it to say the same about their cricket grounds. New Plymouth is as picturesque a place for playing cricket as anywhere in the world, but the Test grounds are mostly rugby stadiums, specially sited for the wind-tunnel effect. It can be very hot, and it can also be bloody perishing. Dunedin, for example, is where Captain Scott had his final net practice, and I wouldn't be surprised if he shot most of the huskies before he even set off for Antarctica. There are also one or two local hazards, otherwise known as umpires. It's more or less the same for both teams, but when the MCC sent New Zealand their original copy of the laws, they must have left out the page stipulating lbw as one of the modes of dismissal. The reason there are so many draws in New Zealand is that you have to take about 17 wickets per innings to get a side out.

That particular tour was more exciting than most, albeit not for anything that took place on the field of play. It was, I suppose, the prototype for the Sex, Drugs and Rock n' Roll stories that the cricket press (or to be more accurate the news reporters now more or less permanently attached to the England team) have grown so fond of. The tour went downhill from the very first evening, with a curious case of mistaken identity involving Willis, Botham and Lamb. Now you may find it hard to believe that a hotel bar in New Zealand can contain three characters bearing a passable resemblance to that trio, but I can assure you that on this occasion there was, and we subsequently got to know these guys very well. Anyway, Willis, Botham and Lamb had a longish session in the bar, but did in fact go to bed early that evening. This wasn't always the case, I grant you, but that night they did. However, the three lookalikes were a good bit later, and a day or two after there was a lurid account in the press that three of England's finest cricketers had a riotous evening in the bar at the Sheraton Hotel in Auckland. It was rightly denied by the three involved, and we later found out that although there had indeed been some poorish behaviour that night, it had actually come from these three other guys, who were up in Auckland from Wellington on business.

It was an unfortunate start to say the least and turned out to be an ominous portent of things to come. As I say, we got to know the three from Wellington fairly well, and on closer acquaintance it became clear that they were not averse to a good time. When we got to Wellington, one of them held a party for us at his house somewhere in the suburbs, and with not a lot on the cricketing agenda the next day, it turned out to be quite an interesting evening. It also co-incided with A.C.'s birthday, so we invited him along with the rest of the management. A cake had been baked to mark the occasion. Nothing much in that, you might think, although it would be erroneous to say that there was nothing much in the cake. Some of the ingredients, I have to say, would not have been in the Delia Smith cookbook, and although A.C. – with all his diplomatic experience – managed to avoid having a slice of it, one or two of the players decided that it would be impolite to refuse. I'll say no more, other than to mention that the revolving eyeball count was fairly high – high being the operative word. Talking of A.C.'s diplomacy, he was the manager on the tour of the West Indies in 1980-81 and responsible at a press conference for the following line: 'If I have to say anything, which I don't, my only comment would be "No comment", but don't quote me.'

It was a fairly harmless evening, and with the press failing to get wind of it, all that was written about in Wellington, where we gave a pretty good account of ourselves in a drawn first Test, was the cricket. The second Test in Christchurch, however, was a long way from being England's finest hour, where we managed to lose by an innings and plenty in a shade under twelve hours playing time. Having looked at the pitch we thought it might be an interesting game and, having put the Kiwis in, one delivery in Willis's opening over hit a crack only just short of a length and cleared John Wright's head by some margin. It became immediately clear that 300 runs might be a good aggregate for the entire game never mind the New Zealand innings, and when they got that many we were struggling. They gave it a slog, and Hadlee thrashed us all over the place for 99. We then batted like complete drains, Gatting top scoring in the first innings with 19, and Randall in the second with 25. I remember padding up to a ball from Hadlee that was so straight it had to be lbw even in New Zealand. I was so upset that I was then done for driving the car through a red light on the way back to the hotel. The policeman was very polite and asked me if I knew what I had done wrong. 'Left a straight one from Hadlee,' did not seem to be the answer he was looking for, but he kindly let me off with a caution.

Although we lost, as I say, in less than twelve hours, the game itself spanned the best part of three days because of the weather, and it was what we were allegedly doing while waiting for the rain to stop that formed the basis of the next attack by the press. Part of the reason for this ridiculously poor performance, according to the newspapers, was that far from psyching ourselves up in the dressing room while it was raining, we had in fact closed all the doors, stuffed all the cracks with wet towels, and were puffing away on substances that were not be found on sale at your average tobacconists. It was also suggested that the captain's positioning of Lamb at third man had less to do with his fielding prowess in that area, than its proximity to the boundary enabling him to take possession of packets of white powder – for distribution, can you believe, to players on the field. Investigative journalism can be very imaginative at times. It did not surprise us that the press found it impossible to believe that a team could be playing as badly as we were without some kind of sinister reason, but some of the stories were so absurd that we were falling about laughing.

However, we were now unable to shake off the tag of debauched playboys with a taste for illegal substances, and after drawing the final Test in Auckland, things took another turn for the worse. We were all invited to an Elton John concert, and thence back to the Sheraton – where Elton had taken over the entire top floor – for a party. It was a fairly lively do, topped off by 'Foxy' Fowler (who has a better head for heights than he has for alcohol) giving us his Spiderman impression outside one of the windows. Nothing outrageous happened, not in my presence anyhow, but everything was fair game for the press now, and they went to town on pot-smoking, women in rooms, drinking things that wouldn't be found in the standard off-licence, etc. So as we flew out of the country to Pakistan for the next stage of the tour, the management gave us a coaching clinic on what to expect from the press when we got there. Basically, don't even stand in a hotel lobby chatting next to a plant pot, because there would probably be a tape recorder in it. When we got to Lahore we bumped into press men we had never heard of or seen before, sent there purely to dredge up anything they could on the team, and it led to the bizarre situation in which we were told not to talk to anyone – careless talk costs lives, that sort of stuff.

It was the first instance any of us had experienced of this kind of news reporter being attached to a cricket tour. After that it became almost common practice. Even when the newspapers did not send their own men, they hired local journalists from whichever country we were in, and there was one rather amusing incident early on Mike Gatting's tour to Australia in 1986-87. There we were three weeks into the tour, and not a scandal in sight (unless you included our batting in that). However, Lamb and Wilf Slack were working out in the hotel gymnasium in Brisbane when they were engaged in conversation by two Australians. Lamb, with South African accent, and West Indian born Slack, were not as obviously identifiable as English cricketers as, say, me and Botham, and when Lamb asked them whether they were in the hotel on business, one of them replied, 'Nah, mate, we're journos. Here to dig some dirt on this Pommy cricket team. If you hear of anything we'll make it worth your while ...' Exit Lamb and Slack.

Likewise, when we were in Pakistan, it was difficult for the players to identify a tourist from a journalist, especially in places like the Lahore Hilton and the Holiday Inn, Karachi. Faisalabad was a little easier, as there are not so many tourists there (we even had our food transported from Lahore during the Test) but suspicion was generally the order of the day. At the same time we were signing more affidavits than we were autographs, mostly for Botham's solicitor. In the course of this, we were also required to play some cricket, so perhaps it was no great surprise when we lost the first Test in Karachi. It was a good game. I got a couple of fifties, and although they wanted only 60-odd to win in their second innings, they lost seven wickets getting there.

We drew the other two Tests to lose the series 1-0, but on a personal level it was a very good series. I made two scores of over 150 in those games, and also captained the side when Willis went down (and eventually home) with a mystery illness. I think it was diagnosed as hepatitis in the end. Botham didn't survive either. He flew home to have a knee operation, during the course of which he made life a good bit easier for those still there by describing Pakistan as a good place to send your mother-in-law. (I should point out, by the way, that Jan – the mother-in-law in question – is a delightful lady, a big supporter of Ian's, and, like a White Horse, can be taken anywhere.) The Pakistani parliament actually met to discuss this insult, and they took it so badly in Lahore that it struck home in the culinary department. Our food at the ground was brought to the ground and cooked there by the staff at the Hilton, but they withdrew the service in protest. We were down to toast and baked beans at one stage, with Bernard Thomas as head chef.

So we weren't the most popular side to tour Pakistan, and it took a good deal of diplomatic effort to keep the thing on a relatively even keel. For all that, we came reasonably close to forcing a victory in the last Test after setting them a gettable target, and we left Pakistan on a high note. The sex and drugs thing smouldered on when we got home, but by and large it centred on Both's alleged pot-smoking, which eventually he admitted. It had all been made a lot more uncomfortable, of course, by the understandable reaction of wives and girlfriends back home to all the press stories. For example, there were allegations about girls in Lamb's room, and I was with him a couple of times when he was desperately trying to get through to his wife, Lindsay, in England. In Pakistan it is not always that easy to get a connection, and to be on the wrong end of an almighty earful when you do can be more than just frustrating.

By the start of 1984, Willis had just about recovered from his illness, but the selectors appointed me captain for the home series against the West Indies. It threatened to be a difficult baptism, given the nature of the opposition and because some of our best players were still doing penance for the South African Breweries tour. It was one of those delicate handovers from a bloke who had basically been sacked, despite the illness and signs of understandable wear and tear, and while he did not say so as such, when he phoned to wish me luck I detected just a hint of, 'And by God, you'll need it.'

My season did not begin very well as within a week of the opening match I was in hospital with a severe case of blood-poisoning. For what had started as a slight graze to the knuckle became a much swollen and very painful hand. Two days later it was so infected that the specialists who answered my calls began phoning hospitals for rooms. I spent the next two weeks doing pin-cushion impressions, as any amount of anti-biotics were pumped into the system and lakes of blood came out for analysis. It is no exaggeration to say that twenty years earlier the infection might have proved fatal, and it took a few weeks to get back to playing again. Even then the finger that had been originally infected remained very stiff and sore throughout the rest of the season – it still doesn't bend as easily as the corresponding finger on the other hand.

The England side also started with a painful experience at Edgbaston, during which Andy Lloyd managed to add the words 'never been out against the West Indies' to his curriculum vitae, albeit not 'never been knocked out'. A ball from Marshall thudded into the helmet, and he never played again. Retired hurt 10, and absent hurt.

The next match at Lord's was, of course, the one in which I made a name for myself as a captain by becoming the first England skipper since 1948 to declare and lose. Someone called Bradman made 173 not out on that occasion, and when I did it, Gordon Greenidge made 214 not out. As they required 340 plus to win in less than three sessions, I thought we were fairly well insured against defeat, but I had not bargained for us bowling total crap, not to put too fine a point on it. I did not so much get stick in the press for losing the match for that declaration, as for the events of the fourth evening when we were batting and came off for bad light.

We were over 300 ahead with Lamb and Downton going well

when the light went dim. The umpires offered it, and when they peered up at what was just about detectable as an empty balcony they realized that no assistance was forthcoming from that direction and decided to come off. The press wanted to know next morning why I had not been up there waving at my players to stay out and crack on for more quick runs. Had they known that I was sitting inside watching Wimbledon on the TV, I dread to think what might have been written. But when you are playing the West Indies, the new ball is due and it's dark, I don't consider that it is really my place to order a senior batsman to stay out there. Had I done so, and one of them finished up like Andy Lloyd, or worse, the press would probably have demanded my arraignment on a manslaughter charge. As for getting the declaration wrong (and if you end up losing I suppose it's hard to argue that you haven't) there were one or two inside the dressing room who thought we should have declared overnight. In fact, if I'm not mistaken, one of them was the chairman of selectors. Peter May – P.B.H. – would not have pressed the point too hard, though, because he was never one for the dictatorial style. I never saw him in the dressing room very much – he'd pop in early for a few quiet words, but that was about it. The only time he got close to animation was over the press. He used to refer to them as 'those dreadful press chaps', probably because he was very sensitive to some of the criticism he came in for from the media.

P.B.H. and I were fairly friendly, without having much depth to the relationship, and it was really quite hard to get to know the man because he was very shy. I would talk far more to Willis than May before selection meetings, which were somewhat fraught in that series. We made God knows how many changes, what with all the injuries and the fact that we were getting stuffed, something like twenty-two players all told. I was criticized in the first Test for dropping down a place in the order and batting Derek Randall at No 3, which was probably a fair comment as things turned out. I wanted a bit of breathing space as captain, and at No 3 against the West Indies, you tend to see the new ball a little earlier than you would like. Derek was a very fine player, but probably tended to hop around even more frantically than normal against quick bowling at that time. Anyway, the plan was not a major success for either of us.

He was dropped after nought and one in the first Test, and I had a bad series both with the bat and as captain.

Chris Broad was one good recruit, as was Graeme Fowler, but apart from winning the second one-day international at Trent Bridge it was defeat all the way. Even during that victory I remember getting the first taste of criticism that captaincy attracts, especially when I was trying to get the balance right between containment and trying to get people out. Geoff Miller was bowling well, and when Clive Lloyd came in I decided to bring in a close fielder to add to the pressure – putting him at silly point rather than first slip. Almost immediately, of course, Clive nicked one to where slip would have been, and I took some more stick for that. By and large, though, the media were relatively sympathetic in that I was still the young apprentice, not to mention the fact that we were playing the West Indies. Also in that Lord's match, when Greenidge played one of the great knocks, I was taken to task for not setting more defensive fields to slow down the scoring rate. As it was a Test match I had not really considered it, but looking back I realize I could have made them work harder for the runs.

At the end of the Old Trafford Test, by which time we had played four and lost four, I had something of a heart to heart with the press at the post-match conference in the downstairs dressing room. Even if most of the writers disappeared to hack out their customary 'England Disaster' pieces, some stayed behind and we chatted off the record for the best part of an hour. I think it did some good in that I managed to get across one or two of the mitigating circumstances, and also my own personal thoughts having had what by any standards was a traumatic introduction to the job on a full-time basis. I wasn't scoring runs, so I couldn't cheer myself up that way, and quite frankly I wondered whether I wouldn't be better off back in the trenches rather than trying to lead what was by now a pretty dispirited set of troops.

In fairness to P.B.H. and the rest of the management team, I was not short of support from higher up, and when I thought more deeply about the situation I was not completely despondent: I remember sitting up in the BBC radio box just after the 'blackwash' had been completed, chatting to the likes of Johnston and Blofeld, and not only delivering the standard line on these occasions – i.e.

'Things are not quite as bad as they look' – but also believing it. There had, I said, been one or two positive features to the series, and I singled out Broad as being one of the larger ones. Obviously encouraged by the skipper's vote of confidence Chris went out and got 80 odd in the final Test of the summer against Sri Lanka, whereupon, he was dropped for the winter tour to India!

Broad was left out because of his perceived deficiencies against spin bowling, of which there is rather a lot in India, but he was clearly something of a find, and I was being honest – both with the media and myself – when I said that the picture was not all doom and gloom. There are occasions, I admit, when you offer platitudes for public consumption, particularly before a Test match. You will be familiar with the sort of remark – 'Yes, I know we've lost our last 50 matches against them, but it's only 11 against 11, and if we play to our full potential we have a good chance of winning.' Graham Gooch will say, 'Of course we think we can win, there's no point turning up if you don't think you've got a chance,' and I've said something similar on occasions myself when we're obviously up against it. Meantime, back in the dressing room we're saying, 'Look, they're better than we are, but let's give it a crack anyway.' But for public consumption, you are usually a couple of steps more optimistic than perhaps you really are.

Press interviews are more often than not highly predictable, stunningly boring and wholly formulated. Wednesday afternoon: 'Can we win this one, skipper?' 'Yes, we can.' Saturday evening: 'Can we save this one, skipper.' 'Yes, we can.' The slight variation on the latter being when you add, 'especially if it pisses down for two days'. Mostly, the real honesty comes through in the form of black humour – and you don't hit people with black humour before you've even tossed up.

Talking to the press, however, is a long way from being the captain's worst off-the-field duty. Telling people that they are not playing is the hardest part of the job, although through the course of that particular summer I got plenty of practice at it. One of the tougher ones was telephoning David Bairstow, who had played as wicketkeeper-batsman in the one-day series, to tell him that he was not in the Test side. We thought that Downton was the better keeper, and this was probably the right decision – probably better thought out than one or two other decisions that summer, at any rate – but it scarcely made the job any easier. You come up with the usual line: 'Thanks very much, marvellous job, blah, blah ... But sorry, you're not playing in the Test match.' There's really no way of dressing it up, and Bluey took it very badly. He was really a very emotional character and very proud of every England cap he earned, a long way removed from both the public image of barrel-chested hardnut, and indeed how he played much of his cricket. He was very upset, and when you eventually put the phone down after making a call like that, you don't feel very good.

I was still in charge when we sat down to select the squad for India, although my stock could not have been too high as I was out-voted on the question of Broad's inclusion in the party. On the other hand, I did get my way on the two semi-controversial choices: Edmonds as one of the spinners, and Gatting as vice-captain. Nick Cook, Geoff Miller and Pat Pocock had been the spinners used during the West Indies series, and Edmonds – who has never been over-reticent in these matters – tackled me fairly volubly on the subject during the Leicestershire-Middlesex match at Grace Road. In any event, I did want him for India, but there was a certain amount of opposition given his reputation for being a difficult character.

Gatting had not been picked for England since the previous tour to India in 1981-82 and had not done very much in that series, but I thought enough of him to want him as my second-in-command. This prompted some animated debate, but after eventually accommodating Edmonds and Gatting, the other selectors offered an impenetrable forward defensive on Broad. Tim Robinson was regarded as a better player of spin, and as he got a lot of runs in India, the horses for courses option turned out to be the right one. Broad was doubly unlucky in that we held the selection meeting right at the end of the season. When I tried to get in touch with him, he had disappeared off to Cornwall for a short break, and he only found out via the newspapers over his breakfast table. Broady being a forthright sort of character, I feared the worse when I did finally make contact at a benefit match in Uxbridge a week or so later, but in fact he was very good about it.

In contrast to the previous winter, India was a very happy tour. Drug-free, scandal-free, and we also won the Test series – no mean achievement over there. It was not a very happy start, mind you, because when we cruised into Delhi airport at about four in the morning, it was only three hours or so before the Sikhs assassinated Mrs Gandhi. We had a scheduled press conference at ten o'clock in the morning which began with the manager, Tony Brown, reading out a statement of regret, which I recall causing a certain amount of consternation among the Indian journalists who had clearly not heard the news. Information, like most things in India, can take days to filter through. We then spent most of that day collaborating with the British High Commission, and although we took the view that what had happened did not directly involve us, we discovered that we could not get on with anything because everything in India had shut down. You are hard pressed to know what's working and what's not in India at the best of times, but on this occasion absolutely everything had come to a total standstill.

We made a token trip down to the cricket ground, only to be told, not unreasonably in the prevailing circumstances, that nets had been cancelled during a period of national mourning. The thought did occur briefly that had the Indians known of my non-consuming passion for net practice, I might have been rounded up along with the other suspects. We used the grounds of the High Commission as a combination of sanctuary and a place to run around and train a bit, which is where we sustained our own first casualty of the tour. Vic Marks made the early, and somewhat painful, discovery that fielding out of an Indian sky is not as straightforward as it is at Taunton (not that Vic has ever been the greatest poucher of skiers) and was led away with blood gushing out of his nose.

With the political situation not improving much over the next few days, we managed to get away to Sri Lanka to play some cricket until India returned to some semblance of normality. When we did get back, the first Test match in Bombay was not too far away, and from my previous experience of India on Keith Fletcher's tour, I was anxious about the erratic preparation that had been forced upon us. If you lose the first Test in India, and they don't want you to get back into the series, there is precious little you can do about it. Five-and-a-half-hour days, flat pitches, slow over-rates ... We were completely stuffed on the 1981-82 tour after going one down, and I made this point pretty forcibly.

However, more bad news was just around the corner. We were invited to the Bombay High Commissioner's residence for a semi-official party a couple of days before the match, the sort of function that can be several hours of rhubarb and lingering death, but this one was one of the best I've ever been to. The atmosphere was brilliant and it re-emphasized the excellent spirit that the team was in for all the earlier difficulties. Next morning, we were just about to convene for the official tour photograph in the gardens by the swimming pool at the Taj Mahal Hotel, when the phone rang in my room. It was Percy Pocock, who had enjoyed himself so much the night before that he had just phoned the High Commission to thank Percy Norris for the party, only to be given the news that he had just been shot. Now at this stage, the mood of the team certainly began to change. We had had considerable sympathy for the death of Mrs Gandhi, but our own High Commissioner was a bit closer to home than their Prime Minister. We were high-profile Englishmen abroad in a volatile country, and naturally wanted to know whether the Norris shooting was connected to any anti-British feeling. The Commission told us that it was probably no more than a case of the wrong man in the wrong place at the wrong time, but meantime the press were telling us that all British businesses had been advised to close down, and that British Airways had put their shutters up for the day. So we held a series of meetings in the hotel to decide whether we wanted to carry on.

In the end, myself and the management decided to be very British and gung-ho about it (having been assured by the High Commission), and the first thing to do with the Test almost upon us was to get in some decent preparation. This meant leaving the security of the hotel, and when I put my head around Graeme Fowler's door and said, 'Come on, Foxy, we're off to practice,' he hit me with a slice of that dry wit of his. 'What sort of practice would that be then, captain? Target practice?' I can't pretend that our minds were very well focused when we got to the nets, and there were one or two players within the team who still felt strongly about going home. This was a growing mood within the camp, which filtered through to me, so we had another meeting at which Tony Brown lost his cool a bit and said, 'Right, if anyone doesn't like it, they can collect their passports and get the hell out of it. The rest of us are staying.' No-one took him up on this, but it did not dispel the feeling among one of two of us that we were about to play in front of 50,000 people and one sniper.

Someone attempted to lighten the tension by recalling that on Tony Greig's tour to India in 1976-77, when there was similar anti-Brit feeling, Keith Fletcher decided to walk in from slip to make himself a slightly harder target. I'm not sure it raised much of a laugh, though, and it came as no great surprise to me when we lost the match. Quite apart from all the distractions, we came up against a leg-spinner we had never seen before, Sivaramakrishnan, and an umpire, Swaroop Kishen, that we never wanted to see again. Siva started the rot by getting Fowler with a full toss, and ended up with twelve wickets. Swaroop didn't bowl, but he must have run Siva close as India's man of the match. I had seen Swaroop before, and regarded him as quite a decent umpire, but this time, not to put too fine a point on it, he had a shocker. However hard done by we might have felt, the situation I had most feared – one down after one in India – had duly come about. On Fletcher's tour there had been six Test matches, and the last five produced some of the most tedious games of cricket you could possibly imagine. The scenario I then conjured up made out far more of a case for taking up Tony Brown's passport offer and heading straight for the airport, but the good news was that not many of the squad had been on Fletcher's tour, and were therefore not as pessimistic as I felt straight after that Test match.

We were mentally in much better shape when we moved on to Delhi, and took a first innings lead of about 100 or so. Nevertheless, they had plenty of batting left when we went into lunch on the final day. There then followed one of the rare documented cases of the Gower fuse blowing. It was only a short explosion, as we were due to leave the dressing room for the post-lunch session, and was brought on by the apparent apathy of the players to our chances of bowling India out. Somehow, though, it seemed to work. I made a decision to keep the spinners on instead of taking the new ball, which also worked, partly thanks to Kapil having one of his occasional brainstorms and slogging one to long-on. The dressing room was a good place to be that night – we had not only ended a (then) record sequence of thirteen Tests without a win, but I was heading for a

87

winner's press conference for the first time after eleven Tests as captain.

We then drew a tedious match in Calcutta, before going 2-1 ahead with one to play in Madras. Neil Foster bowled India out in both innings, and we got 600-plus with Gatting and Fowler both scoring double centuries. Even the press, especially those who had spent Fletcher's tour face down in their inkwells, were excited, and on production of the entrance fee (a bottle of French champagne) we invited them back to our team-room celebrations that night. There was more of the same when we comfortably drew the final Test in Kanpur to win the series.

The team-room is a major feature of a tour to the sub-continent, far more so than somewhere like Australia, where there is so much entertainment on tap outside the hotel front door, and players disappear in all manner of different directions. When things are going badly it can perhaps be a double-edged sword, as it tends to promote a siege-like atmosphere and one of the many diplomatic incidents on the Gatting tour to Pakistan in 1987 apparently (I wasn't on that tour) revolved around an exasperated Dilley kicking the door closed on the fingers of a retreating autograph hunter. However, when things are going well it throws all the players together and is a definite plus for team spirit.

Even when the cricket being played is dire, there is no shortage of fun off-the-field in India. On the 1981-82 we flew into Jammu one morning just as dawn was breaking – Lord knows why we were arriving at that time, but Indian Airlines schedules are, to put it as politely as possible, subject to minor alteration – to what looked like a very boring town indeed. Jammu is a long way north (you could see the foothills of the Himalayas as we were coming in to land) and it was bloody cold. So much so, that the rooms in what appeared to be the only hotel in town were all provided with single element fires – and as soon as we arrived, everyone, but everyone, turned them on. This, of course, resulted in the entire establishment being plunged into darkness, so I decided to turn on the shower to try and get warm that way. To my great joy, not to mention utter amazement, it actually dispensed copious quantities of hot water, although the slight drawback was that once on, it refused to go off. So I phoned downstairs to reception, and in the fullness of time a man with a spanner arrived to be confronted by this mini Niagara in the bathroom. He wrenched away at all the various knobs, before turning round to announce: 'Shower, sir. It is not turning off.' 'Brilliant, Holmes,' say I, whereupon he starts hammering away while I attempt to make a phone call home. This is another exercise not to be attempted in India without a decent supply of valium, particularly if you have to go through the hotel operator. Tony Lewis, the writer and broadcaster, tells a nice story of 1001 abortive attempts to get through to London, culminating in an exasperated, 'Look now, let's go through this again ...' whereupon the operator replies, 'Ah, you want Lucknow!' It was a bit like that on this occasion. I eventually got a lot of encouraging clicking and whirring noises on the line, and a voice crackled down the receiver, 'Hotel laundry, how am I helping you please?'

The whole visit was a novel experience, zero temperatures by night, one hundred by day, and after the match the hotel threw a party for us in a marquee around the back. It wasn't supposed to be fancy dress, but J.K. Lever had taken himself off to the market and equipped himself with a long black wig, dress, bra ... standard transvestite kit, and he swept into the tent looking suitably vampish and tarty. There was a fourpiece band playing live (or live-ish) music, and one scratched Bee Gees record when the band took a break. But no women. So most of the lads decided to take J.K. for a dance. This was all good fun, until one strapping Sikh gentleman, emboldened by the local fire-water, and not seeing too clearly, fell hopelessly in love with our left arm seamer with somewhat embarrassing results. J.K. attempted to warn him off with 'I'm not that sort of girl, and anyway my husband will be here any minute,' but eventually it took a large crowbar to separate them.

There were some classic moments on the field, too, like the one I had on that trip to Jammu. I managed to get myself run out in partnership with Lamb, and while we were having lunch the umpire came up to me and said, in all seriousness, 'If you had run faster, you wouldn't have been out.' It reminded me of the time Mike Brearley was in Pakistan, also during a lunch, when the umpire approached him with an earnest look on his face. 'Mr Brearley, I am terribly sorry. I know you were not out, but I felt my arm going up and I just couldn't stop it.'

When we went to Hyderabad on my tour, we stayed at a hotel which was right next door to a small ornamental lake studded with water fountains. They also had four shikaras, a sort of Indian gondola, which was piloted by a member of staff upon application at the porter's desk. You would sit quietly in the back while he took you out for a gentle twenty minute glide. However, I thought it would be quite good fun to put these things to more energetic use, and I challenged the press to a shikara race – two boats per side, two circuits of the fountains, and no rules. An added diversion was the presence on the top balcony of the hotel of Fowler and Pocock, two of the better arms in the team, armed with a vast crate of oranges purchased at minimal expense from the local market. We took an early lead, by virtue of the Gower-Bruce French vessel ramming the *Daily Express* amidships, survived the fusillade of oranges, and declared ourselves the winners. Meantime, Fowler and Pocock had run out of ammunition, and were by now using water bombs whose flight path, unfortunately, crossed the dining area reserved for hotel guests. One of these was a Danish scientist who was apparently running some sort of project for the Indian government. When a defective water bomb exploded in mid-air and cascaded down on to his soup, he exploded as well. He was the unhappiest Dane I've seen since Ole Mortensen had an lbw turned down, and something of an international incident ensued. He stormed into the hotel management claiming that he had been hit by flying ice, and while my men assured me that it was only water, an apology was clearly in order. However, as in the Gatting-Rana business a few years later, he wanted a written one, and I was busy doing that when the hotel management began jumping up and down and pointing to various holes in their boats. This one was finally settled with a whip-round and more apologies. It all got a bit out of hand, for sure, but it was basically pretty harmless stuff – and managements in those days apparently didn't feel the urge to dish out £1000 fines. Team spirit was very good, and there was none of the regimentation that seems to be deemed to be good for morale nowadays. We also happened to win.

I've always believed that a team that is allowed to develop its own character will respond to the responsibility of playing important cricket. Fowler told me later how much he had enjoyed that tour to

India, and one of the reasons he gave was that he had been allowed to feel as though he was a responsible human being. In other words, if you say to a player, 'Do you think you need a net this morning?' as opposed to saying, 'Nets, 10 a.m. sharp', you give a guy responsibility for himself as opposed to making him feel like an overgrown schoolboy. On the tour to the West Indies in 1985-86, the same theory of treating people like adult individuals was applied, and this time, frankly, it fell on its arse. Ergo, the advent of a full-time sergeant-major in Micky Stewart by the time the winter of 1986-87 came around. The prelude to that disastrous trip to the Caribbean was D.I. Gower standing on a balcony at the Oval informing the nation that the West Indies were probably 'quaking in their boots' at the prospects of facing us, which was of course semi-jocular, but none the less had more than a little to do with the elation I was feeling at that particular moment because the Australian summer of 1985 was, quite simply, the highlight of my career.

We came back from India very much on a high, beat the Australians 3-1 and I got a lot of runs in the process. If you can combine winning and performing to a high level yourself, especially against the Aussies, nothing could be better. I'd go so far as to say that I have never played as well over the course of a summer.

It started off as a tight series – we won fairly conclusively at Headingley, but then Bob Holland bowled us out in the second innings at Lord's to enable them to square it up at 1-1. Just for a moment in that game horrible memories of 1981 came flooding back for the Australians when they were 65 for 5 chasing 120-odd, but they eventually won by four wickets. Trent Bridge was a high-scoring draw, Border rescued them from defeat at Old Trafford with a big hundred, and then came that memorable match at Edgbaston when we won by a mile in terms of runs, but only squeaked home against the clock. They had a decent first day, but then we got nearly 600 very quickly, my double century taking me past Denis Compton's previous record of runs in a series against Australia, and Botham's little cameo just before the declaration when he launched into McDermott swung the psychological balance further in our direction. Ellison then got four wickets in a great spell late on the fourth day, only for us to wake up on the Tuesday morning with rain spattering down the window. I remember Border giggling away and offering me mock commiserations, but we finally got out there and won the game after one of the more unusual dismissals in Test cricket.

Wayne Phillips had been holding us up for some time when he cracked a short ball from Edmonds out on the offside, where Lamb and myself were standing in close catching positions. As neither of us subscribe to the Brian Close theory of 'sticking out your chin and head it to slip if necessary' we had both turned away and were in the eyes closed semi-foetal position when the ball thudded into Lamb's instep. I uncoiled myself just in time to see it coming gently down in my direction, and Phillips was given out. The Australians were pretty unhappy about it, arguing that neither umpire could have been sure, and because David Shepherd had to consult with David Constant at square leg, they might have had a point. How clearly Connie saw it, only he can say, but the fielders close to the bat were in little doubt, and Lamb's instep was in no doubt at all.

We went on to win the match with something like eleven overs to spare, and it was then on to the Oval for the final Test, leading 2-1 in the series, requiring only a draw to regain the Ashes that we had lost in Sydney in 1983. We batted first, and when Gooch and myself put on 351 for the second wicket, I thought we might get 1000. However, thanks to the fact that no-one else got more than sixteen, we only ended up with 464. It was, though, more than enough. We bowled them out twice to win by an innings, and it was tremendous to finish the series in such style. It was a wonderful series to be captain in, and I have never before or since had more cooperation from a group of players. My hardest task was making bowling changes, because everyone wanted to bowl.

The only difficult moment I had in six Test matches came in the third at Nottingham, which was played on a track that was too dead to produce a really good game of cricket, but towards the end of one day's play there was an electrifying period involving Ian Botham. Graeme Wood and Greg Ritchie were both going well when 'Both' snatched the ball, and for the next twenty minutes he raced in as quickly as he has done in his career. He had Ritchie caught at third man, a great diving catch from Edmonds, only for it to be adjudged a no-ball by Alan Whitehead. Both will tell you that he never bowls no-balls, and having bent his back to get one up to around shoulder height on a lifeless pitch, he was a long way from being impressed. A feeling he duly conveyed to Whitehead. I had to step in smartly to defuse the operation, and thought at the time that I'd done a fairly good job in placating both bowler and umpire. We found out after the game that Whitehead had reported Botham, which meant we had to go through all the rigmarole of an official disciplinary hearing. In my view, it was both unnecessary and unwarranted. Whitehead is a good umpire, and as Test cricket these days has the potential to boil over, a commendably strict one. On this occasion, though, he was far too inflexible over a small incident during a spell of Test cricket at its most compelling.

We all ended up sitting in a room at Lord's – players, captains, umpires, disciplinary committee – wasting each other's time in short. At the end of the whole pointless exercise, Ian got a reprimand. It was the one slightly deflating note in an otherwise perfect summer, although I do recall being slightly miffed at the official award ceremony on the Oval balcony. I took possession of a replica of the Ashes, which I misconstrued as a personal and permanent memento, but no sooner had I mentioned that it would look nice on the mantelpiece at home than it was whisked smartly back to the Lord's Museum.

CHAPTER EIGHT

A total mess

I THINK most people realized that my reference to the West Indies as 'quaking in the boots' was tongue in cheek – a long way removed from the Greig 'grovel' school of pre-series oratory, anyway – but we did feel that we could achieve something in the Caribbean that winter. One of the points that seemed to be in our favour was that the players now had a four month break in which to re-charge the batteries – although as we now know, we somehow managed to re-charge them to the extent that we scarcely looked capable of powering a pencil torch.

I whiled away a relaxing month or two before deciding that perhaps the best way to prepare to bat against the West Indies would be to do something a good deal less dangerous – such as hang gliding or the Cresta Run. My friend Simon Strong suggested the Cresta, so off we went to St Moritz via (in order to get in some net practice before the real thing) Cervinia in Italy. It was there that I ran into a reporter from the *News of the World*, whose newspaper had decided that the England captain hurtling down bobsleigh runs was perhaps not the ideal way to be carrying on before an overseas tour, and was worth a mention. The fact that I was about to tackle the Cresta was picked up by the rest of the media the next day, and it was even suggested to P.B.H. that he should order me home on the next plane. This he sensibly ignored, and from where I was lying the odds on a plaster cast and a stack of get-well-soon cards were considerably longer for a tobogganist than someone standing twenty-two yards away from Marshall and Holding. In any event, we ended up riding with the British No 1 and No 2 bobsleigh teams in Cervinia, tucked

A memorable start to Test cricket as the first ball goes for four – even if it was a rank long-hop!

This shot off Stephen Boock took me to 99, one away from my first Test hundred, against New Zealand at The Oval in 1978.

A year later and another hook, this time off India's Karsan Ghavri, on the way to a first Test double century.

Two of the great fast bowlers, both much respected opponents and good mates: Dennis Lillee (left) and Malcolm Marshall (below) were amongst the quickest in their day and always knew exactly what they were doing with a cricket ball in their hand.

1985 – the year everything went right. At Edgbaston we went 2-1 up against Australia. I scored 215, and also ended up catching Wayne Phillips via Allan Lamb's boot – the crucial dismissal in Australia's second innings.

In Australia under Mike Gatting in 1986–87, we retained the Ashes with a 3-1 series win. My best contribution came at Perth with an innings of 135.

I have just reached my century at the Oval in the final Test of the 1985 summer. Our second-wicket partnership of 351 set us on the road to a decisive victory, with Graham Gooch eventually making 196.

This was a special moment, 'joining the party' with 157 not out against India in 1990 to help save the Oval Test, and ensure a fifth major tour to Australia, where two more hundreds followed.

in behind the driver, and then went down the Cresta solo.

We were still buzzing on the day we prepared to fly home, when I received news that took me from high to low more drastically than at any time in my life. The day we left Switzerland was also the day my mother died. The tour management team of Willis, Brown, Gatting and myself was scheduled to meet at Lord's that evening, which is where I went after arriving in London, but there was obviously no way I could stay and I soon found myself heading north on the M1 with misty vision and a head full of sad and reflective thoughts. There was only a week before the team flew out to the West Indies in which to arrange the funeral, tidy up the legal side of things and clear out my mother's house in Loughborough. It was not a pleasant week.

I was still fairly zombified when I attended the pre-tour press conference, which is not the worst frame of mind to be in on these occasions. You try your best to answer the questions, but it's mostly an exercise in platitudes. 'Yes, we'll be trying hard ... yes, of course we hope to do better than last time ... [we didn't of course] yes, they're a good side, but ...' all the usual stuff. Ninety per cent of what you say is wholly predictable, and whatever you come up with is soon rendered obsolete by events in any case. Graham Gooch has been known to kick off a press conference with something along the lines of, 'I don't know why you all bother. You know what I'm going to say. Same as last time. It's all so boring.' But the ritual is gone through just the same.

Let me say at this stage that even though the ritual can seem tedious to both sides, player and press, what everyone must do is accept it. Press conferences can be what they were originally designed to be, an opportunity for the cricketer or manager to provide the information that will assist the pundits in making an assessment based on some sort of fact and not just pure guesswork or intuition. For a captain to make best use of these meetings, he must keep a cool head and maintain the utmost confidence in his own judgement at all times, even when the side is doing badly. Unfortunately, emotion does enter into all this, quite naturally, and I would be the first to admit that I could never stick to this idea in all my dealings with the media for all my good intentions. Perhaps the best way to look at it all is to regard the press conference as part of the game and to play it accordingly.

' "WE'LL GET HUGE STUFFING" SAYS GOWER.' Now that would be a story, but you wouldn't say it even if you thought it. 'WE HOPE TO DO WELL' is usually about the size of it, followed by yards of quotes that, upon close examination, don't reveal much about anything. You sometimes come away from these things thinking about tomorrow's newspaper and wondering whether half the population will be found slumped head-down in the cornflakes. You soon discover that the press boys, or some of them, have a marvellous talent for improving even the most tedious of quotes. 'Tickling it up a bit' is what they call it in the trade. So blandly stating the obvious does not necessarily mean that this is the treatment it will get. 'Yes of course I think we've got a chance ...' becomes 'Gung-ho England skipper David Gower yesterday warned the mighty Windies: "We're out to get you, Viv." ' You rarely find you've simply said something. You've insisted it, or blasted it. You can talk like whispering Ted Lowe with a sore throat and still discover that you've fumed, snarled and stormed.

It's a shame that these things have to get exaggerated or 'tickled up' so much, because when you actually have something worthwhile to say, the public is so used to everything sounding mega-important, it rather loses its impetus. Where the pre-tour press conference does serve a purpose, however, is in focusing public attention on the impending battle, and (standard answers to standard questions or not) it also has a kind of therapeutic value for the tour captain himself. Part of the psyche of doing well is the inner belief that you are going to do so, and attending a press conference to make a public affirmation of that does not do any harm at all. Having said that, it is the private affirmation that really counts, or at least it did until that 1985-86 West Indies tour. A lot of us (if not all) genuinely believed that we would do well – maybe not by winning the series, but at least in showing a major improvement on 1984 in England. We had a stronger side, with Gooch, Emburey and Willey back after their three year bans – Willey a horses for courses selection for the fast bowling.

The mistake we made, though, was in spending the best part of four months basking in the delectable aftermath of beating Australia, without putting too much thought or effort into the Caribbean tour until it was more or less on top of us. I told Lord's that when they sacked me the following summer, which is one reason they employed much of the same four month period before the 1990 tour to the West Indies (for which, of course, I was surplus to requirements) sweating away at places like Lilleshall. Ironic, isn't it? Here I was in later years supposed to be the very antithesis of the Stewart-Gooch way of doing things, and yet I can say that I was in at the conception of the winter training and preparation programme.

We also discovered on that tour that the idea of practising before we got to the West Indies was an even better idea given that practice facilities out there did not exist. We had a couple of reasonable nets when we arrived in Barbados, but were not aware that we would scarcely see another decent turf wicket for the next three months. It is not quite true to say that I have a tendency to break out into a rash if I get too close to a net. In point of fact, I have always believed in having them available for the work each individual feels he needs. To have stepped into some of the nets we encountered on that tour was not so much to invite a rash but to contemplate popping your teeth into a glass before turning out the light for the rest of your life. It is now, however, common knowledge that in the opening match of that tour, the England captain had opted to rule out the possibility of rashes and broken teeth for himself, and bravely gone to risk the dangers of ocean wind-burn instead. The flaw in the captain's thinking was that the opening match in St Vincent, to a Windward Islands side rated as the weakest in the Caribbean, was lost. At the time, taking the first game off did not seem to me to be in any way irresponsible, especially as the two weeks since my mother's death had been so fraught and breathless, and as there were only three games before we were into the first one-day international, as captain there was a fair chance I would playing almost all the games from thereon in, and frankly I felt tired and run down. So I said to myself: 'Right, let's take a bit of a breather before the cricket gets too serious,' and on much the same principle, I gave Botham the first match off as well. Anyway, on the second night of the game some of us strolled down from the Sunset Shores Hotel to one of the local bars down the road, and I ran into an old acquaintance by the name of Bjorn. I'd met him a couple of years before during a Fred Rumsey cricket festival out there, and had chartered his yacht – along with

Fred, Robin Askwith, and our three partners – for a week's island hopping at the end of the trip.

After a beer or two, Bjorn invited Ian and I out for a day's sailing the following morning, and not unnaturally we accepted. Things did not quite go according to plan, which was always a possibility with Bjorn. He was lovely man, but as ocean going captains go, neither he nor his crew modelled themselves on the Captain Bligh school of whip-cracking discipline. We had discovered all that on our earlier trip from Bjorn's crewman – a character called Kennet – who had an interesting approach to the job to say the least. If we ever went ashore at night, we'd invariably arrive back at the boat to find the cabin full of blue smoke and Kennet completely out of it. He was just as hopeless in the mornings, which invariably began with him pointing to an elastic bandage that seemed to shuffle between either elbow and either knee. A moveable pain, and far too acute of course to allow him to take part in anything as physical as sheet-hauling, so Askwith and myself (who weren't too lively of a morning ourselves) ended up doing most of the work. On this occasion we did not get off to a flier either. We took a dinghy out to his boat at 9 a.m., only to find a good deal of poking and peering at engines in progress. Bjorn had three engines, all of which were knackered, and we needed some man-made power to get through the strong currents running through the entrance to the bay. So we settled for sitting around on the sun deck with a few beers while the lads set to work on the engines (we eventually got out for about an hour) and in an idle moment turned on the radio. The Windwards had never before beaten a touring side and we had begun the third day in a good position. However, from the moment we switched on the radio we lost wickets faster than we raided the cool box. All out for 94, and eventual defeat by seven wickets.

While I was bobbing around on Bjorn's boat, it did not require much in the way of clairvoyancy to predict that my next acquaintance with water would be of the hot variety – not least because we had a press photographer on board. Graham Morris had asked to come along, and being a good friend of both Ian and myself, we happily agreed. This was perhaps a little naive, but in different circumstances he would simply have gone away with a couple of rolls of happy relaxation pictures for use on one of those occasional quiet days on tour when newspapers back at home would be grateful for any kind of variation on the boring old net practice snap.

What happened on this occasion, of course, is that the pictures landed on the sports desks alongside the various 'Day of shame' match reports, and the caption writers duly dipped their quills into a poisoned ink well and went to town. 'Beaming skipper calls for more ice as Titanic goes down in Windwards,' that sort of theme. The only way to avoid this is to prevent the writers and cameramen from getting anywhere near you, which is somewhat impractical, and you have to accept that it is occasionally going to happen to you. Something similar happened on the 1990-91 tour to Australia, when a party that included myself, my girlfriend Thorunn, Lamb and his family, agreed to pose for an Allsport photographer at a man-made lagoon during the match at Cararra up on the Queensland Gold Coast. We sat around sipping various coloured drinks (non-alcoholic) pretending to enjoy ourselves, while he snapped away for the usual batch of off-duty pictures. His job, like Morris's in the West Indies, did not stretch beyond the actual photography, and once again the pictures were used in a negative sense. Here are England having a terrible time in Australia, while Gower and Lamb get stuck into the pina coladas at Surfers Paradise.

I seem to have found myself in this sort of situation more often than most, largely because it runs against the grain for me to wander around looking miserable all the time if the cricket is not going that well. Quite enough time is genuinely taken up with the more serious aspects of living without having to put on face masks as well. It's a sad reflection of the press if a picture of an off-duty cricketer enjoying himself on a tour that is going badly is used in such a way as to suggest he doesn't give a hang about the cricket. If things are going badly for someone at work, what's the point in spending the weekend kicking the cat? By that criterion, no-one would have broken into a smile for three months on that 1985-86 tour. It started badly and it didn't get any better either.

Things were bad enough on the field, but when the press began giving the impression that we were on the same kind of hallucinatory drugs they accused us of using on the New Zealand tour, it really got quite laughable. We had arrived in Jamaica for the island match that preceded the first one-day international and first Test, and while we won that game comfortably, my own form was pretty awful. Nothing higher than 11 in four first-class innings, and in the second innings against Jamaica, Courtney Walsh had me hopping around all over the place before I finally fended one off to gully. When I took my seat for the pre one-day international press conference, therefore, I fully expected – along with the customary,'What's the side going to be … have we got a chance … just the one spinner?' – an inquisition into my own novice performances with the bat. What I was not quite prepared for was: 'We understand you are having an affair with Paul Downton's wife, and would this explain why you are looking a trifle drained on the field?'

This turned out to be a story that had just been floated from London, and was tied in to reports that all was not well with my relationship with my fiancée Vicki. The latter, as it happened, was not the work of fiction that the former undoubtedly was. Things had been very rocky, and only my mother's death had pulled us together shortly before the tour began. She was not planning to come out to join me in the West Indies, but eventually spent so much time under siege from the press back at home in Leicester that we agreed over the telephone that it would be far better for her to fly out, which she did. There were all sorts of stories doing the rounds at that time, most of which were a tribute to the imaginative powers of the fourth estate, and there was one bloke in particular – a freelance hitman – sending back the most remarkable crap. Half of every day was spent receiving faxes of various newspaper back pages, sending back denials and generally peering round curtains to see if you could spot a trilby lurking behind a potted palm. Every non-native face on the island was a potential booby trap, and not even the cricket correspondents could recognize every one of the scandal-seeking merchants despatched by the various news desks.

Given this sort of background, it was scarcely surprising that we were horribly stuffed in both the one-dayer and the Test in Jamaica. Morale was not improved by the fact that, in the one-day match, one of the more unusual examples of a damaged ball was the result of finding a piece of Mike Gatting's nose lodged in the leather after Gatt missed a hook off Malcolm Marshall. It was such a bad injury that he had to fly home for repairs, but if Gatt thought that the consolation prize would be a temporary respite from ludicrous press inquiries, he was very much mistaken. When he flew in, with his nose spread from one ear to the other and covered with elastoplast, he was asked, 'Where exactly did the ball hit you, Mike?'

There was more gallows comedy during the Test, when, leaving aside the problems of facing four of the world's fastest bowlers on a horribly uneven surface, there was also the minor inconvenience of being unable to see the ball until it was halfway through its intended journey from hand to cranium. After the island game, we had asked the authorities to have the sightscreen at the southern end of the ground raised, because it was too low to allow us to pick up the release of the ball from any bowler over six feet. As this applied to everyone in the Test match except Marshall, it was a fairly crucial request, but they turned us down because 200 spectators would not have been able to see properly. It was a comforting thought, humming 'Hail Marys' to yourself as Patterson's arm whirled over from a point comfortably off the radar, that someone had a good view. My first scoring shot of the series was a cut off Holding over third man for six (I was also caught there attempting something similar off Patterson in the second innings) and although Gooch played well in the first innings, and Willey fought a lone battle with 71 in the second, we barely scraped 300 from two knocks. By the time we left Jamaica we had taken such a mental and physical beating, that we never really recovered.

Meantime, the media attention became more and more unbearable. Despite my protestations that our poor start had something to do with the West Indies being a fairly decent side, they were not going to be fobbed off with anything quite as boring as that. We had done very well against Australia the previous summer, and here we were now getting hammered. Therefore, they argued, there must be something sinister behind it. One newspaper would make some startling claim or other, so rival publications would have to top it, and the first thing to hit us after Jamaica was an allegation that Botham had hit such good form off the field – in partnership with a beauty queen – that one of the finest hotel beds in Barbados had been unable to withstand the strain. This was the last straw for 'Both', who from that moment on decided to make hotel bedrooms (i.e. his own) the focal point of his entire tour. He more or less locked himself in for the rest of the trip, which, being such a naturally gregarious animal, did his cricket no good at all.

The only real escape from all this off-the-field pressure, not to mention our best chance of getting the tour back on the rails, lay on the practice ground. The designated net areas, however, had properties considerably closer to corrugated roof iron than the billiard table. Whether the lack of facilities was by accident or design I don't know, but when we started the tour in Barbados conditions were good, and when we got back for the Test match, they were hopeless. In Antigua it is perfectly possible to produce good practice facilities, but they didn't, and the same applied in Jamaica.

So here we were. Ducking and weaving against the West Indies on the field, against our own bowlers on inadequate practice surfaces, and not least against the press when we scuttled back to the hotel. The Caribbean is not an easy place to be when you're losing, as every waiter, bell boy and taxi driver is invariably rubbing it in; neither is it the paradise that some people imagine. There are some places where going out at night looking as though you might have more than a fiver in your back pocket is roughly equivalent to facing the West Indian attack with a blindfold and a floppy hat. On this tour, it was not a good idea to go out at all, because a quiet meal and a glass of wine in a downtown restaurant was invariably interpreted as another wild England orgy in one of the newspapers. There was literally no let-up and on the day Vicki was due in from England I woke up to a faxed Sunday newspaper story containing a vivid account of the England captain cavorting with a British Airways stewardess in a pool in Trinidad. 'This will do a lot for the relationship,' I thought, as I drove out to the airport to meet her, and I duly spent the first couple of hours of the reunion having to explain what rubbish it all was. This was, in fact, one report that wasn't so far away from containing an element of truth, but I didn't regard confession as being good for the soul at that point: it was not worth a perforated eardrum. It had not been anything more than a bit of high-spirited horseplay, but I should have known that it would be easily enough in the atmosphere that prevailed to make a story.

One of the more common criticisms levelled at me down the years has been a tendency to tempt fate, press the self-destruct button if you like, and to be honest it is not an unfair one. This manifested itself after the third Test in Barbados, which we lost even more comprehensively than the first two, and revolved around what came to be known as the 'optional net' syndrome. We were under extra pressure in Barbados, being the main holiday island in the Caribbean, and it was full of British holidaymakers who had come to watch England play a five-day Test match. Correction. Full of disgruntled British holidaymakers who had come in the vain hope of watching England play a five-day Test match. It was all over in three and a bit days, which left them with the sort of spare time they had neither budgeted for nor particularly wanted, and us with extra time on our hands before we flew to Trinidad for another one-day international.

The net pitches that had been substandard before the Test, were now full of holes and totally useless. My views on the value of net practice on this tour have already been documented, and by the time we got to Barbados I recall suggesting to Mike Gatting (by this time back with us after his nose job) that we'd almost be as well organizing a game of soccer on the outfield than engaging in practice that was in many ways counterproductive. So, with what effectively amounted to two days off after the Test defeat, I organized nets on both, but made the first optional. Those who felt it would be beneficial could turn up and practise, those who did not could have the time off. As it happened, only six players decided to cash in their first-day holiday vouchers, and one of the dirty half dozen was the captain. For some unfathomable reason, he had decided that it was just the sort of day to go windsurfing.

I'd bumped into a chap called Stuart Sawyer, who was a fairly big noise in the sport, and he offered to give me a lesson. Too good to miss, I thought, and off we went to the Barbados Windsurfing Club where I had a lot of fun trying (and failing) to become a wind surfer. In fairness to me, the wind was up, the waves were high, and it was a long way from being the relative calm I would have liked. The same, I soon discovered, applied to the atmosphere surrounding the optional net taking place at the Kensington Oval. The press were all there, so were most of the British cricket fans who had found themselves with no cricket to watch. The captain was not, and the old negative syndrome reared its ugly head once again. There wasn't much mileage in writing about a pleasing head count for an optional session when there was a far more enticing head-count inside the

103

guillotine basket, one with a curly mop attached to it. The press let me have both barrels, and I remember thinking how grateful I was that Graham Morris had not been alongside on his own surfboard taking pictures.

By this time there were also rumblings of discontent within the dressing room, which is almost inevitable when a tour is going as badly as this one was. One of the major problems concerned Botham, who in keeping with the successful tour of India, had been allowed a lot of leeway in deciding what was best for himself. Unfortunately he had decided that of all the things that were best for himself, net bowling came a long way down the list, which might have gone down better had he being doing the job out on the field. Which he wasn't. As a result, people like Neil Foster and Les Taylor were doing the majority of the net bowling, while Botham was saying he didn't need the work. I went along with this, hoping that it might bring the best out of Ian. In hindsight it was a mistake. It was a balancing act that went wrong, not least because of the growing dissent it provoked within the camp.

I was also at fault for being slow to pick up the mood of the tour party, which only became apparent to me by whisper and rumour. Having to get this sort of information second and third hand annoyed me more than almost anything on tour, and at a specially convened team meeting before the fourth Test in Trinidad, I blew my top. Why had no-one come to see me face-to-face? I wanted to treat all the players as responsible individuals, yet I felt as though they had let me down with a schoolboyish snigger-and-whinge attitude. Still, there was no denying my contribution to the whole disaster. I blew up at that meeting in Trinidad, but in truth, I knew that it was not only my temper I had lost control of. I had lost control of the entire tour. It would, I think, have been odds against any captain, whatever his methods, to have made the thing work. I have never known, before or since, such concerted outside pressures on a touring side, and we spent as much time trying to dodge the bullets being fired off the field as we did playing cricket.

Where the Botham business went wrong was with him trying to bowl as a strike bowler as he had done against Australia the previous summer – short spells, with as much speed as he could muster. He was neither in the right sort of form, nor, in all honesty, was he fit enough. In those early matches, they splattered him all around the Caribbean. Why, therefore, didn't I act on that sooner? Well, my philosophy has always been to back your bowlers. I've never been a Test bowler, or a bowler of any sort, so I've always trusted those people whose job it is to do what they think they do best. The drawback to this approach, as I painfully discovered, is that when it goes wrong, you end up looking a complete prat.

By the time the fourth Test came around in Trinidad, the other selectors became serious about dropping Ian, but I was loath to be without a player who was still capable of winning a Test with either bat or ball, and managed to hold them off. However, I saw this as an opportunity to get him fired up, so I called him into my hotel room and told him that he had more or less scraped into the team on a split decision. Nothing heavy, just a quiet word. Which is how I think these things should be dealt with. He still didn't get any runs, but he certainly bowled with a lot more zip after that. To a certain extent, we were all guilty of overrating ourselves when we arrived in the West Indies and were physically underprepared, but I think this applied more to Ian than anyone else. He is a fiercely proud man, and an extraordinary competitor, but just occasionally these are qualities that can work against you. For instance, here he was early on the tour bowling filth, but still clinging to the view that the long-hop disappearing in the general direction of Bridgetown Harbour was the best delivery in the world – that some incompetent slogger, by virtue of possessing a good eye, a heavy bat and an outrageous degree of luck, had somehow managed to hoik it over an absurdly short boundary. In his mind, he was still racing in and taking wickets. Botham's self-belief is such that he could shuffle off to slip with figures of 1-0-36-0 wondering what cruel hand of fate had prevented him from doing the double hat-trick. This trademark of his, that he is in his mind always doing, or about to do, great things, is a mixed blessing. When it is going right, everyone knows what remarkable things can happen. When it is going wrong, he doesn't always step back and look closely enough at himself from the outside. The rest of the team were looking closely enough at him all right, and all they could see was someone who hardly bowled in the nets, and was disappearing for five an over in the middle. No wonder they got disgruntled, and however much I might not have cared for the way they got it across to me, I failed to find the right way to get Ian firing as he can.

Man management can be a difficult balancing act, with so many different characters to deal with, as with Phil Edmonds, for example, in India in 1984-85. Philippe was having terrible problems with his run-up out there, a horrible stuttering thing that had the lads giggling out loud on occasions, and it was only his strong upper body and arm action that enabled him to release the ball at all. It was not quite an attack of the yips, the sort that seems to plague left-arm spinners more than any other type of bowler, but it was not a pretty sight. So, one evening while we were up-country in some cockroach hotel with nothing much to do, I decided to take a deep breath and have a word with him on the subject. He was lying on his bed reading when I poked my head round the door to crave audience, whereupon, without so much as a glance up from the book, he said: 'If you've come to talk to me about the run-up, don't bother.' As far as I was concerned, that was all I needed to hear. As long as Phil was happy, so was I. Sure enough, he bowled bloody well throughout the series and was a major factor in our success – and that was a case of getting the man-management right. No heavy hand needed, just an acknowledgement that he was aware of the problem, and would deal with it in his own way. The hands off approach with Botham in the Caribbean was based on the hope that he too would sort out his own problems, but this time it just didn't happen.

Of all the problems we had on that tour, however, I would have to say that the biggest nightmare of the lot involved Graham Gooch. He is not the type to break into a song and dance routine, even when he is scoring triple centuries at Lord's, but on this trip he had the permanent countenance of a bull hound that has just swallowed a wasp. We all knew, given the presence of the previously banned Gooch, Emburey, Willey and Taylor that there would be a certain undercurrent to the tour, but we equally knew that those concerned simply had to ignore what was only ever going to be a mild dose of political windbagging. There were one or two light demonstrations early on in Trinidad, but since Trinidad is the sort of place where they'll demonstrate about anything and everything – between meals almost – the presence of cricketers who had previously been paid to play in South Africa was not a major issue. They were far happier watching cricket than carting placards around, unlike some of the politicians who appeared to imagine that there was some sort of relationship between votes and the amount of hot air that could be spouted without pausing for breath.

One of those politicians who did make a noise was a minuscule and now long-forgotten member of the Antiguan parliament, who was so important that the outlet for his laboured huffings and puffings was some minor free-sheet rag. Graham read it, and as his memory is as elephantine as mine is sieve-like, he never forgot it. So much so, that his one ambition for the rest of the tour appeared to be to wring some sort of apology out of this guy. The longer it went on, and the longer this apology failed to materialize, the more Graham seemed to dissolve into this 'I want to go home' mentality, and it became such a hang-up that the Test and County Cricket Board even flew out a representative, Donald Carr, to try and talk him round. Between Donald and myself we did persuade him to stay, but there is no doubt at all that he allowed himself to be distracted from his cricket by the wafflings of this minor politician in some equally minor island publication. Neither did he appear to grasp the fact that the government of Antigua, never mind a member of the opposition back bench, is not renowned for having a huge sway on world affairs. It's a bit like refusing to play Test cricket in England just because the opposition councillor in Ilford has given him some stick in the *Essex Chronicle*. It was all so trite and silly, and not half as serious as Graham imagined, although in fairness he was singled out from the rest because he had captained the Brewery tour to South Africa. Ironically, he had only led that side because the others had not wanted Boycott as captain.

With Botham already closeted in his hotel room sticking pins in pressmen dolls, here we had another of our best players who had basically withdrawn from public view, feeling hard done by and miserable. Part of Graham's character is that he does hang on doggedly to any principle he feels strongly about, and when it comes to South Africa, he will defend himself to his dying day about freedom of speech, movement, employment, and that there are no guarantees about being picked for England. I can vouch for the latter, but sticking to your guns is all very well until you start regarding minor pin pricks as open wounds. I don't believe that any other member of that touring party, having read the offending paper under the same circumstances, would have done anything other than shrug their shoulders and ignore it. There are times, as with 'Both', as with us all, when character strengths (and determination is one of Graham's very finest qualities as a cricketer) become character flaws instead.

The last straw on that tour (among the million or so we had been clutching at ever since we arrived) was in failing to prevent the blackwash in the final Test in Antigua, when the pitch really played well enough for us to have gone home with something from the wreckage. I was especially annoyed because Gooch and myself were batting easily enough on the final afternoon to bring out the other side of Viv's nature, and that made a pleasant change in itself. He first tried to orchestrate a ball change for one that was not only about thirty overs newer but was also a different make, and having frothed over when my objection was sustained, then began ranting about my gardening expeditions while Harper was bowling. 'If you think I'm going to miss a trick out here when we're 4-0 down, think again,' I told him. 'The more you rant and rave, the less of a hurry I'm going to be in.' So he ranted and raved even more. I was bloody furious about getting out to Harper soon afterwards, and we lost the game with about fourteen overs left. The mood soon changed, though, to one of relief that it was all over. On most tours there is something to look back fondly on, but not this one.

Even though the English season was imminent, I stayed on for a few extra days of relaxation and contemplation, but this was not enough to kick start a numbed brain as the Leicestershire committee discovered on the day I got back. I got home to a mountain of mail and a disconnected telephone, and managed to forget all about the players' pre-season cocktail party. The club captain, fresh from his Caribbean triumph, finally puffed in a good hour late, but profuse apologies all round did not cut much ice with the chairman Charles Palmer, as he made perfectly plain. This was doubly unfortunate as I was waiting on the award of a benefit the following year, which, with a remarkable degree of pettiness, they managed to defer until I had one foot on a plane to Australia the following October. 'Well, Gower,' I thought to myself as I trudged home that night. 'From palm trees to Palmer ... one bloody cock-up after another.'

There is scarcely enough time between the end of a Caribbean tour and a new domestic season for any deep reflection, but neither did it take a genius to work out that the pressure was now on me, and the captaincy, in a very big way. At the end of the 1985 series I had received many encouraging letters, from the likes of A.C. and P.B.H., and even one from Gooch saying that it had been a pleasure to play under me. A few months later and the media was in full cry demanding a change at the top, and the major charge against me was of captaining too much by committee, letting things drift and generally not maintaining a high and angry profile when we were doing so poorly. It was a touch harsh I thought, given the difficulties we encountered on that tour, but when a team is losing, you would be daft not to expect a certain amount of flak from the press.

At the end of the tour, I had a de-briefing meeting with the selectors, during which P.B.H. delivered a pull-your-finger-out message. Nothing specific, just a general intimation of dissatisfaction about my hands-off style of leadership. What irritated me about this was that he appeared to be doing precious little other than imitating various reports he had read in the newspapers. I would have been grateful for more of an opportunity to go into our problems in greater detail, but in another way I was just happy to get another chance, as I really did think that I would come out of that meeting as England's former captain. It wasn't much of a chance – the first Test only in a split summer with India and New Zealand – but I was confident enough of getting the show back on the road against less intimidating opposition.

As things turned out, we could hardly have made a worse start to the summer, losing the one-day series on run-rate after one victory apiece, and then, much worse, the first Test at Lord's by five wickets. India came into that match with an awful Test record, something like one win in their last forty, and as it was also their first victory at Lord's, it made our defeat all the worse. I did not expect to survive if we lost, and I was not wrong, although in the end it was the manner of my dismissal rather than the sack itself that soured things. I had, by all accounts, upset P.B.H. on the fourth day of the game by popping into the sponsors' lunch tent for a drink and a chat on the players' guests table, although why this should have caused offence I don't know. It has been suggested that as we were struggling in the game, I annoyed P.B.H. by being seen in the tent when he thought I should have been on the dressing room balcony making appropriately glum faces for the benefit of the cameras, but if so, it was a fairly good example of double standards. You could barely see the selectors behind a great mountain of salmon and strawberries, and I certainly had no inkling while I was in the tent (and it was only for a few minutes) that I had upset anyone.

It was more than likely that May had also been irked by my response to the national clamour for a more bullish style of captaincy – having thirteen T-shirts run off before the Texacos, one of which had the words 'I'm In Charge' plastered all over the front, and the other twelve 'I'm Not'. It was, I thought, an acceptably light-hearted response, while at the same time acknowledging that I had taken the message on board. This is not to say that I agreed with the criticism, because I still believe that there is more to captaincy than shouting and waving your arms around. I would encourage all the players to come to me at any time and offer the benefit of their opinion, which was sometimes acted upon and sometimes not, but it did get everyone involved and also gave the players status. In the end, of course, because of results, it dissolved into the 'Who the hell is running the team?' type of argument.

At the end of the first Test against India, which we lost around mid-afternoon on the final day, I went up to the balcony to do the usual post-match stuff for the TV, at which point P.B.H. was down below offering the captaincy to Gatting. When I came downstairs to the dressing room, P.B.H. took me into one of the back rooms at Lord's and said something like, 'Thank you for your efforts over the last two years, but we've decided it's time for a change, and we'd like Mike to do the job from now on.' Nothing dramatic, just fairly blunt stuff, and I accepted it without too many words on my own part either. However, when I got back into the changing room, Gatt's initial message of 'bad luck' was quickly followed by commiserations from the rest of the troops, and it was only at that stage that I realized that I had been the last to know, rather than the first. I was not impressed at all by that, but the overriding feeling was more sad than bitter. My last shot at humour that day was to pull off the 'I'm In Charge' T-shirt and throw it at Gatt as he was being interviewed.

I knew it had gone wrong, I knew it was the most likely outcome to losing the game, and a tally of played six lost six since the previous summer was the sort of record that deserved the sack in many ways. It still left me numb. You are never fully prepared for moments such as this. P.B.H.'s handling of the sacking was heavily criticized at the time, which, I suppose, made me feel slightly better about it. I tended to agree with my sympathizers, but it is anything but a lingering grudge, and there is no reason to be anything other than friendly with my ex-chairman nowadays. I missed the following Test at Headingley with a shoulder injury, the result of a fielding collision with the pavilion boundary wall in the Lord's match as opposed to the long-term problem that flared up later, and it was perhaps just as well that I did have a game off. I had been very low since my sacking, and the injury gave me time to reflect on the fact that the end of the world was not yet nigh, and that I'd be far better off getting stuck into my cricket and enjoying it once again.

By the time I returned for the Birmingham Test, I was in a much better frame of mind altogether, and although it felt a little strange not being in charge, I thoroughly enjoyed the game. When I had taken over from Willis, I made a conscious decision to seek out his advice on the field – both as a way of keeping him involved and also because it would have been silly not to draw on his experience – and Gatt did the same with me at Edgbaston. The only odd part of the set-up was Gatt's insistence, probably out of habit, of calling me 'skip'. Conversations would go something like this: 'What do you think, skip?' 'No, Mike. You skip, me Gower.' 'Oh yes, sorry skip. Do you think Dill's good for a couple more overs?' It actually went on for the rest of the summer. There was obviously a certain irony in that I had helped Gatt on the road to his success a couple of years earlier by insisting on taking him as vice-captain to India, and now here we were with him as my boss. I was also told by one or two players that Gatt had always wanted the top job, and had actively connived behind my back to get it. Whether that's true, I have no way of knowing, but I'd like to think not.

There were three Tests left to play against New Zealand, and although I made a half century in the first of them, I gradually dissolved into a hopelessly negative frame of mind and reached the stage – just before the second Test at Trent Bridge – where I had seriously had enough of cricket. Whether this was a delayed reaction to the sacking I don't know, but everything seemed to have got on top of me, and things came to a head in Leicestershire's championship match against Kent at Canterbury when I became as depressed as I had ever been. It began on the first night of the game, when we had about ten minutes to bat after bowling them out for 329, and were 2 for 2 with Dilley on a hat-trick before the bowlers had time to turn on the bath taps. I sent in Jonathan Agnew, nominally as night-watchman, although he appeared to be under the impression that he was going for the fastest century of the season. He hit the hat-trick ball for four, snicked the next one for four more, and then had his stumps re-arranged aiming to smear Alderman over the pavilion. I gave him what can best be described as an old fashioned look as we crossed in the outfield, and although there were only a couple of overs left to negotiate, I could scarcely concentrate any better than Agnew had. I poked and prodded away, and if there had been anyone watching from my old school, they would have left wondering how I had ever been selected for the King's Third XI.

Off I went 6 not out and feeling unutterably miserable, and spent that evening in the team hotel at Chilham chatting to my old chum, the Kent captain, Chris Cowdrey. Normally I will talk about most things except cricket on a Saturday night away from home, but I was so down at the time that we must have spent four hours or so locked together in the sort of conversation that must have resembled a talk to the Samaritans.

Next day, the Sunday League game was washed out by a torrential downpour, which gave me even more time to accumulate negative thoughts, and as the rain beat down on the hotel window, I stared at the bedside phone and began to have serious thoughts about phoning Gatting and pulling out of the final Test the following Thursday. Eventually, I persuaded myself to wait until I had batted on Monday morning before deciding on anything quite so drastic, thinking 'Well, I'll probably go out, cream a glorious century, and wonder what it was all in aid of.' In the event, I lasted five balls, barely looked as though I knew one end of the bat from the other, and trooped off after missing a straight one from Alderman. I thought again about phoning Gatt, but for one reason or another decided not to, and in the end I was marginally perked up by a highly enjoyable game. Phillip DeFreitas scored his maiden century, which probably booked his winter ticket to Australia, and we were only six runs short of victory when our last man, George Ferris, was lbw to Alderman.

It scarcely seemed to matter whether I scored runs or didn't, as I discovered during the final two Tests of that summer. I made 70-odd at Trent Bridge, and a century at the Oval without losing this curious feeling of being, mentally, miles away. Flat wasn't the word for it. I'd gone down faster than a soufflé after someone opening the oven door. I was trying to explain how I felt to Fred Rumsey during that Oval Test when he said, 'If that's how you feel, why don't you ask Leicestershire if you can take the rest of the summer off?' So I did. Mike Turner was very good about it, more or less agreeing straight away that it was perhaps the best thing for both of us, but it wasn't easy explaining to the players that their club captain was too jiggered to see the season out. Still, I left Turner's office with a great feeling of relief, and although I still kept a reasonably high profile around the ground, the rest from playing cricket was all I really wanted. I didn't go on holiday, or anything like that. I watched a bit, slept a bit, reflected a bit.

The decision also gave Leicestershire the chance to reflect on my position at the club, and it was no great surprise when they too decided that a change of leadership might be best for all concerned. When Mike Turner put it to me, I had to agree that whatever difficulties were involved in trying to captain a county side when you are away on Test duty for such long periods, I had not given the club the sort of attention that it required. My mind had too often been elsewhere, even when I was physically on the ground at Grace Road, and Turner wondered whether it would not be in both our interests for me to take a year off from captaining Leicestershire. As I put my boots away that August, I was left to reflect that I had lost two captaincies in the same season.

CHAPTER NINE

A rum tour

FOR the rest of the players, there was only about a month's break between the end of the season and the touring party leaving for Australia, which is not really enough time to recharge the batteries, and our early form that winter was pretty poor. My own feelings were certainly mixed – pleased to be on the tour, especially to the country I enjoyed most, but rather disappointed not to have been appointed vice-captain. I knew quite a bit about the Australian players and the country, and also felt that just because I had been sacked as captain this did not mean that I no longer had anything to offer should anything happen to Gatt out there. On reflection, this was more than a little naive.

Once you have sacked someone from that sort of job, you don't want them to get their hands back on it for two very good reasons: either you are afraid that he will make a hash of it all over again, or else you are even more afraid that he will do it rather well, in which case you will look a mug for sacking him in the first place. So for those reasons it may have been an unrealistic hope on my part. I could also see why they plumped for John Emburey as Gatt's deputy. He was a very good cricketer, with a good cricketing brain, and he at least had some experience of Test cricket in Australia. This did not apply to either the captain, or the guy who had just been appointed the first full-time manager in England's history, Micky Stewart. I knew nothing much about Stewart other than his previous reputation as team manager of Surrey, a job he did not manage to hang onto for that long, but I did happen to know that he held a none too complimentary opinion of me. Surrey had previously passed through Singapore while on a close-season tour, and Stewart had run into an old schoolboy cricketing chum of mine, Chris Kilbee, who was then living and working in the Far East. My name cropped up in conversation, and Chris was left in little doubt that M.J. Stewart regarded me as a professional talent-waster. This duly got back to me, and while I have always tried to judge people as I find them, and not on hearsay, it was not surprising that I regarded him with a modicum of suspicion. I had a fairly gentle honeymoon period with him on that tour, what with him feeling his way in a new job, and the senior players – such as Lamb, Botham and myself – being given a certain amount of latitude. Stewart more or less left us to our own devices in terms of practice and organizing ourselves, reserving the sergeant-major stuff for the likes of Broad and French. However, before the first Test in Brisbane the whole party got their first taste of the soccer-manager style of bullshit for which he became justifiably famous. Part of his pre-match speech, which was a sort of cross between Agincourt and 'Come on the Arsenal', that he expected everyone to be tucked up in bed straight after the players' dinner. At about ten o'clock, in fact. Now, while none of us had plans to bring in the dancing girls and make heavy demands upon the night porter, neither did we visualize the hotel ceiling vibrating to the sound of synchronized snoring ten minutes after the cheeseboard. It took a little while for us to take in precisely what Stewart was saying, but at that point there were howls of protest from Botham and Lamb, followed by a milder objection (but objection none the less) from the captain himself. The issue made from our side of the table was that while no-one was going to advocate finishing dinner and then going off for twenty more beers, there was precious little point in lying in bed staring at the ceiling either. We finally managed to convince Stewart that a few private drinks and a quiet chat before retiring when suitably tired was a decent way to prepare, but it was an early indication of what the manager thought on these occasions.

As I said before, we had a dreadful build-up to that Test match, and while English newspapers are hard to come by in Australia (up-to-date ones anyway) the Aussie press kept us well in touch with what was being written about us back home via what are known as 'quotebacks'. This involves some Reuters man scanning the papers in London, digging out all the juicy quotes, and firing them off to Australia where they are seized upon all the more gleefully if England are doing badly. Which we were. Ergo, lots of 'Pom Press Rubbishes Hapless England' headlines all over the *Sydney Morning Herald* and the like. Relations, therefore, became a touch strained – not least during the flight back to the East coast following the match against Western Australia at Perth. Somewhere along the line, that day's Aussie papers were loaded on board, and Botham – who had just signed for Worcestershire after leaving Somerset – had his attention drawn to an article lifted from the *Evening Standard* in which the author commiserated with Worcestershire for having signed a 'boorish bully'. Botham went mildly potty, steamed down the aisle looking for the offending scribe, and was even more put out to find him sitting next to Gatt playing cards. Peter Lush, the tour manager, had to calm him down, but it was indicative of the strain the tour was already under before the first Test had even begun.

One of the press' criticisms was levelled at the management for not having appointed me to a position of responsibility. I had, it is true, risen to the dizzy heights of chairman of the social committee, but this essentially involves dreaming up silly fines for the players' pool. I was therefore something of a lost soul, and I'm afraid to say I let myself down rather badly in terms of personal behaviour during the very first game of the tour up in Bundaberg. The management had just delivered the customary eve-of-first-game speech along the lines of, 'It may be only a Country XI but let's start as we mean to go on ... etc, etc,' when we attended a reception given by the Bundaberg Cricket Association, at which I made the elementary mistake of getting involved in a drinking session with I.T. Botham. To borrow golfing terms, I'm about a 16 handicap compared to Ian's scratch when it comes to a serious session at the bar, and the situation was made worse by the fact that Bundaberg is famous for only one thing: rum.

Someone had told me that the only way to deal with the Bundy rum, and not wake up the next morning feeling as though you had just been in collision with the Nullabor Express, was by diluting it with large quantities of ginger ale, which I've since discovered is the one sure way to oblivion. Both and I got ourselves ensconced in some quiet corner of the bar, and, as an antidote to the formality of the proceedings around us, got stuck into the Bundy and dry. As usual, 'Both' was a more than adequate opponent for the local firewater, while for me, every visit from my glass to the optic represented a firm push on the self-destruct button.

Eventually it was time to leave, which 'Both' managed under his own steam, but I was literally dragged, giggling and groaning, back to the team bus. Botham and Lamb somehow got me back to my room, where they removed my clothes, stuck me under a shower and attempted to impress upon me that a return to the bar (which is where they were going) would not be a good idea. This I knew, having by now lost the power of speech, but I did make one valiant effort to get two dripping limbs into one trouser leg before falling down in a heap on the carpet. Not surprisingly, I was on the carpet again the following morning, in front of Messrs Lush, Stewart and Gatting attempting to explain away some fairly ordinary behaviour. In the event I got away with a mild reprimand for what, on the Lush/Stewart/Gooch tour four years later would undoubtedly have been viewed as a hanging offence.

The incident may well have convinced the management that they needed to get me more responsibly involved in the decision-making aspects of the tour, as I was clearly not coping well. My form was poor, and in the course of bagging a pair during the WA game at Perth, I remember apologizing to Ken MacLeay for not being in remotely good enough form to get anywhere near his outswingers. Anyway, the suggestion of the press was that I would benefit from more responsibility on the tour was then taken up by the management, who co-opted me onto the selection and tour committees. It was still very much Gatt's tour, of course, but it certainly gave me a renewed sense of purpose, and from then on things certainly began to look up a bit. Gatt, in fact, had been bloody good to me in volunteering to swap places in the order, which meant I was in comparatively calmer waters at No 5, and I also owed a sizeable debt to the WA left-arm bowler Chris Matthews in that first Test. Matthews, fielding in the slips, dropped me on nought in the first innings, which would have made it three zeroes in a row, but after struggling early on, I was eventually back in something like decent form by the time I was finally out for 51. I had always felt that there had been enough plus points from my period as captain for me to be involved as more than just another player, and it was good to regain that feeling of self-worth. Another aid to my rehabilitation was that the team suddenly hit form. After being written off before the Brisbane Test, with good reason, we beat Australia pretty convincingly, and all the good memories of 1985 began to come flooding back. We were chirpy, Border began snapping at people in press conferences, their selectors began to get it in the neck, and even the 'quotebacks' had turned from 'Pathetic Poms' to 'Awful Aussies'. As a touring party, we had split into three distinct groups, captain and management, senior players, and the rest, but it was a chemistry that worked very well once I had managed to sort myself out. The last thing Gatt needed was having to devote a lot of his time to someone like me.

Looking back, I had arrived in Australia more sorry for myself than was either good for me, or necessary. I must have come across as a hopeless case as well, because early on the tour I had a chat with a journalist that threatened to take the form of an obituary. We played in Adelaide before the WA game, and one or two of us thought it would be quite nice to take the train to Perth across the Nullabor Plain instead of yet another aeroplane trip. As the itinerary for that tour was such that I could have won 'Mastermind' with Australian airport lounges as my special subject, thirty-six hours trundling across the outback seemed quite appealing. Phil Edmonds came along, as did Henry Blofeld and Scyld Berry from the press corps, and after several hours of watching nothing but the occasional red bush float past the window, I happily agreed to accommodate Scyld and his notebook for a piece for the *Observer*. I was, though, somewhat startled to find that the theme for his piece was my retirement from cricket – based on observations of my problems and general demeanour since losing the captaincy.

He took great trouble to reassure me that there were still a lot of people who took great pleasure from watching me play, and who would be deeply disappointed if I gave it all up. That was nice to know, but it was still slightly worrying to realize that people suspected I might be thinking of packing it in. It certainly made me stop and think, and the more I thought, the more reassured I was that this was just a temporary phase I was going through. The whole process of transmitting my thoughts to a journalist in conditions of comparative solitude turned out to be highly therapeutic. I had my close friends in the dressing room, but you rarely unburden your innermost cricketing thoughts to colleagues, and this was almost the first time that I had been required to stop and think hard about what had happened to me and where I wanted to go. Looking at the whole thing objectively, I had indeed started to think about life after cricket – albeit without planning too hard – and had realized that I was now on the way down as a top-class cricketer. Wouldn't it be nice, I'd been thinking, if the phone rang tomorrow and I was offered the chairmanship of some public company at £400,000 a year plus perks, and I could just sling the Gray-Nicolls into the ocean and start afresh on some new challenge outside cricket. What that train journey did for me, though, was to focus my mind on life without cricket. And frankly, it was not particularly appealing. Yes, I was still motivated by playing. Yes, I did still want to score runs in Test matches. And yes, despite this lurch into a bout of self-pity, there was still a lot of enjoyment to be had from playing for many more years yet. I was still not thirty, for heaven's sake, and whether or not some people regarded me as a failure, this was what I did best. Emotions come into cricket as in every walk of life, and whatever worries and even fears I might have had at that stage, they suddenly began to seem more trivial.

By the time we played the first Test at Brisbane, my mind was much more uncluttered, and in the second Test at Perth I played as well as I have ever done in scoring 136. True, it was one of the flattest of pitches, and their attack had been nicely blunted by Broad and Athey by the time I got in, but in terms of revitalizing my whole outlook, this innings could not have been more timely. A few weeks earlier, I had been so out of form, I was standing at the crease wondering whether I wouldn't be better off selling encyclopedias for a living. Now, it was 'What an easy game this is,' and I ended up with an average in the fifties by the end of that series. The only motivational problem I encountered later on in the tour, and one or two others as well, was having to wind up again for the World Series Cup matches after we had retained the Ashes. I was already feeling that one-day cricket was not quite the real thing, and I honestly struggled to gear myself up properly all the way through the qualifying matches. We went off at one stage to play the West Indies in Devonport, where the temperature was just above freezing, and the stadium better suited to a game of Icelandic football. It was there that I realized I could no longer kid myself about this form of cricket. There was a game there to be won, but that was about the extent of it. Nothing really tugged at the emotional strings in the way that a Test match still did, and it was only when we qualified for the finals of that one-day competition that I became even remotely fired up to play.

In spite of winning all three competitions that winter, I think I had decided well before the end of the tour that it was now time to take a winter off from cricket. I was in a much better frame of mind than I was when the tour started, but I still felt stale and jaded. Frankly, if it had not been for Lamb and Botham, I don't think I'd have got a run out there. The three of us had played so much cricket together, and socialized so much, that we kept each other going. A mutual piss-taking society, if you like. As you get older, I think you become a little less resilient at coping with the bad times. The exuberance of youth no longer carries you through quite so easily. So 1986 certainly pulled me up short as a year – it was the first in my twenty-nine that I found a struggle. Thrashed by the West Indies, stripped of the captaincy of England, told by Leicestershire (albeit with a touch more compassion) that they too would prefer someone else in charge, so wiped out that I could not bear to see out the domestic season, and losing my mother. Since making my international debut in 1978, I had played in 87 Test matches and getting on for 100 one-day internationals without missing a single overseas tour, and when I failed to get myself properly psyched up for an Ashes tour in Australia, I knew it was time for some serious mental stocktaking. I had reckoned on having another five years or so playing Test cricket, but only if I took a breather. So I had already decided when I flew home that I would not be available for next winter's World Cup and the twin tours to Pakistan and New Zealand.

Before I had left for Australia, Mike Turner had called me in to discuss the possible replacements for club captain the following summer, and by and large it boiled down to two: Nigel Briers, who had been with the club since he was a schoolboy, and vice-captain Peter Willey. Even if I had not been on good terms with the chairman, Charles Palmer, the previous summer, and was still to some extent feeling that the club had hidden behind my forthcoming benefit to take the captaincy off me, I was still on good terms with Mike and keen to help. I recommended Nigel, on the grounds that he was a Leicestershire lad, who had been at the club for a long time, but was still only thirty and had a lot of years left in him. I felt that Peter had done a good job as senior pro, and would remain better suited to that role.

There was another reason for not giving the job to Peter. He was a bluff, forthright character who did not always help to create a harmonious atmosphere. He called a spade a spade, and did not go in for diluting his phraseology when observing the traditional diplomatic niceties. If Will thought that anyone, whether it be junior pro or club president, had behaved like a prat, then the person concerned would be informed of Will's views on the matter in precisely that language. He was respected as a cricketer throughout the whole dressing room, and liked as a character in certain areas of it. Mine included. For a few of our players, however, the unsympathetic side of Will's nature grated away at them. It is fair to say that Peter did not err on the side of the consoling word in the ear when the alternative was to hang you by the jockstrap from a dressing room peg. Yet underneath the hard exterior there lay a more understanding nature than many realized. Some coped well, others did not, and it was at least a partial factor in one or two departures from the club around about that time. Nick Cook had left for Northamptonshire, and although his departure was mainly because he was only considered for first-class cricket, it was no secret that he and Peter did not have a relationship made in heaven.

Willey had left Northamptonshire under a cloud, having appeared for the groundsman in an unfair dismissal case against the club, and was regarded as a bit of a stirrer. However, I enjoyed his contribution to the dressing room. He was still a bloody good cricketer, and was technically a very correct batsman despite that two-eyed stance of his that eventually stopped only just short of turning him into a left-hander. More importantly, though, he made a big effort to fit in for his first season with us and was particularly good at analyzing strengths and weaknesses, both with his own team-mates and the opposition.

He loved playing, hobbling along on a pair of knees that would have finished a lesser character ten years earlier, and his knowledge and input certainly helped my own game. As a senior player, and being the sort of person I am, perhaps I both needed and appreciated his bluntness. If he said, as I'm sure he did a few times, 'Gower that was a crap shot because ...' then I'd listen, but of course there were others with whom it did not work – who would have interpreted plain speaking with unreasonable intolerance – and one of them was Phillip DeFreitas. The potential for that relationship to go wrong was always there when Daffy returned from his first overseas tour to Australia, and it took precisely one match to do so. We opened our Grace Road season against Essex with a cloud of sulphur dioxide hovering over the ground, reportedly from a nearby power station, but quite possibly the by-product of a toxic chemical reaction from mixing one angry Willey with one sulky DeFreitas.

Daffy, who had gone out to Australia as a precocious youngster, had returned as one of the bright hopes for English cricket. He had had a good tour, although he had perhaps been a slight victim of the common media trait of going overboard for a young, inexperienced player with a higher than average degree of talent. As far as Leicestershire were concerned, and Willey in particular, they did not want DeFreitas to be overpowered by his own publicity as it is very easy at that age to have one's head turned by it. What we asked him to do was no more than we had asked of him the previous season, namely to work hard at his game and listen to the advice of senior people. Unfortunately, it went wrong in that very first game when Daffy bowled poorly (he did not take a wicket in the match) and Will cracked down hard on him. Daffy did not appreciate that Will's motives were purely designed to help his development, and the situation gradually disintegrated as the season went on. Daffy was dropped at one stage for disciplinary reasons, and during another match at Grace Road (I was away on Test duty) there was an embarrassing display of the club's dirty washing being hung out to dry in public. Dirty washing in the literal sense, albeit hurled rather than hung out, when Daffy's kit was tossed off the players' balcony and spectators in front of the pavilion were treated to the unusual sight of the rose beds festooned with vests and jock straps.

Jon Agnew was the man responsible, apparently in retaliation to some juvenile act of DeFreitas' with the salt cellar over lunch. Daffy was sufficiently unhinged by this to drive out of the ground in mid-match, pursued by a perspiring Mike Turner, and he was gone for a good two hours. In mental terms, he was gone for the rest of the season – and I had good reason to suspect that something like this was likely to happen after the tour to Australia.

A great deal was made of the fact that Ian Botham took Daffy under his protective wing during that tour, the veteran campaigner looking after the young pretender to his throne, and that Daffy received an invaluable early lesson from one of the world's best all-rounders on the skills, attitudes and tricks of the trade required to make an impact in the high-pressure jungle of international cricket. Now while this was up to a point perfectly true, there was also the adverse effect that Both can have in these sort of circumstances. Ian's methods have always been slightly unorthodox, and his anti-authoritarian views on life in general would probably have been absorbed by Daffy as well. It would be surprising to me, therefore, if the young man – any young man – had not picked up a slightly false perspective of how to harness his talents at this level. They shared a room together in the first week of the tour, which would have been an eye-opener for Daffy in itself, and this might not have been the best of ideas in hindsight. The good news would have been the instant close contact for a young player still perhaps a bit bewildered by it all (after all he barely got his county cap before his England one) but the bad news might have been in exposing some-one who was very impressionable to such a uniquely unorthodox character. Neither, in a different way, was Mike Gatting a wholly good influence on DeFreitas. The skipper, as did we all, formed the opinion that here was a young player of boundless potential, and he made it quite plain to Daffy (whose family roots were still in London) that should he want to come back to London, then Middlesex would be more than happy to give him a well paid job. From where I was standing, 'Both' and Gatt represented a pretty dangerous cocktail, and I realized then that Willey's mission to keep Daffy's feet nailed to the ground had already become more difficult.

Having rubbed shoulders with the greats and been tempted by the captain of England, it was enough to turn any young man towards premature thoughts of stardom, and while Willey generally received a poor press in terms of man-management at Leicester, I think on this occasion that he was right to stamp on Daffy from the start. It is a difficult balance when a youngster does well early on. You want him to feel special, to fuel the feeling of being a breed slightly apart, and yet you badly need to make sure that his head will still fit his helmet. All Will was trying to do was remind him that county cricket is a daily grind, involves a lot of hard work, and you owe it to your less talented colleagues to produce your best as often as you can. False gold glittering in the background was at the root of our problems with DeFreitas at Leicester, and they never got resolved. There were occasions when Daffy would steam in bowling his socks off, and others when he appeared to be attempting some kind of off-spin. It raised eyebrows in the dressing room and made life very hard for the captain, particularly if his problem player was complaining that he did not feel quite 100 per cent.

Even though a captain might suspect a player of swinging the lead on occasions, it is unreasonable to expect people to turn it on every day in the form of cricket that we play in this country, and it is more often than not a question of where he draws the line. It just so happens that Peter drew his own line lower than most. I obviously got involved, in that Daffy would complain to me about unsympathetic treatment, and ask me why Will had got it in for him. I tried to assure him that this was not the case, and that all that was required was to provide the captain with more evidence of hard work and commitment, but without a great deal of success. He was only a lad, and it was a very confusing time for him. In the end, it was only sorted out by Daffy leaving the club, which was a great pity. Pete was a hard man, both mentally and, as Both once found out during an impromptu wrestling bout in Jamaica, physically. In terms of sheer strength, I never met anyone to match him other than Brian Davison. Davo rarely lost his temper, but when he did you swiftly made yourself scarce. Roger Tolchard upset him on one occasion, and although Davo partly held back on a thump in the chest, Tolly travelled pretty nearly the length of the dressing room, and when Ken Higgs, who was never exactly a lightweight, moved in to arbitrate, Davo picked him up with one hand. An arm wrestling contest between Davison and Willey would have been worth selling tickets for.

Will's summer as captain did not improve when Paddy Clift

threatened to quit after being left out of a one-day game, and it came as no great surprise when Peter gave the job up that winter. Whether I would have been re-appointed had he made a success of it I don't know, but in the event I was, after one of those rare summers in which I finished with a far higher batting average for Leicestershire than I did for England. I topped the county averages with 56, which was almost double the 29.50 I recorded in the Test series against Pakistan. It was a highly forgettable series all round, so wet that those of us who subscribe to the Darwinian theory of evolution spent our time checking for webbed, rather than athlete's foot, and so cold that not even regular blasts of hot air from Pakistan's manager Hasib Ahsan could penetrate the long johns. We lost, too, with four largely soggy draws and defeat in the third Test at Headingley. The weather, in fact, rendered the game at Leeds almost the first of a three match series, and as ever at this ground, it was a job to know whether to bat first or insert. On this occasion, Gatt's job was made even harder because the groundsman, Keith Boyce, had chosen a brand new pitch, and doubts about its lasting properties prompted him to bat first. Doubts about its lasting properties? By noon we were 31 for 5. It was Headingley's amazing propensity for making the ball swing around under clear skies that did for us. That and some poor shots. In three cases, no shot at all – and I was one of them, bowled off a big inside edge as I shouldered arms, fractionally too late, to Imran.

We were all out by about teatime, and with Imran bowling brilliantly in the second innings, we easily lost the match. There was one highly controversial moment, although we were not to know that in comparison with the return series in Pakistan the following winter it barely amounted to a minor tiff. It involved Botham edging a ball towards their wicketkeeper, Salim Yousuf, who made such a fraudulent appeal for a catch – the ball having clanged out of his gloves, onto the ground, and back into them – that cheating was the word that sprang to most people's lips. Both was not impressed, informing Yousuf fairly bluntly that one handed catches off the bounce did not apply outside the school playground, and included one or two short-syllable words to re-enforce his point. One of the umpires, Kenny Palmer I think, had to step between them when the row simmered on (which was just as well for Yousuf's continued good health) and it was with some amusement that I read the next day that the Pakistanis had lodged a complaint against Botham's language. Imran claimed that they were not used to having words like this directed at them, which was even funnier. Wasim Bari, their previous wicketkeeper, had a vocabulary that made Bernard Manning sound like Mary Whitehouse. He was fluent. When Shakoor Rana and Gatt had their bust-up the following winter, some people found it hard to believe England's account of the expletives flowing from umpire to player, but those of us who have played against Pakistan are well aware of their ability to swear in more than one language, however polite and courteous they might be away from the field of combat.

As for the claimed catch, I felt at the time that it was more reprehensible of the four or five fielders standing next to the keeper (all of whom had a clear view) not to withdraw the appeal. Yousuf was young, if not entirely innocent, and perhaps a little over-enthusiastic. Some of the England players had been just as guilty, such as the occasion when Bob Taylor claimed a catch that probably bounced a foot short of him during the 1978-79 series in Australia. It was a startling event, in that Bob was always one of the honest men of cricket, who for some reason appeared to be unaware of what had happened. However, the umpire raised his finger, and none of the fielders close to the batsman felt inclined to call him back, or query Bob's claim. Because it was Bob Taylor, it did not develop into an issue, but when a Pakistani player becomes involved in something similar, he is labelled a cheat. It is, I think, more of a way of life on the sub-continent, simply because life can be so harsh if you do not cut corners from a very early age. However, there is no cricketing country in the world that can claim to have a clean nose when it comes to trying to con the umpire. I tend not to appeal when I clearly know a bloke is not out, but when you stand at silly-point it is very hard to tell sometimes. You ask the question of the umpire and leave it to him. The big thing, always, is to get on with the game if the decision goes against you. Whatever I might have done wrong as England captain, I always tried to move in smartly if I thought a player was about to show dissent.

Imran let himself down badly in this respect during the final Test that summer. Pakistan had scored more than 700 on a flat pitch at

Allan Border is as much a friend as a rival. In 1985 not even his great batting, such as at Old Trafford where he scored 146 not out with a broken finger (and a bat!), could stop England celebrating at the end of the series, when champagne and XXXX both doubled as shampoo – thanks Ian!

The other side of captaincy – losing. 1984, Old Trafford, and I am on the way to a series 'blackwash' at the hands of the West Indies. With me, looking glum on the balcony, are Chris Broad, Norman Cowans, Graeme Fowler, Paul Terry (nursing a broken arm), Nick Cook, and Ian Botham.

Handing over the reins (and the T-shirt) to Mike Gatting after defeat by India at Lord's in 1986.

In 1989, appointed as captain second time around, I felt very confident at the start of it all. My first press conference of the season at Lord's (above) *was much more relaxed than the Saturday night of the Lord's Test* (below). *Shortly after this photo was taken I had left Micky Stewart on his own to answer any further questions, while I decided that* Anything Goes *at the theatre was a better option. I went.*

I was back at Lord's in 1991 as captain, and a victorious one, only because Mark Nicholas had his knuckles broken by Waqar Younis two days before facing Surrey again in the Nat West final. Man of the match was Robin Smith (below), a much loved adopted son of Hampshire, one of the hardest hitters of a cricket ball ever, and surely destined to be one of England's greats.

the Oval, and we were battling to save the game on the last day when Mudassar claimed a bat-pad catch off Botham. David Constant, who had crossed swords with the Pakistanis before, turned it down and Mudassar and Imran went off like firecrackers. There doesn't seem much point in this sort of thing, because modern-day cricketers do not help the umpire by taking the difficult decisions out of their hands (such as walking), so why should they kick up a fuss when what is a marginal decision goes against them? Walking has almost gone the way of the Dodo and the dinosaur nowadays, and Barry Richards' old joke that 'the only time an Australian walks is when his car runs out of petrol' is still funny, but it's now a bit unfair to single them out.

There was one strange incident in that series, in the fourth Test at Edgbaston, when Pakistan were running up yet another big first innings score, and England almost became the first fielding side in history to be 'timed out'. The umpires, Alan Whitehead and Barry Meyer, had returned to the middle after a brief bad light stoppage in mid-afternoon, and although it is customary for the players to follow, England were conspicuous by their absence. Four or five minutes elapsed, by which time the light had deteriorated sufficiently again for the officials to pursue inquiries along the lines of whether England had officially scratched. Meantime, we were still blissfully unaware of all this, and the one obvious clue – a glance at the TV set – had been missed for the simple reason that it was tuned to the horse-racing at Ascot rather than the cricket at Edgbaston. Peter Lush, the tour manager, spilled the beans somewhat mischievously to the press, and Gatt came in for some tremendous flak in next morning's newspapers. The rest of us found it all rather amusing, but quite why the newspapers made so much of it I don't know. It was scarcely unusual for the players to opt to watch horse-racing as an alternative to a picture of the Edgbaston covers, and the twelfth man had simply fallen down on the job of monitoring the umpires' return to the field. Normally, they would have popped a head around the dressing room door, but Edgbaston is unusual in that the umpires' room is quite a long way from the dressing rooms.

Perhaps it was not surprising that the return series in Pakistan that winter was controversial, although no one would have forecast a scenario that almost eclipsed the Bodyline tour for bad feeling. I, at any rate, had decided early that summer to stick to my plan of taking the winter off, and May and Stewart had both been reasonably sympathetic when I brought the subject up with them. I would have liked to have played in the World Cup, but overall, what with the explosion in Faisalabad and a dreary post-Christmas P.S. in New Zealand, it turned out to be a good winter to miss.

The first two or three months of the winter I spent on the benefit, which was hard work but therapeutic – it did the bank balance a fair amount of good. Having done all that, I then cleared the decks for the period of fun and relaxation I had promised myself. I went to Africa, did some skiing in Europe, and also took the opportunity to attend the Winter Olympics in Calgary. Looking back, it was while I was away on the piste, that the embers of my second coming as captain were being stoked.

CHAPTER TEN

A new board game: spot the England captain

I WAS as surprised as everyone else when Faisalabad hit the newspapers. The last time I had been to Pakistan I had ended up captaining the side after Willis went home, with Gatt as my second in command, and things had gone reasonably well. Mike knew the score out there (especially as he had been lbw twice to Shakoor on his England debut in Karachi in 1978) and whatever the provocation it did not seem possible for things to come quite so badly off the rails. There is seldom smoke (most of which appeared to be pouring from Gatt's ears) without fire, and I am quite sure that a certain amount of sympathy was in order. However, where the side – and therefore the captain – may have lost sympathy, was in the award of that £1000 per man hardship bonus. Again, without being there, it is difficult to make a definitive judgement, but I was definitely among those people who thought it an extraordinary decision. Also, by the end of that winter, England's confirmed reputation under Gatt (plus Stewart, let's not forget) was that of a bolshy side. Broad had refused to leave the field in Lahore, then whacked his stumps over in the Bicentenary Test in Sydney en route to New Zealand, and in Christchurch Dilley had been fined for a burst of expletives over the umpiring. Gatt has never been one to hide his feelings on the field, neither would he have taken much notice of what was being written about England in the press at that time. He has never had much time for newspaper reports on the game, although it was an appearance on the front pages rather than the back ones that finally blew the wheels off.

Whatever had gone wrong in the winter of 1987-88, however, the

World Cup had almost been won in Calcutta, and it was no huge surprise when the selectors stuck to much the same nucleus of players for the Texaco Trophy series against the West Indies, even though it meant disappointment for both myself and Ian Botham. Neither Both, who had also taken the winter off, nor myself were included, and P.B.H. and Co. came in for a fair amount of stick. The chairman must have been delighted, therefore, when he made them grovel, in this instance, referring to the press rather than the West Indies.

England won all three matches in the series, and P.B.H. must have felt even more smug when Derek Pringle, whose selection was written off by the press as proof of the chairman's urgent need of a straitjacket, proved to be one of their best players. Personally I was delighted for Pring, who always seemed to be the butt of the press and spectators, and had not had a very good World Cup. One unkind story that came out from that competition involved Ray Illingworth, out there as a BBC commentator, recalling over the breakfast table in Rawalpindi Keith Fletcher's comment when Pring was originally picked for the World Cup. 'Fletch,' said Raymond, 'described him as a banker with both bat and ball.' To which someone replied: 'Are you sure he said banker?' Pring, though, routed the critics, and even had the Headingley crowd chanting for him. As for Gatt, P.B.H. and Micky, any pressure they might have felt from the winter seemed to have been lifted.

I was quite relieved to be back in the squad when the team for the first Test was announced, or as pleased as any batsman can be when selected to face the likes of Marshall and Ambrose. Marshall, who had been described as getting a touch portly and avuncular beforehand, did not seem any less mean from where I was standing, while Ambrose delivered his usual mixture of throat balls and toe crushers. We collapsed against those two from 125 for 0 to 245 all out, and it triggered off an amusing and somewhat curious outburst against the press by Micky Stewart. There had been a photograph in the *Independent* on the morning of the match, taken on the 1984 tour, depicting me in the airborne position attempting to locate (or to be more accurate, avoid) a West Indian bouncer. Micky described this as 'disgraceful journalism', claiming that it was somehow non-patriotic, and not the sort of thing to fill the lads with confidence before a West Indies Test. If this wasn't overreaction, I don't know what is. I liked the photo so much I ordered a copy.

In the end, we drew the Test with reasonable comfort, ending with a big second innings partnership between Gooch and myself. But as the troops disappeared for either a three-day break or one of the two Benson and Hedges semi-finals the following day, the storm was about to break over Gatt. There was, according to a couple of journalists I spoke to later, an amusing episode involving Stewart and the way he found out about the barmaid allegations on the morning after the Test. He was down in Swansea for the B & H semi between Glamorgan and Derbyshire, combining some talent spotting with the man of the match adjudication, and was staying in the same hotel on the Mumbles as two of the cricket correspondents. The two pressmen arrived in the breakfast room before him, and had just been choking on their toast at the front page of *The Sun* when Micky walked in, bade them a cheery good morning (he would still have been in a good mood after the Test) and sat down at a nearby table.

One of the journalists, slightly mischievously, asked Stewart who he thought the England captain would be for the Lord's Test, which brought forth the obvious response of, 'What are you talking about?' The scribe then walked over and plonked *The Sun* onto the manager's table, whereupon a large amount of coughing and spluttering ensued. The headline which went something along the lines of 'Test Skipper In Girl In Room Romp'. Stewart hastily dismissed the waitress, scuttled out to find a telephone, and set off not for the cricket ground at St Helens, but the committee room at Lord's.

I had been booked into the Rothley Court Hotel for the Test match, which is about twenty-five minutes drive from Trent Bridge, but as my house in Leicester was only forty-five minutes from the ground, I had not spent every night at the hotel. I was not there on the Saturday night in question, and as there had been nothing in the dressing-room conversation to suggest that anything out of the ordinary had gone on, the newspaper article took me totally by surprise. It did not surprise me that some of the boys had been in the pub which was alleged to have been the pick-up point for one or two local girls, as it was a favourite watering hole for the players.

Everything else, however, was pretty startling. Gatt was supposed to have taken a barmaid back to his room, and the whole story seemed like a set-up. Why Lord's did not dismiss the whole thing as a mucky newspaper story not worth giving the time of day to, I don't know, but they allowed the whole thing to blow up out of all proportion by dragging the captain and several other players implicated in the article up to London to explain themselves. Gatt admitted the girl in the room, but denied any impropriety – which produced the laughable reaction from P.B.H. of 'Yes, Gatt, we believe you' on the one hand, and 'By the way, you're fired' on the other. It hardly suggested that they believed him at all. The players were stunned by what had happened, and as you can imagine, morale went from something approaching good to rock bottom overnight.

Still, the search for a new captain was on, and I got a couple of press inquiries along the lines of whether I considered myself back in the frame. I said that I thought it likely that I would step back into the job over the dead body of one P.B.H. May, and that in any event I was myself involved in potential disciplinary matters over such weighty matters as the colour of my cricket socks. I had taken possession, courtesy of my tennis partner and Leicester sports shop owner, Tim Ayling, of a number of very comfortable pairs of socks, in every colour you could possibly mention. Except white, that is. I had chosen, partly for a bit of fun, partly because they were more comfortable than any of my regulation cricket socks, to wear a nice patriotic navy blue pair at Trent Bridge. I made 88 not out in them against Marshall, Ambrose and the rest, and as you know what a superstitious lot we cricketers are, had already decided to wear them again. No harm, I thought. Apparently not.

Having not only had the helmet removed by Curtly, but also declined the chance to bat on into the final half hour when I was 12 runs short of a century, I felt I had done my bit for my country, an impression I was swiftly relieved of when I was invited for a small conversation by the England manager before the next Test match. He voiced his concern that the England cricket team was being cheapened by people training and playing in non-white socks, and how worried he was about the hundreds of thousands of potential England cricketers thrusting up their hands in the school classroom and saying: 'Sir, sir, why is Mr Gower wearing blue socks?'

Pompous stuff like the heritage of the game was bandied around, and he made it perfectly plain that he did not care too much for my choice of colour scheme. I replied that I had made quite a few runs in them at Trent Bridge, and would feel very much happier if I had them on again. 'Okay,' he said, 'you can bat in them, but you have to field in grey ones.' I thanked him for his wisdom and sagacity, and left the room wondering how it was, with the England cricket team in turmoil, that the manager came to be immersing himself in such crucial issues as the colour of my socks.

Meantime, there were five names being bandied around as possible replacement as captain. Chris Cowdrey of Kent, Mark Nicholas of Hampshire, Kim Barnett of Derbyshire, Graham Gooch of Essex, and John Emburey, Gatting's vice-captain both with England and at Middlesex. Embers it was who got the call, and he might well have been appointed ahead of Gatt in the first place had it not been for the South African rebel tour in 1982. Part of John's punishment at that time was to be relieved of the Middlesex vice-captaincy, and the captaincy then passed to Gatting when Mike Brearley retired in 1983. Embers was always a loyal lieutenant, having orchestrated the threat of a player strike if Gatt had been forced to resign in Faisalabad, and he was actually playing in a benefit game for Gatt when he got the summons to Lord's. Embers, who accepted the nomination while still in his flannels, was then told that the key model of trouser for the England cricketer from now on would be pyjamas.

Having been thwarted in his attempt to impose a curfew in Brisbane, Stewart was not to be denied this time. Following the business with Gatt, who had asked not to be picked for the Lord's Test, we were told that we were not to be seen in public after ten o'clock. Given the West Indies' over-rate, this left us with an outside chance of being fined for this offence while actually still on the field of play, and on one day of the Lord's match, the last ball was bowled at something like a quarter to eight. This 'cannot be seen anywhere after ten o'clock' edict basically meant that we had to be inside our rooms by that time, and on the eve of the Test there were two or three of us having a drink at the hotel bar, counting down the minutes and seconds as the clock ticked round.

It left me, therefore, with a curious mixture of delight and horror when we bowled out the West Indies next day for 209. On the one hand we were congratulating Dilley and Small, and on the other we were cursing them for condemning us to a life of Dandelion and Burdock and bedtime stories from Micky Stewart. Blanket success for the curfew, you might say, and even I had a hand in this triumph for the early to bed routine by taking a blinding catch at short backward square. However, for those of us who did not much care for the prospect of overdosing on Horlicks, salvation was at hand. By the rest day, it became clear that all these early nights were beginning to catch up with us. The West Indies still managed to take a first innings lead – Marshall bowled us out – and by Saturday night they were 354 for 5 in their second innings. Embers thus became the latest in a long line of England captains for whom the first question at the Saturday night press conference was: 'Can we save it?'

Whatever the answer was, we didn't, and despite the fact that the Manchester weather did its best for us at Old Trafford, we lost that one as well. Gatt was back, but a combination of failure with the bat and the fact that he was still seething about what Lord's had done to him made him withdraw his services again. As for Embers, he must have known he was under pressure, particularly as the next Test was at Headingley. He had recommended playing only one spinner against Pakistan at Leeds the previous summer – which ironically backfired on him when Gatt left him out of the twelve rather than Edmonds – and with his place as a player, never mind as captain, under threat, he must have half expected the 'Dear John' letter. Actually, it was a phone call to the Middlesex team hotel in Nottingham that brought the news, and the nation was once again plunged into debate about the identity of the next victim.

As is customary in this country, a certain amount of black humour prevailed, and one cricket correspondent suggested that the selectors stick an ad in the Situations Vacant column. 'Join our third-rate team. Working conditions dicey (Headingley), no previous experience necessary, perks include company carphone for early notification of the sack.' The press themselves had an internal book on the runners and riders, and during one late night session at the bar (no curfew for them) the name of Christopher Cowdrey popped up at 100/1. Hence the smiling journalist who told me before play at Leeds that he had thrown away a tenner on this improbable longshot, or so he had thought, and was now £1000 better off. Whoever gave those odds, however, must have had a couple too many. Chris, who was a very good friend of mine, was by no means the most unlikely candidate at that time. Kent, who had fairly limited resources, were leading the championship table, and Chris had built up an impressive and deserved reputation as a leader, not least for his ability to get the best out of modest talent, and the way he encouraged his players to enjoy the game.

Chris never had any restrictive attitudes towards the game, striking just the right balance of effort, input and fun: the work hard play hard philosophy. He was, I know, slightly apprehensive about the size of this particular task, and his only previous international experience had been under me in India on the 1984 tour. He had only been expected to figure in the one-day matches out there, but to his surprise, and to that of most people I think, I played him in all five Tests. He was very much aware of his own limitations as a player, but he did, as I say, have this marvellously infectious good humour, which was very important in a place like India. The story has been told before, but is worth telling again, about when he came on to bowl in one of the Tests and was asked whether he wanted Gatting a bit wider. 'If Gatt gets any wider,' he said, 'he'll burst.' At which point, of course, we all burst.

England's problems in the summer of 1988, however, were such that even Chris was slightly low-key at the pre-match dinner. It was a long way from being a tub-thumping speech: although P.B.H. – his godfather – had appointed him with the words, 'We believe that Chris Cowdrey's dynamic style of leadership is what is now required,' Chris himself was not quite as secure in that belief. In the event, we lost the match as badly – if not more so – than the previous two, and Chris contributed next to nothing with the bat. But he had, I thought, led the side very well, and the mood in the dressing room was not, all things considered, too bad. My own mood was a bit of a mixture, in that I had concluded my 100th Test match bang on 7000 runs – landmarks I was reasonably proud of. On the other hand, I did not expect Test match No 101 to come around in too much of a hurry, as I had not played particularly well. In that, at least, I was proved correct.

One plus point for England in that game was Robin Smith. It was his first Test, and I remember sitting on the balcony with him while he was waiting to bat attempting to calm his nerves a little bit. Whether the chat helped or not, he played very well in partnership with Lamby on his debut, and it was only when Allan ripped a calf muscle and had to retire hurt that we went rapidly downhill in that match. My one other memory of that game is of receiving a commemorative medal to mark my 100th Test, and chatting to Brian Johnston about it in a radio interview on the Saturday morning. He asked me whether I would like to have any two words erased from my career ('laid back' being the two he had in mind) and I said, 'Yes, "caught Dujon".' This was both historic and prophetic, because he had already caught me off Winston Benjamin in the first innings, and did so again off Marshall in the second. As I feared, it was too much for the selectors, and it fell to my old mate Cowdrey to tell me that I was dropped for the Oval Test. He naturally enough felt sorry for me at the time, but it was only a day or two later when he began to feel a good deal sorrier for himself.

Cowdrey had been hit on the foot while batting against Adrian Jones of Somerset, and both he and Lamb were struggling to be fit for the Oval. By this time both P.B.H. and Micky were beginning to have doubts about their original casting of Chris as the saviour of English cricket, and this came across in the differing nature of telephone calls from the England manager to his two wounded men. The gist of Stewart's call to Cowdrey, on the Tuesday before the game, was: 'Look, if you're not fully fit now, it may be best if you withdraw. We can always get Gooch to captain the side.' At the same time he was telling Lamb: 'Come down to practice tomorrow and give it a try out, but we can always leave it until Thursday morning.' So we had this bizarre situation in which the captain of England was being persuaded to drop out two days before the match, while the No 4 batsman was given up until half past ten on the morning of the game to let the selectors know whether he was fit and available. It goes some way towards explaining Cowdrey's outburst in *The Sun* after he was omitted from the final Test of the summer against Sri Lanka. His opinion of Stewart after that episode was not a great deal higher than mine.

Gooch duly led the side to another defeat against the West Indies at the Oval, in which Derek Pringle also did a lengthy stint as captain

– the fifth of the summer – after Gooch dislocated a finger. We used twenty-eight players in the six Tests that summer (Sri Lanka included) and while there was ample evidence to suggest that Marshall, Ambrose, Richards and Logie represented formidable opposition, there was a certain amount of irresponsibility in the England camp. I was involved in yet another high turnover of players in the 1989 series against Australia, so can testify (albeit against myself) that it is not a good way to go about building a successful side. Four captains in five Tests was not calculated to improve morale, neither was the Clouseau-like investigation into the barmaid incident.

For me, at least, the season ended on a happier note with a torrent of runs for Leicestershire, including two very good centuries against Notts and Essex. I opened the innings on both occasions, partly because we were struggling in that area, and partly to give myself an extra challenge, and I ended up with over 1000 runs and top of the county averages. Poor old Cowdrey ended up losing the championship by a point, and getting carpeted for complaining of 'shabby treatment' after Gooch's appointment as captain for the winter tour to India. I thought he had put it rather kindly.

The speculation at that time was that Gooch, who had already signed a contract with Western Province in South Africa for the winter, had been talked by Stewart into getting himself released in order to captain England in India. Whether or not that was true, I don't know, but it would have been no great surprise had Stewart worked hard to ensure that Gooch took the team on tour rather than Cowdrey. Chris was more a captain in my own mould, keen to give players more individual latitude, and less consumed by the regimented side of things. He would also have felt, as I did, that the captain was far higher profile than the manager, and all of this would have filtered through to Stewart. In short, Stewart would have less authority, and less opportunity to run things the way he instinctively liked alongside Cowdrey than he would with Gooch. Whichever way Gooch's appointment came about it was to result in the tour never taking place.

The more cynical would say that it was because India were to host the Commonwealth Games in Delhi that they acted as they did after the tour party was announced. The prospect of a mass boycott from other athletics nations clearly did not appeal to the Indian government, so England in general, and Gooch in particular, were objected to. Lots of wrangling ensued, but in the end we were left with a cancelled tour, and a winter off on two-thirds pay. Horrid, I thought. Off to St Moritz again on the TCCB's money. Actually, having had the previous winter off, and finished the summer in good form, I was disappointed when India fell through. The cancellation of the tour came about at the same time as Peter May's resignation as chairman of selectors – he had decided that enough was more than enough.

As the winter wore on, it appeared that the job was no longer to be an honorary one (possibly on the grounds that anyone volunteering to become a national Aunt Sally at least deserves getting paid for it) and various rumours surrounded the likely identity of the new man. Even Stewart was touted for promotion in some areas, which made me shudder a bit, but in the end it turned out to be Ted Dexter. I thought at the time that England's style of leadership was certainly about to change. Peter May, of the neutral suits, minimal communication and whose fluctuations of unease were reflected by the speed with which he revolved loose change in his pocket, had been replaced by a dasher quite capable of arriving at the Grace Gates on a 1000 c.c. motorbike, and who had stated in his inaugural address that he would prefer any barmaids who got involved with England players (presumably single ones) to be 'attractive'. Even if England are just as hopeless under Dexter, I thought, they at least wouldn't be dull.

The talk about my possible re-instatement as captain began almost at once. Ted, who I hardly knew at all, made one or two flattering comments about me, while poor old Graham had the 'wet fish' thing plastered all over one of the newspapers. Ted had previously contributed a newspaper column on cricket, and one of the tabloids enterprisingly dug out of the archives one of his articles which likened Gooch's charisma to being hit in the face by a wet fish. Gower and Dexter, on the other hand were being promoted as some kind of 'dream ticket', although the way things turned out perhaps 'nightmare ticket' would have been more appropriate. Still, it was great to know that I might be in the frame, and the prospect of a second term of office genuinely excited me.

Despite Ted's less than flattering remarks about Gooch, I still assumed that the incumbent captain would be very much in with a chance, although I soon found out that it was a two horse race involving myself and Gatting. We both got interviews while Gooch did not. I got the call one Sunday morning, with Ted inviting me down to his residence in Ealing, and even if I was slightly put out to find Stewart there as well, it was not entirely surprising. It started off with the standard formula. 'Yes I am keen to do the job again. Yes, I do think the team can do well under me ...' that kind of thing. However, the events of the previous twelve months or so quickly brought us round to overtones not directly related to playing the game, such as were there any skeletons in the cupboard that might be dragged out by the press within twenty-four hours of the appointment, and did I have any plans to augment my bank account with South African krugerrands? The answers were 'no' and 'no'. Gatt presumably went through the same sort of thing, with a slight variation perhaps in that his skeletons were already out of the cupboard. That was it, really. There was nothing terribly heavy, and I suppose it was mostly an exercise in giving and receiving the right vibrations. As I drove home, I truthfully had no idea of how the afternoon had gone, but in the event the phone rang a week or so later, and Ted offered me the job. I said, 'Thanks very much, chairman, that's very good news,' and the time between the phone going down and the cork coming out of a bottle of Bollinger was, I have to say, not huge.

As I worked my way through the bubbly, my thoughts were all positive. I told myself that I would not get distracted by the media, and that if things did not go according to plan I will still enjoy it. I think it was this state of mind, the early euphoria of it all that led me to disregard rumours I had picked up a few days earlier that Gatt had been reappointed. Later on in the season, of course, I did indeed discover that he had been, only to be blackballed by Ossie Wheatley's veto. At the time of the appointment, however, I gave little or no thought to it, neither did I pick up any negative vibes at my first press conference.

Micky was quiet, stern faced, and barely said a word. Then, when Ted was asked whether the decision to appoint me had been unanimous, he circumnavigated the question in a manner befitting a former parliamentary candidate. 'After a long discussion,' he said, 'David was the committee's choice.' If this clear get-out clause suggested anything at all, it was only that Stewart might have voted against me, and that would neither have surprised nor bothered me. Had I known, or even suspected, that Ted had not initially voted for me either, I suspect my mood might not have been quite so upbeat. The press conference itself went well, given that everyone wanted to put the events of the previous summer behind them, and there was undoubtedly a honeymoon atmosphere.

We had an early players get-together, mostly comprising of those who had been picked for the India tour, and the only person missing as we gathered at Lord's was Gatting. We had still not spoken about the captaincy decision, and I was keen to do so, but when he phoned and asked me if he could turn up late in order to keep a lunch appointment, I readily agreed. Firstly, I have always believed that senior players should be allowed more latitude; secondly, I wanted to chat to Mike in as cordial an atmosphere as possible; and thirdly, it takes a brave man to come between Gatt and his lunch. My other priority at that gathering was to sit down somewhere quiet with the manager, and sort out our terms of reference. We were on nothing like the same wavelength as he and Gatt had been, so it was important to find out where we stood. It was Stewart who came up to me, in fact, and said, 'How do you want to do this?' and we spent half an hour or so trying to establish the nuts and bolts of the operation. I told him that I would value his support behind the scenes, but in terms of the team itself, and the tactics on the field, then I wanted to run the show. The whole justification for a manager is to take some of the burden off the captain. I suppose, to put it unkindly, to organize some of the more tedious aspects of the job. The clear inference to him was to stay low profile, and I can't imagine that pleased him a great deal. I had formed the view that the team could only be successful on an equal mix of input from captain and manager if those two characters had a great deal of empathy and rapport. The extent of my rapport with Micky could have been accommodated on a postage stamp, and while it was always my hope and intention to keep the relationship as harmonious as possible, I think we both knew that there were certain areas on which we could not agree. I don't know whether it occurred to me at that stage that by taking much the higher-profile stance of the two, I would be the one carrying the can if things went wrong. However, even if it had, it would not have changed anything. I was quite happy to lead from the front, so to speak, as I was truly confident of beating the Australians.

My optimism was scarcely diminished by opening the season with a double century for Leicestershire against Glamorgan. There were the usual two men and a dog huddled together against the April cold, but for once the rather less than motivating effect of pulling on more sweaters than there were people on the ground did not apply. My mood was entirely positive, and every time I swung the bat the ball seemed to disappear for four. This sunny disposition remained unaltered even when my first meeting with Allan Border resulted in a huge defeat for the Duchess of Norfolk's XI in the traditional pipe-opener at Arundel. Before long, the Texaco Trophy series was upon us. Normally, I would not have been able to fill an eggcup with adrenalin at the prospect of three one-dayers, but the new-broom atmosphere, and the weight of public expectation, made this series different. It is customary for the winning captain to claim a psychological boost for the forthcoming Test series, and for the losing one to claim that it has no relevance whatever – but I think both Border and myself realized that this particular Texaco would be of a higher octane than most. Border had been a good friend down the years, and still is, but there was a significantly harder edge to him from the moment he arrived on this tour. He had come in for some flak back at home for not playing the game ruthlessly enough, from the likes of Ian Chappell in particular, and it was clear from the outset that this was not to be a friendly visit. It is an important point, because while no Ashes series is ever akin to taking tea with the vicar, there has always been a tradition of mixing with the opposition afterwards. Not on this tour. The Aussies went out of their way to be unsociable, and the atmosphere on the field was as unpleasant as many of our players could recall. Robin Smith thought it was as nasty as he had ever experienced, and they don't play for fun in the Currie Cup. We rarely saw any of them for a drink after play, the notable exception being Carl Rackemann, who hardly played that summer anyway. Not that we had any plans to give anything away to the opposition, as the chairman made perfectly plain before the first Texaco at Manchester. I had already decided to open, and when I was asked at the press conference who would be going in first with Gooch, I said something along the lines of, 'Don't be too surprised if it's a left-hander.' Ted immediately bristled, and as soon as I was asked which bowler would be left out, the chairman nipped in smartly with a speech that made it clear that he did not approve of alerting the enemy to anything before it was entirely necessary. I was suitably chastened, but not so much that I allowed myself to be talked into bowling by Gooch and Stewart when I won the toss. The pitch had a tinge of green, but I have seen them like that at Old Trafford before, and all that had happened was that they got lower and slower. So bat we did, and we won by a landslide. It was a great start, and although we then went on to win the trophy through some clause in the competition small print after a tie at Trent Bridge, there was one controversial incident that did nothing to lighten the atmosphere for the Ashes series still to come.

It also had a high element of farce. With the match boiling up to a breathless finish, Ian Healy had just acquired a runner (Dean Jones) because of a knee injury sustained in the course of Steve Waugh's run out. The incident began when Healy, Jones, and the other batsman, Tim May, all completed a frantic two, with the wounded Healy, who must have been his school's three-legged champion, scorching home first by several lengths. I suggested to the umpires (and on occasions such as this it is pre-ordained that Dickie Bird should be one of them) that Healy did not quite appear to be an amputation case, and amidst general flapping all round, Jones got the red card. I thought it was all highly amusing, and put my arm around Jones as he walked off and said, 'Thanks for popping in.' Jones replied in less friendly terms, and I later discovered that Border had been foaming at the mouth about it at the press conference after the game. Border's not unnatural concern was that his No 1 wicketkeeper might have done himself some permanent damage before the Test series, while from where I was standing, someone who could hare up and down slightly quicker than Carl Lewis was probably not that badly injured. I had a chat to Border about it before the third match at Lord's, and it was clearly still rankling with him.

I approached A.B. again at the end of the series, when he was in a slightly better mood after Australia's victory, but overall his attitude was completely different to that on the 1985 tour. He batted very well in '85, but was generally out of control as captain, and from the moment he arrived in '89 he set out his stall to be as mean as possible. He was mean to the opposition, the press, and indeed to his own players. He sledged pretty fiercely, too, which is something that doesn't normally bother me too much, although on this tour it was hyper unfriendly. There was one potentially amusing incident involving Robin Smith and Merv Hughes, when Hughes, having had Robin in trouble, snorted at him: 'Smith, you can't ——ing bat.' Next ball, Robin smashed him for four, and as he was turning at the non-striker's end, looked at Merv and said: 'Make a good pair don't we? I can't ——ing bat, and you can't ——ing bowl.' This could have been a nice safety valve, but it merely set Merv's moustache revolving at an even greater rate of knots. It illustrated, in a way, how determined they were not to get involved in any friendly banter. As I said, they barely socialized, and the only time that summer that I had any real social contact with A.B. was when I invited him, Geoff Marsh and Geoff Lawson home for a barbecue during the tourist match at Grace Road. By that time they had already regained the Ashes, so he was considerably more relaxed of course, and he did admit to me once the season was over that he had set out his stall to be as hard and unfriendly as he could. He wasn't going to let anything distract him until he finished the job, and he was as good as his word.

He said to me, 'David, the last time we came here I was a nice guy who came last. I've been through all sorts of downs with my team, but this time I thought we had a bloody good chance to win and I was prepared to be as ruthless as it takes to stuff you. I didn't mind upsetting anyone, my own team-mates included, as long as we got the right result.' As for being gruff and uncompromising on the field, as opposed to off it, the Australians were not unveiling anything new. If they knew an opponent liked a chat, they didn't say a word. Derek Randall, who would talk to himself if no-one else would, used to come in for the silent treatment, and the same has applied to me. I've always enjoyed a chinwag, and I've even been sent to Coventry in county cricket. I remember Geoff Miller muttering out of the side of his mouth from mid-on, 'Sorry, Lubo, I'm not allowed to talk to you.' It's all part of the psychological game within a game.

The atmosphere when we got to Headingley for the first Test was as tense as I have ever known it. We were all aware of the importance of this first match, particularly on a ground where a result was almost guaranteed given a fair crack from the weather, and it galls me to think even now that the game was partially lost on placing undue reliance on Michael Fish's isobar chart on Breakfast TV. You organize your life around English weather forecasts at your peril – it had not been that long since predictions of a gentle breeze were accompanied by falling trees and flying roof tiles – but after watching TV on the morning of the game, Ted had begun to talk in terms of a three-and-a-half-day match. As such, he reasoned, an all-seam attack bowling first would represent our best chance of winning, and this idea gathered momentum when management and senior players gathered at the nets on that opening morning.

My own feeling was the need for a more balanced attack, which meant including John Emburey, and if I wanted backing for that viewpoint I needed to go no further than Keith Boyce, the Headingley groundsman. It looked a good wicket, and Keith confidently predicted a belter, but as Keith's predictions down the years had been even less reliable than the BBC weather bureau, I eventually allowed myself to be talked round towards Ted's point of view. Embers was despatched to Abergavenny for a county match, I put them in after winning the toss, and by close of play Australia were 207 for 3. Boyce, on this occasion, had got his forecast right, and we ended the day looking pretty silly. To give credit to Border and Simpson, they had managed to rid themselves of the negative thoughts that Headingley invariably encourages, and would have batted first anyway had they won the toss. We, on the other hand, were caught up with too much history, and made the wrong decision. Even then there was no reason to think that we would bowl quite as badly as we did, or that one individual would have a total nightmare.

We had cast our thoughts back to 1985, when Richard Ellison's away swing had proved so decisive, and with Phil Newport having already demolished the tourists with a similar type of bowling at Worcester, we thought he was an ideal pick for Headingley. Unfortunately, Newport bowled gunbarrel straight, and the only time the ball swung through the air was en route to the advertising boards. Foster, Pringle and DeFreitas also bowled poorly, and although I ran around attempting to offer words of quiet encouragement, a captain is pretty well rendered impotent when every single one of his bowlers is off form. The second day was total carnage, with Steve Waugh murdering us through the offside, and the final humiliation was Merv Hughes scoring 60-odd in the final session. They eventually declared at 601. When Lamb and Smith played well to take us past the follow-on mark, it should not have been beyond an ordinary county side to go on to draw the match. Unfortunately, our performance on the final day would almost have been an insult to an ordinary county side.

Australia began it 329 runs ahead with seven second innings wickets in hand, and I could not see Border being able to declare until most of the first session had gone. If our bowling had been poor in the first day, however, it was indescribable on the last. There was a certain element of them having a dart at everything and getting away with it, but even so it was a nightmare period as Australia were able to declare after adding 72 in 9.5 overs. While survival should still have been well within our compass, this sort of carnage scarcely buoyed us up for the task ahead. In a nutshell, we were required to bat for 83 overs, and managed to get bowled out in 55. The atmosphere in the dressing room was not improved by the sound of wild celebrations going on next door, and the press conference was a little traumatic. I felt it fair to mention the injuries to Botham, Dilley and Gatting, but otherwise pleaded a fair cop. I felt even more depressed by the knowledge that my chronic shoulder complaint had now deteriorated to the extent that I was due to undergo an exploratory operation between the Test matches. It had not been affecting my batting, even though I was comprehensively rubbished in the press for twice getting caught behind down the legside at Headingley, but I could scarcely throw at all by now. As it happened, the operation went very well, and the cortisone injection that accompanied it certainly helped to lift my spirits for the Lord's Test.

If anyone should have had any hang-ups about Headingley it should have been Australia, not us. There was 1981 for them to remember. But they approached the match more positively than we did, and made all the right moves. We made all the wrong ones, and they came out of it so far ahead in mental terms that a lot of damage had been done to us. On the other hand, I still believed we could turn it round. If they can win at Headingley, I thought, where history pointed to us, then we can win at Lord's, where history pointed to them. There was no point in thinking otherwise.

If there were grounds for optimism, this ground – Lord's – was not one of them. Of the 21 Ashes Tests played there since the turn of the century, we had won only once. That was in 1934, the year the driving test was introduced, and one or two of the wags were saying that we would now settle for one or two competent blockers never mind drivers. What was it about Lord's that fired up Australia? The sight of all those MCC ties perhaps. Whatever, they led 8-1 in 20th-century Test matches there, and by the end of this one they had made it 9-1. I had led England to defeat for the eighth consecutive time as captain, and the tabloid cartoonists variously depicted me with a dunce's cap on my head, and a noose around my neck. I began to view the second coming as a poisoned chalice.

This time, despite an ominous cloud cover, I decided to bat first on a good looking pitch, and we were bowled out in a day for 286. It was a curious innings, in that we were either losing wickets or smashing boundaries everywhere, but by Friday night we still had a narrow lead with just four more first innings wickets to take. Then came Saturday, which, in its way, was even more horrific than the last day at Leeds. Australia's tail end, marshalled by Waugh, put on another 252 runs, 74 of them from Lawson at No 10, and by stumps we were 58 for 3. Gooch, for 0, Barnett and Broad all gone. It had been a wretched day, bowling, fielding and batting, and the last thing I wanted to do was attend the statutory Saturday night press conference. As I walked towards the tent with the media relations manager Peter Smith, I was looking for any excuse not to have to go in, and was not at all sure I could keep control of my emotions. Contrary to public opinion, the view that the half-raised eyebrow is the summit of my passion has always been a major misconception, and I was well aware that my fuse was in danger of blowing. However, on lifting the flap, and spotting the empty chair reserved for me next to Micky Stewart, I took a deep breath and resolved to get through the thing as calmly, painlessly, and politely as I could. I not only failed, but failed in spectacular style.

I got off to a bad start, because although I was trying hard to be semi-humorous, I could detect the inner tension coming through in my voice. My opening address was along the lines of: 'Righto, I've not much to say. All the questions you asked last time still apply, and the answers are all the same too. If you consult your (Headingley) notebooks, it will save us all a lot of time.' I sat down with a wry smile, gazed out upon the assembled newspaper and TV hacks, and realized what I had said had gone down like a lead balloon. The first question was, 'What have you got to say to all those people who have bought tickets for Monday?' and I handled it pretty poorly. 'We'll be trying our bollocks off. If that's what you want me to say, I'll say it.' The mood was going from bad to worse.

Compared to the next question, however, this proved to be – given the mood I was in – a gentle half-volley. 'Tell me, David,' inquired Phil Edmonds, who was working for one of the Sunday papers, 'why did you bowl everyone from the wrong end?' Mike Selvey of the *Guardian*, another former Middlesex bowler, wanted to know specifically why Neil Foster had been operating from the Pavilion End when, on Friday, he had been more effective from the Nursery End. When troubled waters are flowing, Philippe is not slow to volunteer to pour the oil, and I knew he was being mischievous. But it was precisely the sort of question (as opposed to the pointless 'Can you save it?') that press conferences should be designed for. Tactical decisions not always apparent from the press box can be explained, and on this occasion the answer was simple. I had agreed with Fozzie before play that he would start at the Pavilion End, but when I offered him the chance to switch after four overs or so, he told me he was happy to carry on as he was. However, before I could explain this, the growing air of hostility all around the tent got to me, and the brain fused. Micky attempted to move in on my behalf at this stage, but mentally I was miles away, and, I thought, it was now time to go in person. Up I got, announced that I had both a theatre engagement awaiting and a taxi meter running, and swept out of the tent with as much dignity as I could muster.

As soon as I was outside, my mood was instantly transformed. I whistled my way back to the team hotel, jumped into the cab with one or two of the other lads who were going, and had a thoroughly enjoyable evening at the Prince Edward Theatre watching Tim

Rice's production of *Anything Goes*. I was, on the other hand, well aware that I had made a total hash of the press conference, and that I had certainly not heard the last of it. When the phone rang in my hotel room on Sunday morning, I more or less said 'Hello, Ted' without waiting to find out who it was, and sure enough, the chairman was on the line. I gave him the background to the walkout, and while he was very sympathetic, he made it clear that some kind of placatory offering was essential in order to quieten things down a little. My own statement, half explanation, half apology, was actually prepared by Ted himself, while he issued his own statement that was, in effect, a mild reprimand. He was very supportive, and told me that if I felt the need to get away from it all, I would be more than welcome to join him for lunch at his golf club, Sunningdale. It was a nice gesture, but I had already arranged to watch some tennis at the Hurlingham Club, where, of course, I was tracked down by the press. I could see the benefit of a spot of bridge rebuilding, and went through a series of interviews as best I could. It was all very polite, and I didn't walk out of one of them. Monday morning dawned, and it occurred to me as I resumed my innings on 15 not out, that I had never needed a century more than I needed one that day. Happily, that's how it worked out.

If there was no prospect of the Queen superseding George V as the last monarch to shake hands with a winning England captain against Australia at Lord's that year, it was pretty important for there still to be a match in progress when she arrived at teatime. Thanks partly to my century (and I was deeply moved when the whole ground rose to greet it) there was, and the mood was certainly brighter when the teams shook hands. Contrary to the speculation in one newspaper, she did not ask me why I had bowled Foster from the wrong end. We were, in the end, still playing at five o'clock on the final day thanks to a much more disciplined batting display – Robin Smith got 96 – and Foster taking three wickets in a superb spell from the 'wrong' end again. Although defeat by six wickets was comparatively respectable after Saturday, the fact remained that historically sides did not come back from two down after two Test matches. The mood of national expectation had been spectacularly transformed into one of doom and gloom, and, as is usually the case in this country, black humour was now the order of the day for the

England cricket team. No one captured this better than the satirical magazine, *Private Eye*, with a cruel but highly witty spoof.

MR EDWARD DEXTER AND MR DAVID GOWER – AN APOLOGY.

In common with all other newspapers, we recently published a number of articles about the prospects for the England cricket team under such headlines as 'LORD TED'S TEST TONIC' and 'IT'S SUPER-ENGLAND AS WONDER GOWER RETURNS IN TRIUMPH.' These articles may have given the impression that we thought that the appointment of Mr Dexter to the post of Chairman of Selectors was in some way likely to lead to an improvement in the performance of England's cricketers, and, further, that his choice of Mr Gower to return as captain indicated the possibility that we might win a Test match at some stage in the future. The passage 'Make no mistake – Dave and Ted will stuff the Aussies this summer. Border's boys can XXXX off back down under' may in particular have given rise to the unintentional inference that we in some way believed that Mr Dexter and Mr Gower would somehow play a part in a revival of England's cricketing fortunes. We now accept that Mr Dexter is nothing more than a loud-mouthed PR man who has done for English cricket what Mr Michael Foot did for the Labour Party. We further accept that Mr David Gower is a public school twit whose so-called 'laid-back' approach to the game amounts in reality to nothing more than an obsessive desire to be caught behind off a half-hearted parody of a leg glance at every available opportunity. We apologize to all English cricket lovers for any distress that may have been caused by our earlier articles, which we now unreservedly withdraw.

TEST MATCH LATEST Australia 790-3 dec. (Wargs 291 not out, Pringle 0-416. England 23 all out (Gower ct behind 0, DeFreitas 21) and 19-7 (Gower ct behind 0, extras 19).

If I had a cheery thought in my head at this stage, it was in thinking that nothing much more could possibly go wrong. No sooner had the thought, occurred, of course, than everything did. Smith, who had damaged a hamstring during his 96 at Lord's, telephoned Micky to say he would be unfit for Edgbaston, and the phone was scarcely back on the hook when Lamb called to say that he had torn some shoulder fibres fielding in a Sunday League match. Then, in keeping with the tradition that these things invariably come along in threes,

Stewart's next message came from Horsham, where Foster had burst a finger blister on his bowling hand. All this took place while I was playing for Leicestershire at Hinckley, a homely club ground, but not exactly the communications capital of the county circuit, and Ted was very nearly a fourth casualty – with a burst blood vessel – trying to get through. We had already made changes in an attempt to turn things around, and to lose three players of that calibre was not what we wanted at that precise moment. Then, when we arrived at Edgbaston for the usual Wednesday afternoon practice session, Gatting made a routine phone call home and discovered that his mother-in-law had died. He naturally rushed away, and in deciding that we could not blood a newcomer in such circumstances, sent out an SOS to Somerset for Chris Tavaré.

The match would have been more or less ruined by the weather but for the fact that, even in the short time available, we made a concerted attempt to lose it. It was not a good toss for me to lose, and although Angus Fraser – twelfth man at Lord's – turned in a good performance on his debut, Australia were 391 for 7 after the first three days, in which less than four sessions of playing time had been possible. Saturday night was press conference night, of course, and while I managed to last the distance this time, it wasn't easy. Q: 'How do you feel now you can't possibly win?' A: 'Ecstatic.' Q: 'What can you do on Monday?' A: 'Make 800 in four hours and put them under pressure.' Q: 'Did you think about playing two spinners on Thursday morning?' A: 'No. We only had one on the ground.' Well, what can you say to questions like that? I ended up doing a Basil Fawlty and banging my head on the interview table, which is more or less what I was doing in the dressing room on Monday when we were 75 for 5 and 150 short of the follow-on.

Fortunately, Ian Botham, who had been ruled out of the first two Tests after breaking a cheekbone batting against Glamorgan at Worcester, was back in harness, and his fighting qualities came through in an innings of 46 to help us out of trouble. We still came close to making a bodge of it, and with the last pair at the wicket on the final morning, required ten more runs to avoid having to bat again. Paul Jarvis smeared a four to save us, and I have scarcely felt more relieved.

CHAPTER ELEVEN

Steward Micky, Malcolm Devon, and sacked again

IT was after the Edgbaston Test, during the Benson and Hedges Cup final I think, that Ted and myself had a further chat about the problems the team was having, and he suggested that I worked a bit closer with Stewart. I had more or less kept Micky in the background, and the chairman wondered whether it might be an idea for captain and manager to communicate more during the day's play. It was a reasonable theory, but unless you respect the other bloke's opinion, you are not exactly keen to seek it. In fairness to Micky, all the available evidence pointed to him feeling precisely the same way. He probably spent all day thinking to himself, 'What's that prat doing out there now? Why isn't Gatt captain?' As I have hinted previously, we never really hit it off from the outset, largely I think because our views on man management differ so much. I like to treat people as individuals, while Micky would prefer a team of subbuteo players all programmed to do things by numbers. The combination of wanting players to be seen and not heard, and his mistrust of the press, came together in Perth on the last Ashes tour in 1990-91 when Mike Atherton was left out of the one-day team. Stewart informed the press that Mike felt he was out of sorts with his game, which came as news to the player, who had never said anything of the sort. On a broader basis, the role of manager before Stewart was appointed full time, was confined to overseas tours. I toured under people like Barrington and Gifford, who were both good in their own way, organizing nets, taking on the admin duties and generally taking some of the pressure off the captain.

There have always been conflicts between captain and manager,

Brearley and Barrington being a case in point. Brears did not always appreciate what Kenny was trying to do with the players, but I saw him very much as an ally; a solid, dependable, rock-like father figure, who would advise when asked, and generally took a paternal interest in what you were doing. He always commanded great respect, because of his track record as an England player, and the strength of character he had shown in switching from being a dasher in his early days, to a rather dourer, more Boycott-like figure in the search for greater consistency. He certainly wasn't in the business of attempting to clone players – he was a dispenser of wisdom as and when it was required. To an extent he lived and died the game for you, and almost without a doubt the passion he put into the job contributed to his fatal heart attack in the West Indies in 1981. He was always genial, and never less than one of the boys. He was famous for his malapropisms (when Brian Rose was worrying about his technique on the 1980-81 tour to the West Indies Kenny advised him that he was 'getting caught in two-man's land' and a Smorgasbord buffet was known as the Smog or Gas Board), but perhaps not so well known for being easy to wind up. Before the Trinidad Test in 1981 we had our dinner in a private room at the Hilton Hotel, during which a succession of players kept slipping out to the house phone and putting calls through to Kenny. We put on West Indian accents that should have been entirely detectable, claiming to be representatives from the team's official coach couriers, Batoo Brothers.

As pranks go, it was fairly predictable. 'Man, we got a bit of problem wid de bus for tomorrow, de steering gone, man ...' and Kenny would puff back into the room saying: 'Cor, blimey, the Batoos have cobbled it up again. Looks like cabs in the morning, boys.' And we'd put a call through about every ten minutes, saying that the steering was now okay but the wheels had fallen off, then they'd fixed the wheels but the brakes had gone and the bus was now embedded in a wall, and so on and so on. Lord knows how many times Kenny left the table, and when he finally twigged he found it funnier than anyone. He was a lovely man, straight as a die. Giff, too, was well liked and respected by the players. If you wanted a net with Giff at midnight, he'd be there. Neither had the scope that the England manager's job now entails, which embraces selection, policy, press conferences, and year-long involvement in a much more highly pressured way. It was a much lesser role before Stewart took it on, and much less accountable, although if you look at some periods of Micky's tenure, you wonder whether it was ever accountable.

The players' first introduction to Micky would have been at the airport hotel before we flew out on Gatt's tour to Australia, and I think one or two of us would have wondered about his appointment in as much as he had been eased away from the dressing room during his previous role with Surrey. In other words he had gone from hands-on involvement to an office down the corridor, and the major influence inside the dressing room had passed back to the captain. In amongst all that there had been other candidates for the England job who had reportedly turned it down on the grounds that it didn't come with enough autonomy, including the likes of Illy, although I have to say I thought it was a flawed concept from the outset. A full-time paid manager, in my view, makes for a muddled sense of priorities. You have a manager who gets a long term contract, and a captain who does not, but who obviously wants to run the show in the way he wants to. Therefore, the captain becomes the senior man, and the whole thing gets very confusing. In an ideal world, manager and captain will see eye to eye on everything, but in practice this is not always the case.

As you would expect, Micky was quite low key to begin with, although we could all see – and admire, I have to say – how enthusiastic he was. We slightly baulked at his enthusiasm for us going to bed at ten o'clock before the first Test, as I've said, but you couldn't quibble over his urge for us to be as well prepared as possible for the game. As it happened, Micky must have been a very worried man before Brisbane, because it had been one of the worst build-ups to an overseas Test series that any England side can ever have experienced. It may have slipped one or two memories, but we were written off before we even arrived in Australia, and the way we did our best to prove it in those early matches must have made Micky wonder whether he'd still be in a job when we got back.

However, we picked our game up as soon as the cricket became serious, Australia fell apart, Gatt was cock a hoop, and Micky, basking in the reflected glory, no doubt came home thinking that the job was a piece of cake. Opinions differed as to Micky's part in it all. He put in a lot of work with Chris Broad, who had a phenomenal tour, but he also did the same with James Whitaker, who went out as a young, uninhibited strokeplayer, and came back, temporarily at any rate, riddled with theory and retarded by several months. My own relationship with Micky at that stage was alright, and I've never thought that his heart was anything other than in the right place. But as he grew into the job, it became clear to me that his methods were fairly inflexible, and it looked very much as though conformity to Micky's system was going to be the road to prosperity – echoes of Bob Simpson and the Australian team. If you could conform, and do a lot of fielding practice at the same time, you didn't need to score quite so many runs or take quite so many wickets to stay in his good books.

If Micky had one player to deal with, rather than a team, he would have been magnificent. The problem with having a team to deal with is that there are eleven different people in it, or, on a tour, sixteen. One of my particular memories of the 1990-91 tour to Australia was of Micky shouting at Devon Malcolm during practice sessions. Devon had been pigeonholed as lazy, and also didn't answer back, so he was marked down as fair game. Another one was how much time he appeared to spend bowling cricket balls in the nets, very slowly, at England captains. Yet his limitations at bringing the best out of individuals were exposed on that tour when it came to Robin Smith. Here was a player of immense value to England, having a very average time, and experiencing all sorts of technical problems with his batting. Micky couldn't sort him out, and it was only when his brother Chris (who to be fair knows Robin's game a good deal better) arrived in Sydney that the situation began to improve.

We had a daily routine with everyone getting together for stretching exercises, warm ups and fielding practice. If you wanted a net, you had to do so either beforehand or afterwards. We were in Perth for the final Test of the tour, and Robin, who still hadn't got a decent score, was batting in one of the nets. He was ordered to take off his pads and join in the physical jerks. Naturally, he regarded this intrusion into the work he was devoting to his technique as both unnecessary and dispiriting. Stewart's tactical input was nothing to write home about either. He would usually come out with the standard stuff, telling the batsmen to play straight, and the bowlers to deliver it down the 'channel of uncertainty', one of his favourite phrases. You would not necessarily knock that, as we all need reminding of the basics from time to time, but there was nothing that startled you into sitting up and thinking, 'Here's a chunk of wisdom I dare not miss.'

His team talks on that tour were basically meaningless. They certainly did not impart anything new, put it that way. For example, Geoff Marsh played against us in the Western Australia match, and was soon, as was his custom, hitting everything through gully. So, before the Test, Micky told us to watch out for Marsh hitting everything through gully. Again, there is a certain value in stating the obvious, but as a pre-match orator, I found him less than convincing. One of my bugbears throughout the tour was the fact that all the pre-match meetings were little more than a naming of the side and an exhortation to go out and do your best. By contrast, on many of my previous tours, there was much more of an opportunity to bounce ideas around the players. There was always the slight risk of going on too long (hatching up various masterplans that would by and large be forgotten by the next morning) but I always felt that by getting everyone involved a much keener sense of team spirit developed. It gave individuals a greater sense of their own worth, and made them feel that they were something more than just pawns, that we were genuine international cricketers who had a say in our destiny, and were able to contribute to what both we and the team were going to do. On this particular tour, people felt like chess pieces waiting to be plonked somewhere on the board.

I did in fact talk to Graham about this in Adelaide. We had played dreadfully in the first World Series match against New Zealand, when Micky justifiably blew his top, and we were equally justifiably ordered down to 'naughty boy' nets the following morning. At some stage during the net, I told the captain that I thought we had to get things going a bit more during team meetings. I said that if we could get people more involved, and thinking for themselves, I was sure it would have a positive effect. To Graham's credit, he did make the next meeting more open, but by then, I think, the mood had been too far established for things to change very much. The players had been so conditioned that they did not quite know how to utilize this freedom of speech, and so the idea more or less died at birth. If all you get from a team meeting is, 'This is the side, and this is what you are going to do,' you are in great danger of ending up with an us and them, employer-employee situation. You are losing something in terms of team morale and identity. The same applies when practice is carried out in an unremitting way, without variety. You wait until you are told to bat or bowl, and you feel as though if you dare to be individual, or speak out against anything, then you are marked down as a bad egg – a dissident. This is the area in which I did not fit in too well. I did not actually say too much, but attitude is also perceived and I'm afraid the old body language gave me away once or twice.

This sort of thing builds up, of course, and over the years my relationship with Micky undoubtedly deteriorated because of it. I fell into more bad odour on the third morning of the Sydney Test, after we had been in the field for the best part of the first two days while Australia clocked up 500. I had spent a restless night thinking about batting, and turned up at the ground looking forward to it. In short, I was in a highly positive frame of mind. We did a few exercises before gathering on the outfield for Graham's talk, the gist of which was: 'We've had two bad days ... not bowled very well ... not fielded very well ... not the sort of performance ... really got to battle harder ...' all negative stuff. Well, we got through that, even though I was starting to bridle a bit, and then it was Micky's turn. "We've had two bad days ... not bowled very well ... not fielded very well ...' It was like listening to a bloody tape recording. At which point I piped up and asked whether it might be at all possible to have some positive input. I duly got the 'quiet at the back of the class there, boy' treatment, and while I did shut up, I was quietly steaming inside. Okay, we had lost both the opening Test matches, had some bad results in the one-dayers and it was perfectly obvious that we were not playing well. But it was high time we developed a more positive approach, I thought, and that there had been nothing productive in the tone of that morning's conversation. Quite the reverse. For what it's worth, four, maybe five senior players took the chance (out of earshot of the management) to agree with me, although it did not improve my mood greatly.

Something else that bothered me on the tour was that after

coming off the field at six o'clock, half the side was out of the dressing room by quarter past and heading back for the hotel. It was as if the office had closed, and there was nothing to be gained from winding down a bit more slowly and talking about the game for a few minutes. There's always the opportunity for a bit of privacy in the dressing room, the beer is there in the fridge for you, and it's a perfect atmosphere for quiet chat. Or a noisy one, if it comes to that. Yet here we were a good two-thirds of the way through the tour, and it wasn't happening. I once found myself in the dressing room talking to the three or four players who were left – Eddie Hemmings was one, I remember – wondering why it was that the team just disappeared every night. There must have been a lot of people at that stage harbouring doubts, grievances and disappointments, and we were not taking the opportunity to share them round and get a few things out into the open. Spirit was not dead by a long way, but I felt it was a worthwhile exercise to have a bash at getting the whole team talking about any little niggles and problems that people might have and I helped set up a kind of forum after practice the next morning.

We touched on various matters, with Micky reiterating his opinion that he thought he and Graham were doing things the right way, but it did not really work. It was too formal. We'd have been much better off doing it after play with a few beers inside us. That just about summed up the tour. No spontaneity, no individuality – and no wonder we did so badly.

The D.I. Gower glasnost approach had not been working too well in the 1989 series, of course, and as we approached the fourth Test at Old Trafford 2-0 down my confidence had switched from full flow to full ebb. I could not even unwind at home too much, as my relationship with Vicki was considerably more parlous than two down with three to play, and by way of variation on a depressing theme, we had lost one of our key players before, rather than after, selection. Lamb broke a finger playing in the same county match as myself at Leicester, and in deciding that our best chance of getting back into the series lay with experienced players, I replaced him (amidst predictable howls of protest from a press corps demanding new blood) with Tim Robinson. Robbo was my personal choice, and however badly things were going on the field, I was still getting my own way – more or less – in selection. Ted chipped in with ideas, and while Micky invariably came staggering through the door with an armful of dossiers, he did not attempt to overturn the early ground rules whereby the captain carried most weight in picking players. It is ironic to think now that Robbo was selected knowing that he had already agreed to join a 'rebel' tour to South Africa that winter, and that the news would undoubtedly break during this Test match.

The South Africa business had been rumbling on for most of the summer of 1989, and press speculation grew with the news that Gatting had declared himself unavailable for England's tour to the West Indies. Gatt had cited family reasons, plus what he considered to be a 'totally unrealistic' TCCB offer of £2500 for six weeks in India for a one-day competition in October and November. Could a family booking for a well paid winter in the Cape sunshine, and a further offer of the captaincy, have had something to do with Gatt's withdrawal? Whatever Ted and Micky knew, it was a rand to a penny that they knew more than I did. In fact, I suspect I was the last person in the England dressing room to know. The South Africans had, by all accounts, been recruiting since the beginning of the year, and the captain of England would have been the last person they wanted to alert. The only time South Africa had directly entered my thoughts was when I received the standard TCCB letter before the Old Trafford Test asking me whether I was available to tour with England that winter. The selectors had chosen thirty players as likely candidates, and what bothered me was the fact that I was one of the selectors. I had not been consulted about their choices, and while this might simply have been an innocent matter of routine, I did wonder whether they were trying to drop me a hint that while I had half a chance of touring the West Indies as a player, I had none at all as a captain.

Still, South Africa was well down the list of personal worries as the Test approached, and I was not best pleased to find out on the Sunday before the match that cricket correspondents were now in the business of mind-reading as well as reporting. I picked up the *News of the World* to discover a story saying that I would quit the captaincy if we lost the Test, and, by definition, the Ashes. It was a good story admittedly, and would have been an even better one had it been true. I had dragged myself out of the shower to answer a call from David Norrie, their cricket correspondent, on the Saturday morning, who asked me whether I would consider my position if we lost. I told him that I would, which was not quite the same as saying I would definitely be going. It was cleverly done, but in this case, two and two made four and a half. What bothered me far more was one of the tackier tabloid dailies amusing itself with line drawings of me and other England players wearing dunces' caps, and it occurred to me, not for the first time, that cricket writing had altered somewhat in recent years.

Unfortunately, I gave them some more material to sink their teeth into on the Saturday of the game. The same old record had been playing – England bowled out for 260, Australia heading for 400, and as I ended up on my knees having grabbed at a possible bat-pad off Nick Cook that was out of my reach anyway, I received an uncomplimentary word from a lone heckler behind me. I responded with a fleeting and playful 'V' sign behind my back, picked myself up and thought no more about it. It had been another depressing three days, and my mood became even darker when I heard that ITN had caught the V sign on film, and were running it on their Saturday night bulletins. I thought at the time, and still do, that this was a cheap shot, and I knew how the rat pack from the tabloids would gobble it up. I was not disappointed in myself, but I certainly was in the chairman, who phoned me – as he had at Lord's after the walkout – on the Sunday morning. Another problem, said Ted. We have to make another statement. At this point, I blew. Lord's was one thing, but this was giving credence to a piffling piece of nonsense, and for the next few seconds I suspect that Ted had the phone some distance away from his ear. He insisted, though, that he had to say something even if I did not, and I banged down the phone in frustration. I had already given the management some evidence of my deepening gloom during play on the second afternoon, when I came back into the dressing room at tea and said to Micky, 'How did you think the session went?' 'I don't know,' he replied, 'I've been in a meeting with Ted all afternoon.' So I said (a bit richly, considering that I scarcely gave much credence to his opinions anyway), 'If you're going to manage, bloody well manage.' That outburst may have had a bearing on Micky and Peter Smith approaching me on the Saturday night and telling me not to bother with the pre-rest day conference. I was grateful not to have to go, but I later discovered that they were panic stricken in case I went in and turned in an explosive resignation speech.

I would not have done, but after that Sunday morning conversation with Ted, I seriously felt like packing the whole thing in there and then. If I had been on my own for the rest day, I think I might have done, but I managed to partially unwind over lunch out in the Cheshire countryside, and then spent a totally relaxing afternoon with friends in Hale. I was still in a much better frame of mind by close of play on Monday, even though we were staring at defeat, and a stimulating evening with Bob Willis stiffened my resolve not to give up the job until I had at least seen the summer through to the bitter end. Twenty-four hours later the Ashes were back with Australia, and I was as happy as I had been in weeks. The series had gone, so some of the pressure had been lifted. But far more significant was the fact that the South African tour party had been announced that morning. At last we would be able to look to the future instead of behind our backs. The air of resignation, both on the field and in terms of the captaincy, was suddenly blown away. Ted stood with me on the outfield, told me he wanted me to carry on, and with the rebuilding operation already under way in a sense, I was suddenly looking forward to enjoying the job again.

I was not terribly pleased with Ted in another sense, in that he and Micky had gathered considerable surveillance material on likely South African defectors over the summer, and had not seen fit at any stage to take me into their confidence. Perhaps it would have seemed less surprising had I known that I had not been their original choice as captain, and I remember around this time John Emburey hinting to me that Gatt had originally been told he had got the job. I was slightly taken aback that Gatt was going to South Africa, although had he indeed been promised the captaincy back, and then seen it go to me, his sense of grievance with the TCCB would have made it that much easier for the South Africans to tempt him. Neil Foster's decision to go surprised me far less, as there was a limit to how much longer his dodgy knees could hold out, but Fozzie's sense of patriotism also runs very deep, and he could scarcely bowl for tears on that final afternoon at Old Trafford.

I thought of Gatt again when we pitched up at Nottingham for the fifth Test and signed the register at the Royal Hotel in the centre of town. The previous chairman, P.B.H., well aware of Nottingham's well deserved reputation for nightlife, had moved us out into the country, safely out of the way of all temptation. The hotel he chose was called the Rothley Court and it was the episode at that hotel, and his dismissal as captain soon after, that had a very large bearing on Gatt ending up in South Africa. It had been decided, not unnaturally, that no-one on the flight to Johannesburg would be chosen for this match, and so, with Gooch having also requested a rehabilitatory spell in county cricket away from Alderman, we were able to experiment. The two new caps were Mike Atherton, who I knew all about, and Devon Malcolm, an unknown to me, and very much Ted and Micky's choice.

Before the match, Leicestershire had played the tourists at Grace Road, which was just what I needed at that stage, and Mike Turner – astute as ever – had pre-empted my thoughts by calling me at home and saying, 'Don't even think about pulling out.' I wondered whether I might get annoyed by scoring a century against them when I could have saved it for a Test match, but I didn't have to worry on that score. At least it felt like a Test match – we lost by nine wickets. There was not even much consolation in watching one of our bowlers take 7 for 54 against them, as his name was Winston Benjamin, and he played for the West Indies. As for our Test attack, we lost our bowler before the game when Gladstone Small dropped out injured, and on the opening day two opening batsmen went right through to stumps without being parted. It is hardly necessary to add that England were bowling. It was, apparently, the first time that this had ever been done in a full day's play in this country, but as for our part in making history, we felt a bit like Malcolm Nash must have done watching the last of Garry Sobers' six sixes clattering down the Mumbles Road. Late in the day, with Marsh and Taylor still going strong towards their eventual 301 for 0, I decided to give vent to a sense of humour that had last been sighted disappearing over Headingley, and waved on the twelfth man Greg Thomas. Greg looked a bit puzzled, then burst out laughing, and ran off again. I had asked him to run over to the press box and ask the experts what I ought to do next.

We made a brilliant start in pursuit of their 602 for 6 declared – 1 for 2 after one over – and although Robin Smith scored a fine century, we were following on by Monday morning. I went in first in the second innings, partly to give Moxon a chance away from Alderman and the new ball, and partly for reasons for which Peter Smith was despatched on an informatory mission to the press box. Smudge came back with tears rolling down his cheeks, and I (bowled Lawson 5) was already back in the dressing room when he returned. The media relations manager had addressed the scribes thus. 'Botham's finger injury means that he would be batting, at best, at No 9, Moxon would be required to bolster the middle order, and the captain thought it might be a good idea to open with a left [long pause for raucous laughter] and right hand combination.' The long pause, apparently, had been prompted by the sight of the left-hander's off stump leaning back. We lost by an innings and 180 runs, Australia's highest winning margin in this country, and I had now captained England to defeat ten times in eleven Tests. Even Ted was shellshocked by now, and when he was asked for some plus points in the press conference afterwards, he said, 'Who can forget Malcolm Devon.' So much for the fresh start.

I drove home, not exactly bubbling over, but not in a total trough either. I had decided that even if it was quite possible – even probable – that I would get the sack at the end of the summer, I had had enough anyway. I had always tried to enjoy life, and I was not prepared to put up with this miserable existence any longer. I had made up my mind. Sad though it was, I would resign after the Oval Test. It was in this frame of mind, although I kept it to myself, that I entered my final selection meeting, and the best part about it was the fact that I did not have too far to travel. It was held in my own kitchen – an appropriate setting, one might say, given the presence of several choices of knife. We replaced Moxon and Curtis with Hussain and Stephenson, but no sooner was the team released, than the usual business of people dropping out started up all over again. Malcolm went in the back, Fraser did his knee, and DeFreitas, called in as a replacement having reversed his original decision to go to South Africa, pulled a hamstring. We replaced DeFreitas with Greg Thomas, who then said, 'Sorry, I'm DeFreitas' replacement for South Africa.' Norman Cowans and Ricardo Ellcock were both contacted at Middlesex, and both reported unfit, and Glamorgan's Steve Watkin was described as being too jiggered to stand up for five days. I'm not sure whether I laughed or cried. We eventually ended up with two bowling places still to be filled the day before the game, and to add to the confusion Ted, Micky and myself all came up with two different names. Eventually, through a combination of phone calls, and me handing over the final pick to Micky out of sheer exasperation, we settled on Pringle and Alan Igglesden of Kent. This brought us up to thirty-one players for the series, and if there had been any plans for an end-of-term dinner, we would probably have had to cancel for the lack of a big enough restaurant. Morale, as you might have expected, was not exactly sky high, nor was it greatly enhanced when Micky, at the pre-match press conference, described Igglesden as our seventeenth choice seamer. Armed with this magnificent vote of confidence, Igglesden actually did pretty well. England did pretty well too. We drew. We were close to following on, and were in another mess on the final afternoon, so as draws go, it was a long way from glorious. It was, however, at least a small piece saved from the wreckage. Ted signed off by telling the press that he was not aware of any errors he might have made, while I kept thinking back to that very first Test, and the biggest error of all that I made. If I could have turned back the clock and changed just one thing, I would have had Emburey in the side at Headingley. I had allowed myself to be talked out of it, and it had gnawed away at me all summer. It was now time to resign. Or was it?

I still thought it was right to bite on the cyanide capsule, although I had been slightly confused (albeit flattered) by the many people who had taken the trouble to get in touch and urge me to stick with it. So, when I met Ted and Micky at the chairman's house on the eve of the NatWest final, I was prepared to think about staying on if that was what they wanted. It soon became clear, to me at any rate, that this was the last thing they wanted. Having had a short discussion between themselves before I arrived, they told me that they now felt it was time for a change of direction. If there was any doubt at all that this meant the sack, Micky then suggested a variety of excuses that could be put forward as ways of 'softening the blow'. His particular favourite appeared to be fitness, as I was due to have proper surgery on the shoulder in October, but I said that I would

163

prefer a straight red card. They then asked me if I had any ideas for the West Indies that winter (little knowing at the time that one of their own ideas was to leave me out of it altogether) and I reiterated the need to make sure that we did not remain inactive between the end of the summer and leaving for the Caribbean in January. After that it was 'Thanks very much, sorry it didn't work out, etc, etc,' and as the decision was not due to be ratified by the full committee for a few days, I was asked to keep the outcome secret.

I then disappeared to Portugal for a short break away from it all, but disappeared is a relative word with the press, and before I knew it I was confronted by a journalist from the *Daily Mirror* asking me to confirm a story in the *News of the World* that I had resigned. I said, 'No, I can't confirm that I've resigned, because I haven't. As far as I'm aware, I've been sacked.' Perhaps I should have left it at the flat denial, but by that time I wanted the record straight. This caused a major flap in the general area of Ted and Micky, who denied that I had been sacked, and I suppose it was technically true until it had been ratified. However, I knew and they knew that I had been given my cards. Shortly afterwards the news was out of Gooch's appointment for the Nehru Cup competition in India and the tour to the West Indies, although it might have occurred to Ted to let me know before I saw it on the Teletext at home. No matter, I thought, it had ceased to be an issue for me from the moment I last went through Ted's front door. I then decided, in an attempt to prevent the phone from ringing every ten seconds, to hold a press conference at Grace Road, during which I wished Graham well and looked forward to playing under him in the Caribbean. At that very moment, however, Graham was sitting in on a meeting that made that last remark look a little silly. The tour parties were finalized that afternoon, and by some quirk of the fixture list Essex were due at Grace Road the following day for a county match. A good chance for the photographers to take some 'out with the old, in with the new' shots, although I dare say even they did not realize just how far the selectors had gone.

I was at the ground much earlier than is normally my custom for a meeting with Mike Turner, and we were chatting about various club issues when I was summoned to the phone in his secretary's office across the corridor to take a call from Ted. I assumed it was some minor matter concerning the captaincy, but it was far worse than that. He immediately said that I was not in the winter tour party, and I could scarcely believe what I was hearing. I asked for some clarification, and he said something about inconsistency and injury. It was all a bit vague, and my mind wasn't really taking it in anyway. When he had talked to me a week or so earlier about a 'change of direction', I had not imagined that the arrow could be pointing towards the gangplank as well as away from the captain's cabin. I wandered back into Mike's office in a bit of a daze, but as that was not an unusual early morning expression for me, he simply carried on with our chat.

Not long afterwards, Graham arrived at the ground, and took me aside for a private conversation. He talked me through the decision as best he could, inferring that my omission had more or less been presented to him. I didn't comment on that, but it would be hard to believe that he had not felt a certain sympathy with the decision. However quickly things happen (he was captain one minute and selector the next) if you are strong enough in your feeling that you want someone to play, then you usually get your way. Whichever way he wanted to couch it, the fact is that they all got up at the end of the meeting having agreed upon sixteen names, of which mine was not among them. It's funny how things work out, I thought, as I adjourned to the changing room. Having captained Gooch a week ago, here he was telling me I was not wanted in his team.

It was raining when play was scheduled to start, so I thought I might as well go downstairs and accede to the press clamour taking place in the members' enclosure. I felt genuinely emotional, but had no wish to do a Kim Hughes and dissolve into tears, and managed to get through it somehow. I spent a miserable night at home, and an even more miserable one the next night after I had been lbw to Pringle for 0. 'Bloody game,' I thought, as I lay in the bath, lying there for so long that I ended up with wrinkled skin to go along with the grey hairs I had picked up during the summer. I rediscovered some lost youth – not to mention self-belief – with a second innings century before sitting down to sort out plans for an unexpectedly vacant winter. Two months later there was a final postscript to my second period as captain, when the summer rumours that Gatting had been the original selection were confirmed. It seemed as though

I had been Ted's original choice, but Micky, to my complete lack of surprise, had talked him into Gatt instead. Ossie Wheatley, the chairman of the cricket committee, was armed with a veto, and had applied it. I cast my mind back to the April inauguration, at which Ted had announced that I had been the 'committee's choice'. Only one thing wrong with that, I thought. He missed out the word 'second' between 'committee's' and 'choice'. At least we now knew why he had claimed not to have made any errors after the series. He had not voted for me in the first place.

The first part of my winter off was a mixture of pleasure and pain, a trip to Hong Kong with the Lord's Taverners, followed by one to hospital for another operation on the shoulder. The operation was to relieve what is known as decompression. In layman's terms it meant that the bone running along the top of the shoulder was rubbing on the tendons that lay beneath, making any movement like throwing or serving at tennis suitably painful. Having opened up the affected area, the surgeon's task was to carve away some of the bone to create space for the tendons to move freely. Believe me, the physiotherapy after the operation alerted me to new levels of pain and had me wondering briefly if it was all worthwhile.

When I arrived for the pre-med, I asked the surgeon, Ian Bayley, whether it might be possible to kill two birds with one stone, as I was suffering from another condition not conducive to playing cricket at the highest level (or whatever level the selectors now had in mind for me) known as Dupytren's Contractures. It sounds weird, but actually involves a build-up of scar tissue along the tendon, drawing the fingers in towards the palm of the hand in a kind of claw-like way. It is not terribly good for fielding, nor indeed for clutching a glass. He was suitably sympathetic, and a degree of success ensued – in that I was able to pour the champagne sent to the hospital by thoughtful friends – although a further operation was necessary at the end of the 1991 summer. During my five-day convalescence, I had plenty of time to mull over the future, and decided that there were two things that could not be put off much longer. The first was my cricketing future, and whether I would now benefit from a change of county, and the second was my private life, which had deteriorated to the point where it was affecting my cricket.

I had already made it known to Mike Turner that I was thinking of moving on, and while he made it clear that he was not terribly happy and did not feel that it was the solution to my problems, he did not apply any pressure on me at all. Mike could be an intransigent man in some areas, but we had built up a very good relationship down the years, and in viewing him as a friend as well as an employer, it did not make it any easier to break the ties with Grace Road. In order to clear my head, I first needed to relinquish the captaincy. I would probably have done so in any event, because I had become increasingly frustrated by my inability to get on top of the dressing room niggles that were contributing to Leicestershire's reputation as under-achievers. I had made more of an effort during this second term of office to stay more closely in touch with club affairs while I was away on England duty, and will be the first to admit that I had been a touch lacking in that area first time round. Rightly or wrongly, I felt that I had to give England my full attention while I was with them, and that Leicestershire ought to be capable of ticking over in the hands of deputies appointed for the purpose. In practice, though, I would often come back to an assortment of problems and individual grumbles, and in 1989 we had had an especially disappointing year.

There had been a major dust-up during one match at Scarborough, again while I had been away with England, when our overseas player Winston Benjamin was accused by several team-mates of not trying. This surprised me, as it would have been out of character for Benjy, but when I tackled him he merely said that when others had not tried their best during the season there had not been anything like the same fuss. It was a depressing answer, and it was clear that things were worse than I could have imagined. After speaking to other players, I realized that there was an undercurrent of ill-feeling all round that was not going to go away in a hurry, and I felt so impotent that the job was probably not worth the hassle. County captaincy, especially when you are trying to carry it out from long range much of the time, is a much more trying business than many people appreciate, and by the end of 1989 I doubt whether I would have continued in the job even if I had had no thoughts of moving county.

CHAPTER TWELVE

On thin ice, and pressed into service

*T*HE captaincy at Leicester was handed over to Nigel Briers, and I then jetted off to South Africa before Christmas for a round of speaking engagements combined with a week's solitude out in the bush. It was a therapeutic trip, not least for one terrific social evening in the company of my boyhood hero Graeme Pollock, but when I arrived back at Heathrow, another wave of depression washed over me. It had nothing to do with the England situation, as I had more or less got over that blow, and was in any case looking forward to working in the Caribbean – having signed up to contribute both to *The Times* newspaper and BBC radio – from the other side of the fence. I had been with the same girl, Vicki Stewart, for twelve years, and also been engaged for several of them, but things were becoming increasingly painful at home, and the situation was not enhanced by a front-page story in the *Daily Express* just before Christmas. At that stage, we had decided to split up. I was spending a lot of time with friends in London, trying to avoid the less than friendly atmosphere prevalent when I was at home, and also attempting to find somewhere suitable for Vicki to live in Leicester. We did, however, regard this as an essentially private matter – which was rather foolish, I suppose – and did not much enjoy reading that not only had we already gone our separate ways (on the right lines) but that I had already signed for Hampshire (incorrect) and bought a house in the county (also incorrect). Cue siege of house by a variety of newshounds, and although I was able to throw them partially off the scent by stating (correctly) that we were spending Christmas together, our privacy was badly invaded. We were both feeling fairly sorry for ourselves anyway, but when you've got people marching down your driveway demanding photographs, telling you that they know you've got a new woman stashed away upstairs, and basically behaving like total dickheads, it gets a touch annoying.

In the end, it became such a trial that we decided that the only way to return the bottom of our drive from something resembling Hyde Park Corner back to one of the sleepier parts of Leicester, was to issue some kind of public statement. We opted for the personal columns of *The Times*, partly because we wanted to do it with a bit of style, and partly because they were employing me that winter. Happily, it more or less achieved its purpose of persuading the media that it was no longer much of a story. 'DAVID Gower and Vicki Stewart would like to put themselves and their friends out of their misery and confirm that sadly they have decided to separate as amicably as possible and go their own ways. As the matter has already been the subject of speculation by some members of the press, they hope that this brief announcement will obviate the need for further comment. (Fat chance!).'

It was a sad time, because we had come so far together since we met on a Young England tour of the West Indies in 1976. The team had not been welcome at all the major venues because of one or two South African connections in the party, so we also played in places like Montserrat and Grenada, which is where we met. Vicki's father was working in the islands as an agricultural adviser – he was a specialist at making things grow in hot climates – and she had flown out to join her family during the school holidays. It has to be said that there was not a vast reservoir of suitably aged talent on the island, which was a bit unlucky for Vicks, who rather copped the brunt of all of us. She was a good hostess, taking us around the island and generally entertaining us for three days, and although I put myself forward as a contender for, shall we say, more of a one-to-one relationship, I did not make much of an impression on her. It was quite clear, in fact, that she was far less taken with me than the captain, Chris Cowdrey, and she pursued him to our next venue in Trinidad (where we were playing a mini Test against Young West Indies) by stowing away, or begging passage, on an old cargo boat.

It was a brave venture for a sixteen-year-old girl, verging on the foolhardy in fact, but she somehow managed to clear customs despite having none of the relevant entry forms, and booked herself into a place called the Pelican Inn overlooking the Port of Spain savanna. It was much livelier than our hotel, the Queen's Park, which was perhaps not surprising given the fact that she turned out to be sharing the place with an Irish rugby team, and we spent most of our evenings down at the Pelican generally having a good time. However, she was still firmly attached to Cowdrey, and I had made no further progress by the time we said our farewells and returned to England. I had a steady, or steadyish, girlfriend by the name of Louise in London, and used to travel down at weekends from Loughborough to see her. I had, though, managed to prise Vicki's address (near Reading) from her, and began to drop in on her on my way home.

I got another hefty clue as to the extent of her passion for me by the fact that, whenever I arrived, she would scuttle off to her room leaving me to talk to her mother. Nice lady though her mother was, this was not quite the idea, but persistence finally won the day. Who said I never had the patience to build an innings? We set up house a couple of years later, and I was very much in love with her. We spent a lot of time apart, of course, especially with me being away for large chunks of every winter, and she undoubtedly got bored a lot of the time. She got one or two part-time jobs without finding anything she enjoyed greatly, which contributed to the boredom, and although she would come out for parts of a tour, we inevitably spent long periods apart. There was also the customary problem of fidelity – which young single cricketers tend not to find that easy to stick to – and I was no exception. It was not that great a problem, in that I worked pretty hard at being discreet, although the occasional slip-up was unavoidable. As you can imagine, this did not go down too well, and there is an inevitable erosion of trust when you are found out. At that time, though, we were close enough to survive the one or two rocky patches. It would be hypocritical of me to pretend that the professional cricketer does not encounter potential favours from the opposite sex on his travels, and there are some girls who are so keen to get on the scoreboard that it would take even Bill Frindall a long time to work out the averages. In all honesty, though, I have never been attracted by the so-called groupie set – the notch on a bedstead brigade. I can't handle the feeling of wondering, 'How many other flannelled fools have you known, my dear?' and I have largely shied away from the obvious, horribly available targets.

Being away from home so much also creates its own problems in that you invariably prefer quiet nights in when you are at home, although here again this did not greatly affect our relationship in that Vicks was quite a homebird. Two of her more enjoyable pursuits were cooking and gardening. We thought a couple of times about actually going ahead and getting married, but the other women business eventually became too divisive. You can perhaps handle it once, even twice, but eventually it wore us down, and perhaps we went too long without getting married. The relationship deteriorated, slowly at first, but the arguments eventually outnumbered the good times. It was a slow death, and in the end both of us knew that it was time to call it a day. So, having broken up on amicable terms, and also having got the press off our backs with the announcement in *The Times*, it was no mean achievement for me to cause, with one fell swoop, a further row with Vicki and have the press scrambling for their typewriters following a particularly poor piece of behaviour early in that New Year.

I had flown out to St Moritz with, among others, Allan Lamb, to have another crack at the Cresta Run, and the *Daily Mirror* had sent along a reporter and photographer to record an attempt at a personal best. I failed (by about one and a half seconds) but did manage to record another personal best (by about 100 fathoms) in the less well known winter sport of hired-car rallying on a frozen lake. It ended with my involuntary research into whether an Opel Vectra could double as a submarine (it couldn't) and another burst of bizarre publicity in the national press. I had been out to dinner in St Moritz, followed by a visit to a night club with the two *Mirror* men and the two sons of Lynn Wilson, chairman of Northants, whom Lamby had invited out to sample the delights of the resort. To tell the truth, we had been for a joyride on the lake, during which I had indulged myself in a spot of power-sliding and various other winter rallying techniques. Having had twenty minutes of this it was time to drop the men from the *Mirror* back at the Palace Hotel , and this is where I should have called it a night. However, we opted instead for a final burst of rallying across the lake, and I rather lost my bearings. There is a point, where the lake joins the river, at which the ice is conspicuously thinner, and I found it. I did receive some warning when the ice turned an entirely different shade in the headlights, but an emergency stop is not terribly easy on ice, and we only finally came to a halt when the wheels cracked through the surface, and the car settled in about a foot of water. Of all the ways of sobering up quickly, I can honestly say that this method is more effective than any I had previously experienced, and I abandoned the car in a high state of panic. After sloshing through the water, I managed to scramble back onto the ice, and paused for a minute both to lower my pulse rate and take stock of the situation. A call to the A.A., I reckoned, was not high on the list of possibilities, so we rescued the ski bag and chains from the boot, and set off on the half-hour slither back to town. I hailed a taxi driver outside the Palace, who told me that there was a garage opening at 7.30 in the morning, and that they might have a tow truck. We splashed our way back to our own hotel, booked a call for 7.15, and I went to bed wondering how best to extricate ourselves from this delicate situation.

I slept through the alarm, and shortly after 9 a.m., enlisted the aid of some of the hotel staff to check on the car. 'What car?' was the gist of their message, and, sure enough, it had gone. I tried to think of an explanation that would satisfy the St Moritz constabulary and failed. I tried to imagine the head of the hire-car company smiling forgivingly when I told him that their vehicle was ready for collection – assuming they happened to have a team of frogmen and a crane handy – but couldn't. What I needed, I thought, was a lawyer, so together with the two others who had hired the car with me, the ever-present Simon Strong, and one Mark Horne, we contacted a Cresta member – Urs Nater – who was qualified in this particular field.

His advice, not surprisingly, was to inform both the police and the hire-car company of what had taken place (with one or two minor alterations to detail) although it transpired that the law had already been investigating the large hole in the lake. By and large, having promised to meet all salvage costs, I got away with it – except for one thing. Part of Herr Nater's advice had been that because there was a possible charge of endangering life under Swiss law – and with two passengers in the car, it could have been applied to me – it was thought best to suggest I had been alone at the time. This was a cunning plan which was unfortunately complicated by the fact that the local Poirots had spotted that there appeared to be more than one set of footprints emerging from the hole in the lake. When the press got to hear of this, they could not resist coming to a conclusion that added titillation to what was already a fairly useful story. The extra footprints must, of course, have been made by a woman, which was an added bonus for me when the newspaper boy plopped his delivery through Vicki's letterbox. The press had then laid siege to Vicki at the house, either unaware, or simply not caring, that she was the one person who knew nothing at all about what had happened. A chill far worse than had been present on the St Moritz ice descended when I arrived home. I got a bollocking not only for doing it, but also for not telling her before the papers got hold of it. On top of which, protestations that I had been flying solo that night, and not with a ravishing blonde co-pilot, appeared to fall on deaf ears.

By this time, I was looking to make a decision on my cricketing home for the following summer, and had narrowed the options down to two. I wanted to be close to London, where most of my friends were based, and the attraction of playing under one or other of two of my closest cricketing chums, Chris Cowdrey and Mark Nicholas, left me with either Kent or Hampshire. To be honest, had it simply been a question of which captain to choose, it would have been Chris, the older and closer friend. Furthermore, having been born in Tunbridge Wells, and spent most of my schooldays in Kent, there was obviously a strong pull in that direction, but the more I thought about it, the more I gravitated towards Hampshire. There were selfish reasons involved, in that Hampshire were undeniably the stronger side, and I would certainly have more chance both of winning things and remaining high profile at Southampton rather than at Canterbury. On top of this, I thought that too much might be expected of me in a struggling team. I had still not made a decision when I took myself off to the Hertfordshire health resort, Champneys, in mid-January. My association with them had begun towards the end of the summer, when I agreed to feature in an advertisement that provided one of the more amusing spin-offs to the Ashes series.

Although I realized that they had me in mind as a 'before' in one of those 'before and after' ads, a picture of a gaunt and haggard-looking Gower appeared under their name, with great timing, in the

Daily Telegraph on the morning of the final Test match. One or two of the newspapers had a go at me for this, for reasons I cannot quite fathom, but part of the deal was a complimentary weekend at the resort which I now took up and turned into a week of fitness work and physiotherapy on the shoulder. It was a peaceful stay, and helped concentrate my mind on the pressing business of making a choice between Hampshire and Kent. I eventually told Mark over dinner in London that I had decided on Hampshire, which seemed to please him, and I then had the difficult job of telling Mike Turner I was leaving.

I was sad to be going, because Grace Road had been my home for fifteen years, and while there had inevitably been grouses from those members who felt that I had underachieved for my county in comparison to my country, the tone of the many letters I received on announcing my departure was almost 100 per cent supportive. This is more than could be said, of course, for the England committee and Ted in particular. He made particular mention of my shoulder injury at the press conference to announce the West Indies tour party, but there was never a hint of this when he phoned to tell me I'd been omitted. He made it quite clear that the omission was performance related, citing the old chestnut of inconsistency. I was well aware, in the snakes and ladders environment of professional sport, that I had slithered down a particularly long serpent. This 'inconsistency' charge had always rankled with me. It is like a computer virus, and once it is applied to you, it takes a fair amount of flushing out. I had not defended myself against the charge when Ted phoned, partly because I was too stunned, and partly because it is not in my nature to argue the toss in such circumstances. If I can be permitted a burst of another quality I am supposed to be heavily endowed with, vagueness, I will confess to be inconsistently inconsistent.

I'm aware that I can be frustrating for my supporters, those people who like to see me do well, and that I have given fuel to my detractors over the years. There has been scope, I admit, to channel my ability a touch more cold-bloodedly, and to have been a degree or two more professional in my overall outlook, but my own nature has precluded it. I am what I am. Some people would say that if Boycott and myself swapped half of our brains, you would have the

174

ideal batsman. Gooch will run miles back to his hotel from a training session; I take a cab. We are all different, and I firmly believe that if you change the character, you change the player. By its very nature, cricket is the kind of game that will allow a spectator, or any kind of observer, to make a very well informed guess as to an individual player's nature. For instance, when a West Indian fast bowler is walking back to his mark there is plenty of time for a batsman to kill, and while someone like Jack Russell will hop, skip and bend all the way to square leg and back, you are more likely to spot me attempting to engage Dujon (assuming my voice can carry that far back) in some vital topic like claret, or the best seafood joint on the island. It does not mean to say that I care any less about the game than Jack – it merely represents our differing approaches to uncluttering the head before the next delivery, while some fast bowler is sauntering back to a mark a good deal closer to the boundary rope than the umpire. One or two people have managed to change their game. Glenn Turner went from being captain of the Bore's XI to a D'Artagnan, and Kenny Barrington went the other way because of pressure applied by the England selectors. Most of us make minor adjustments along the way, either to suit changing circumstances or the advance of old age, but very few swing radically away from their basic nature.

Professional cricketers, in my experience, do not like to admit to weaknesses, and I am no exception. We are aware of them, deep down, but mostly we attempt to dwell on the positive aspects, which is no bad thing. For my part, the key to my game is feeling good when I go out to bat. If I feel in proper fettle, both mentally and physically, then the way I play is good enough. Concentration is no problem, and I expect to get runs. Big runs. If, on the other hand, I am below par for some reason, then the onus is on me to battle it out – a quality that my detractors will say is absent from my game. This is partially true, in that my boredom threshold is not terribly high, and I can get tempted by a wide ball while I am still trying to get to grips with my batting. However, I do battle it out more than many people give me credit for, and it is irksome when much the same stroke is described as either 'languidly brilliant' or 'typically lazy' depending on whether the ball finishes across the rope at extra cover or in the hands of third slip.

I have been accused of regarding nets as some kind of torture chamber; as though I have an allergy to the things. *Nettus nervosus*, to invent a term. Again, there is partial justification for this judgement, without it being wholly accurate. I always do what I think is best for my game, and if a long period in the nets is what I decide is required, then the nets is where you will find me. When I was badly out of form for Hampshire in the 1991 season, I spent a lot of time in the nets trying to work on a few things, and generally build confidence. That is what they are there for. Each individual must do what he thinks is best for his own game. Generally speaking, I have never regarded slavish net practice as being any good at all for my own, but when I think I have needed them, I spend as much time practising as anyone. The two sides to any performance are the mental and the physical, and the mental is often the biggest problem. If you are in good nick, performing well, and comfortable in both mind and body, then a net sometimes does more harm than good because what you lack in a net is the sense of competition and adrenalin. It is an important option to have, but you should never be carried away by a net performance. I've lost count of the number of times I've holed every putt on the practice green before a round of golf and then three-putted every green in competition, and on other occasions the reverse has been true. In simple terms, my philosophy has been: if you need the practice, go for it; if you don't, then there is no point in doing it for the sake of it. If this is misunderstood, and has been partially responsible for my being pigeon-holed as a dilettante by some people, there is not much I can do about it – but it is not an attitude that I apologize for. I will confess here and now that I am an intrinsically lazy person. If I see a signpost saying 'Assault Course' one way and 'Beach' the other, then I am not naturally inclined to take the former route. When my tombstone is eventually chiselled out, it will not read 'Here lies (or lies back) David Gower. This boy was dedicated.'

On the other hand, I don't think I'm doing myself down by admitting to this. I am not instinctively dedicated in the sense that I cannot say to myself, 'If I get out and run three miles every morning for the next six months I will be a better player.' I think to myself, no, I've got this to do, that to do, and in any case it's too cold. However, I will always argue that to have achieved what I have done

– even if it doesn't necessarily match the expectations of England selectors or the great British public, and even if there is still scope for the argument that 'it could have been better and he could have done more with an extra degree of dedication and application' – could not have been done without a large slice of both those qualities, not to mention mental toughness. Professional cricket is a hard learning process, and it has not been any easier for me than it has for anyone else. When people say I make the game look easy, it is a nice compliment in one way, but in all honesty I have never found this game easy. It is a constant mental battle. I might go out to bat, feeling sharp and alert, and immediately start middling the ball. Fine. The next problem, though, is to learn how to keep that going. When I think back to the early days, people would say to me, 'You've got some very nice twenties and thirties lately.' This was not a compliment, and part of the learning process in those days was to get over that early excitement at the start of an innings, the slight draining of adrenalin that inevitably follows, and make sure you concentrate hard enough to go on and make big scores. You can play bloody well for an hour, and the natural instinct is to say to yourself 'Well, we haven't done too badly so far have we?' The trick is to resist the little man in your head, not to allow any feelings of satisfaction to creep in, and my success rate in this area has certainly been below average. If my critics accuse me of lacking a killer instinct, pure greed and hunger for runs, then I would not disagree with them. Whatever it is that drives the true champions, the real greats of sport, has been dished out to me in less than liberal quantities. I have worked as hard as I can in cricket, but within my own mental limitations. I'm not Boycott, Gooch or Gavaskar, I'm Gower. Some people love me, others tear their hair out.

Mental toughness is a vital attribute for all sports, even when it crosses the border into self-delusion. Peter Roebuck tells a nice story of the time when, as a comparative youngster still feeling his way in the game, he was batting with Brian Close on a difficult pitch at Taunton. For some reason, he was in superb nick that day, middling everything, while poor old Closey could scarcely lay a bat on it at the other end. At the end of one over, Roebuck was doing some gardening in his crease when he saw Closey walking down the pitch clearly intent on conversation, at which point Roebuck puffed up with pride thinking that his skipper was going to congratulate him on playing so well. 'Eh lad,' said Closey, 'I don't know what to make of this daft, bloody game sometimes. They're bowling unplayable stuff to me, and total bloody tripe to you.'

To be able to con yourself in this way is quite an attribute, and one I have never really mastered. I tend to take the brutally honest approach on these occasions and say to myself: 'Gower, old son, you haven't got a price today. Your left foot is moving when your right should be moving, your right foot is moving when your left should be moving, your hands are the wrong way round and someone's put your eyes in back to front.' And the instinctive temptation is to say, 'Bugger this. I'll come back tomorrow and see if I can do any better.' The true grit attitude, of course, is to say to yourself, 'This might look horrible to the spectators, but if you get your nut down you can still get fifty.' One of my faults is supposed to be, to pinch that Oscar Wilde epigram, that I can resist everything but temptation. The feeling is that if I play and miss at a wide one, and stand there with a sheepish grin on my face in acknowledgement that I've done something rather silly and got away with it, then the same picture might still be available to the photographer next ball. It's a reputation that I picked up reasonably early in my career, in some ways fairly, in others not, and if there is one thing that is amazingly difficult to get rid of it's a reputation.

When Graham Gooch got his 300 against India in 1990, even he would admit that the ball passed the outside edge of his bat a number of times in the first session of the game – it often happens. Any batsman, right-or left-handed, can suffer fearful bouts of playing and missing, but because this is the sort of thing that people associate with me, they seem to make a good deal more of it when I play a loose shot. With Gooch it's not a question of, 'Oh, there he goes again,' but with me it is. It would be interesting, for instance, to analyze how much left-handers play and miss by comparison to right-handers. In terms of angles, the bloke who stands the wrong way round has a good deal more scope to play fresh air shots, so we have far more chance of being pigeon-holed as rash than the right-hander does – especially if your natural inclination is to play shots. Towards the latter end of my Test career, I was taken to task for being unable to ignore deliveries deliberately bowled wide of my leg stump, the theory being that I was far more of a potential victim for being bored out than perhaps should have been the case for someone with a Test average of forty plus. I would say it was a question of judgement, as a leg-stump line can be almost as hard to judge as the traditional one around off stump. For an instinctive player like myself, though, I have to admit that the opposition probably finds the trap easier to bait than for the majority. I can say to myself, 'No, I'll ignore all this rubbish until he gets fed up' and suddenly I'll find that I've played the shot almost without realizing I've done it.

I suppose I can comfort myself with the thought that, if it is true that the British public like their heroes to be fallible, then I'm a hero. I think the instinctive type of player will always have his fallibilities highlighted more than others, and if you look at the records, I have had some undeniably poor series. On the other hand, I have had some very successful ones, and I make no apology for trotting out the old cliché that the dividing line between success and failure is not a vast one. Because of the nature of batting, the 'one mistake and you've had it' syndrome, you can go out in wonderful nick, in the most determined mood you've ever been, when bingo, you've suddenly received the only ball that's seamed all day, and you're gone. Another day, you can go out wondering what this strange piece of wood in your hand is for, play and miss as though that was the entire point of the game, and end up with a century.

On reflection, I feel that my own fall from favour towards the end of the eighties had a lot to do with the fact that so much fun had evaporated from Test cricket, that anyone who looked as though he enjoyed it – particularly when things were not going so well – was regarded with a large amount of suspicion. One of the consolations for me towards the end of a generally miserable last Ashes tour to Australia, was a conversation I had with John Wright when we finished off with three one-dayers in New Zealand. John has always been a good man to talk to, and as a cricketer he set a hugely admirable example. He analyzed his game inside out, battled to make his game consistent and productive, and has done a fabulous job for his country over many, many years. We talked cricket when I went to his place for lunch in Auckland, and he told me that the one attribute of mine that he admired over the years was the way that I had never compromised my game, and my way of playing. I realize that it was a double-edged thing, in that it was perhaps partly this lack of compromise that led to my being finally ignored by the Gooch-Stewart regime, but it was meant as a compliment and taken as such. If I had compromised, I might not have scored those centuries in the Melbourne and Sydney Test matches, both of which I thoroughly enjoyed, partly because they were good innings, and partly because of the criticism I had been under early in the tour. Ironically, I don't think they did me much good at all with the hierarchy. Rightly or wrongly, I could sense something – bewilderment is probably the word – from both captain and manager along the lines of, 'How can this bloke be so bad for a month, go out and produce a couple of gems for us, and then go back to being horribly fallible again?'

I did not, of course, get the chance to be either brilliant or hopeless on the West Indies tour in 1989-90, at least not on the cricket field. Armed with my cub reporters' survival kit, which I described to the press in one of my rare flippant moments as corkscrew and spare corkscrew, I took off for Kingston on my twin assignments for *The Times* and the BBC in slight trepidation, but grateful for having something to do.

I knew my way around the BBC radio box, having made the odd contribution to Benson and Hedges and NatWest Cup finals, but my experience of the press box was (despite having a number of good friends within) largely confined to wondering what amount of TNT would be required to blow it up. I had been well used to watching cricket from the dressing room, where the emotions are essentially linked to personal performance, and this was an entirely different mental discipline. The fact that the tour was in the West Indies and we were five hours behind London, made for exhausting days, dashing from commentary to press box to fire off my piece for *The Times* before the close of play. The radio, being live, presented no problems in that direction, although I did discover very early on that there was more to it than saying, 'What a good catch that was,' before passing the microphone back. When you have had five successive maidens, no bowling changes, and no alterations to the field, the pressure can be on you. I was not an old enough hand to waffle on about chocolate cake, and a certain amount of planning before play began was almost essential. As for the press box, it certainly made me more aware of the pressures that the writers operate under, and of the exhausting business that getting paragraphs of turgid prose back to London against the clock can be. But it did not shake my deep-rooted conviction that some of it ought not so much to be phoned to London as sent next door to the gents. Another deep-rooted conviction, that the life of a touring England cricket reporter is not all glamour, was reinforced when a cancelled flight left me stranded in Miami en route to Jamaica, and when I finally struggled into bed at about 3 a.m. it occurred to me that at least, as a cricketer, you have some company when travel arrangements fall apart.

My first day in Kingston was pretty hectic. It began with a friendly reunion with players and pressmen next morning, followed by my first (unghosted) piece for *The Times*, a clear-the-air-meeting with Micky, and a boozy party after which I managed to get myself run over. I was pleased of the chance for a chat with Micky, which took place early on that first evening when he came to my room to take possession of a bag of balls that the TCCB had asked me to bring out. We began with a minute or two of inconsequential banter, before he made the effort to explain selectorial thinking. As I suspected he would, he used the shoulder and fitness to explain it away, and I resisted the temptation to chip in with a 'Come off it, pull the other one' comment. My shoulder, in fact, was throbbing even as he said it, having just tried it out in a game of tennis with Gooch, but I knew it would probably have been fine had I had the incentive of a tour place to chivvy me into a more intensive fitness programme. However, it was an amicable discussion, and I went off to a private party that night along with Lamby and a few of the other players in a good frame of mind.

It was a highly convivial evening, so much so that I was still clutching a glass of rum and ginger when our hostess began reversing her car as a prelude to giving us a lift home. When I realized that this operation did not involve a great deal of reference to the rear-view mirror, the rum had to go, but although an adroit piece of goalkeeping saved me from leaving by ambulance, my foot took quite a hefty blow as her near-side front wheel ran it over. The most amusing part of all was her distress at having apparently cut down one of England's finest cricketers two days before a Test match, and she was suitably relieved to discover that she had done nothing worse that run over a press man. Despite the chat with Micky, and the early revelry with the players, I had already decided to stay away from the dressing room as much as possible, but a certain amount of player contact – on practice days especially – was inevitable, and without actually saying too much, the management did not make me feel over-welcome. For example, when we were in Guyana for the one day's cricket that the monsoons decided not to interfere with, I had contracted the sort of stomach ailment not unfamiliar among visitors to the tip of South America. I knew that one of the more comfortable areas on the ground in which to alleviate my discomfort would be the dressing room, and I was made suitably welcome by everyone except the tour manager, Peter Lush. He put on a very serious face and said to me, 'Don't stay too long, will you?' which was an attitude I found slightly strange.

We had, against all expectation, won that first Test in Jamaica, or should I say, as a neutral press observer, they had won? It had delighted me to hear the taxi drivers muttering about crisis and shock on our trips to and from Sabina Park, but it would be dishonest of me to say that I did not feel the occasional twinge of jealousy. Viv Richards, I felt, captained the West Indies very strangely in that match, which made me think back to the Foster bowling from the wrong end business at Lord's the previous summer. 'Yes,' I thought, 'captaincy is a bloody sight easier from the press box.' I would have loved to have been inside the dressing room at the end, but did not feel it appropriate, and left them to conduct their own well-deserved celebrations at the ground. There was the party to end all parties back at the hotel that evening, to which I was invited, and I had such a good time that I was the last one to leave.

When my brain was finally up to receiving messages the next day, I had to come to terms with the fact that the press were talking about a revolution, and that the key factor was the captain. I comforted myself with an article that had been written by Bobby Simpson after the Ashes series, in which he said that a losing side often needed only a small percentage of improvement to turn itself into a winning one. Kingston was no miracle, just one side playing above itself and the other one below par. On the other hand, the most marked difference between the summer and that game was the standard of our bowling.

What I had failed to get out of them against Australia, Graham had managed here.

Graham, in that modest way of his, declined to take any credit for Jamaica, but it was already obvious that he had forged a very good team spirit since taking over for the Nehru Trophy earlier that winter. He is very much a bloke who leads by example, and is fanatical over his fitness, enjoying nothing better than seeing off the younger guys in that area. When we got to Guyana, he had plenty of opportunity to go running in that there was scarcely any cricket, and as Georgetown, for all its beautiful colonial architecture, is not the most exciting of tourist spots, even I got bored enough to follow the players example and trot along the sea-front. I have never seen rain like it on a tour – and anyone caught fishing outside the off stump at the Bourda Oval would have had to have been in a rowing boat. On one day, the press box was unreachable without snorkel and flippers, and the mini moat that ran around the boundary area was teeming with tadpoles and other tiny creatures. It was perhaps just as well for the journalists (us journalists, shall I say) that there was no Test match, because it is highly unlikely whether anyone would have got a word of it back to London. The communications in Guyana are something else, and during the one-day international (the only day cricket was possible) the BBC radio producer Peter Baxter was in such a lather over the line breaking down that had we been able to broadcast from his ears we would have been going back to steam radio. In the end, Christopher Martin-Jenkins managed to broadcast via a crossed line with the telephone belonging to *The Times*, and it was a further education for me in the problems that the press sometimes have to endure in the remoter outposts of the cricketing world. It was a terrible shame for the Guyanese, who were half-way through their domestic season, and had still not seen a ball bowled in first-class cricket. Trapped in an area of South America that makes Manchester look like an emergency drought zone, they are also below sea-level. This means that the water can only be pumped away at low tide, and, impoverished as they are, the drains are so encrusted with silt that most of it comes rushing back again. Instead of flying straight to Trinidad for the build-up match to the third Test at Port of Spain, I had arranged to take a week's break in Antigua with the new lady in my life, Thorunn Nash. We met in 1985, at a

SPARKS charity ball in London, which she was attending with her boyfriend who had a business connection with the sponsors, Audi-Volkswagen. I was there on my own, and was pleasantly surprised when she asked me for, (a) my autograph, and (b) a dance. It turned out to be a bit of a dare, because she knew nothing at all about cricket, much less who I was, and a girl on her table – a Middlesex fan – had talked her into it. We had a couple of dances, and it's fair to say that I was quite taken. Her mother is Icelandic, hence the Christian name, and her late father was a major in the British Army, hence the surname. There's not much more to say, apart from the fact that we had become very serious about each other at the time of my split with Vicki, and we eventually set up home together in the Hampshire countryside and became engaged just before Christmas in 1991.

After a very pleasant break in Antigua with Bill and Ilse Cooper, friends I had met there on our tour in 1981, we gathered again for the third Test, and it was generally felt that England were due for their come-uppance from a wounded and fairly bad-tempered enemy. In point of fact, they very nearly won again, and would almost certainly have done so but a chain of unfortunate events on the final day. This, in fairness, balanced out the good luck they experienced on the first day in winning the toss. There is no shortage of grass in Trinidad, although the general idea appears to be that you should smoke it. Inside the Queens Park Oval, however, it was being cultivated with the general idea of relieving England of their 1-0 lead, and just for good measure, the pitch was damp as well. I had never been in a Test match in which the single most important captaincy decision was guessing which way a coin might drop, but that was certainly the case here, and within an hour or so of Gooch calling correctly, the West Indies were 29 for 5. Gus Logie, the one player on their side closer to five feet than six, bailed them out with 98, but Gooch's 84 gave England a first innings lead of close on three figures. Then Devon Malcolm blew the door off the hinges with a spectacular spell. On the last day, it all went wrong. Requiring 151 to become the first England side to win consecutive Tests in the West Indies, they were cruising at 73 for 1 from 16 of the maximum 91 overs when rain arrived to deprive them of 45. Then Gooch had his thumb broken by Ezra Moseley, and Desmond Haynes, captaining the side in the absence of Richards, managed to slow things down to such an extent that in 3 hours 35 minutes play, only 33 overs were bowled. England would have done much the same, albeit perhaps less shamelessly, and Bishop and Walsh were threatening life and limb when Gooch finally waved England in for bad light. It was a decision based as much on humanitarian grounds as cricketing ones, but from that moment England's tour took such a violent turn for the worse in terms of injury that they even began recruiting people from the press box.

I had not conceived of any circumstance in which I might be asked to play cricket on this tour. There were all the usual standby players back home in case of emergencies, and I was not in too much doubt that my original omission had as much to do with perceived attitude and commitment as it did with fitness. However, there I was scribbling away in the commentary box at the end of that final day's play in Trinidad when a message arrived from the far side of the ground. 'Gooch wishes to see you urgently,' was the gist of it, and I have to admit that I thought the most likely reason for the summons was my knowledge of some of Port of Spain's better restaurants and night spots. I would not have made any other guess even had I known that Gooch had broken his thumb and would probably play no further part (as turned out to be the case) on the tour. When he told me, I offered my commiserations to him personally as well as to the team, at which point he asked me two pretty startling questions. Was I fit? And if so, did I fancy playing in the next game against Barbados? Having honed my clichés in the press box, you could have knocked me down with a feather.

It turned out that a couple of players badly needed a rest before the final two back-to-back Tests, and although a replacement for Graham was about to be summoned, a place was there for me in the Barbados match if I wanted it. I had not held a bat in anger since September, and the Barbados team was not exactly packed with off-spinners, but once the initial surge of doubt had passed, I began to feel quite excited by the prospect. I needed, of course, to have a proper net before deciding whether I was up to it, and made myself chuckle when I said so. Here's a scoop for *The Times* man, I thought to myself. 'Gower Volunteers For Net In West Indies.' By the following morning, I had already formed the impression (correctly as it turned out) that Graham and Lamby had had to talk Micky round before the manager reluctantly gave his assent, although in point of fact I was still a long way from agreeing myself. Graham felt obliged to have a quiet word to check on whether I was still resentful about being left out in the first place, but I truthfully told him that nothing of the sort had entered my head. I simply wanted to be sure that I would not make a twerp of myself, and I even rang my agent, Jon Holmes, for some good, objective advice from the comfort of his Nottingham office. His advice was simple. Don't let them push you into anything you are not ready for. During the flight to Barbados, I had the curious experience of writing a column about myself.

The net, I need hardly add, was not a private one. The area behind it was wall-to-wall pressmen, plus a not inconsiderable number of understandably curious cricket supporters who had joined the tour for the final two Tests on the two most pleasant Caribbean islands. I began with a weak joke to the assembled throng to camouflage the nerves – 'Can anyone remember which way round I bat?' – but it all went pretty well, and the shoulder felt fine. I was not quite so happy with my touch and timing. Even so, after another knock-up on the morning of the game, I decided to volunteer. In the event, Lamby chose to field first, and I spent the day watching Greenidge carve us to all parts of the Kensington Oval, and England picking up another injury. Rob Bailey was keeping wicket because Jack Russell had been rested and Alec Stewart had a bruised finger, but when Bailey had a finger of his own bruised before lunch, our latest emergency recruit was dragged out of a Bridgetown rum distillery. That, at any rate, is where they located David Bairstow, who was there on a pre-season tour with Yorkshire.

I only got one innings in the match, and did not score very many before being caught at square leg. David Smith of Sussex had by this time arrived as Gooch's replacement, so it was no real surprise when I was pointed back towards the press box with a quiet thank you for my services. I was not disappointed, and had enjoyed slotting back into the dressing room atmosphere with no feelings of being a spare part. Not only that, I had my thirty-third birthday party to celebrate at a French restaurant on the island, before finally taking my leave of both dressing room and press box to join Hampshire's pre-season tour in Barbados.

My confused state of mind at this point was not helped because I was now being introduced to a new set of county colleagues. The people I knew well at the club were elsewhere – Robin Smith and Malcolm Marshall were involved in the Test series, and Mark Nicholas was in a private room in the island's Queen Elizabeth Hospital. Mark had failed to swat a mosquito on the England 'A' tour to Kenya and Zimbabwe, had keeled over on the flight to Bridgetown and was now in their main hospital suffering from malaria. He was, for a time, in a pretty poorly state, which is much the same description that now applied to England. In the one-day international preceding the Barbados Test, poor old David Smith, who had only just arrived, had his thumb broken by the same man who did for Gooch, Ezra Moseley. Angus Fraser was also unfit for the Test with a rib injury, and five other batsmen were nursing an assortment of hand and finger injuries. England, in fact, had so many X-rays in Barbados, that a geiger counter placed close to the visiting dressing room would probably have crackled like a machine gun. In the circumstances, it was not surprising that England lost, although in the end they were only half an hour or so from saving the match. I saw bits and pieces of the game, including some of Lamby's fine first-innings century, but not the incident involving Bailey's dismissal in the second innings when Viv ran from slip as though he had just sat down on a wasps' nest, and poor old Rob was eventually given out caught off what the replays clearly showed was his hip.

I was scheduled to play in another couple of games with Hampshire in Barbados before flying home, but the injury to David Smith, plus the fact all our batsmen now had hands that resembled a rack of spatulas, prompted yet another SOS for me to join the party in Antigua. With hindsight, given that I had already tweaked a thigh muscle playing for Hampshire and was not in any real form with the bat, it would have been a mistake for me to play in that Antigua Test match. However, I came within about half an hour of doing so. There was only one day's break between the Barbados and Antigua Tests, which was absurd in itself, and when I arrived in Antigua I got the firm impression that Lamby wanted me in the side come what may. Graham also gave out positive vibrations, and I went to bed that evening fairly excited by what the next day might hold. I was certainly in the squad, and it probably boiled down to me and Nasser Hussain, who was nursing a wrist injury, for a place in the final XI. I was knocking up on the outfield with Rob Bailey when I saw Lamb, Gooch and Stewart involved in a lengthy discussion on the edge of the square, and it scarcely needed a crystal ball to determine that my name was being bandied around. In the end, Lamby was only a minute or two from having to toss up when they came over to see me, and it was then that they told me I was being left out. It seemed to be a crunch between Lamby, who wanted me to play, and Micky and Graham, who were keener on remaining within the original tour party. I guess they were probably right, and it left me the next couple of weeks to complete my pre-season preparations back in England.

I could see the logic about the danger of fracturing morale by going outside the original squad, and if anyone had lost their place to me in those circumstances, he would have been entitled to complain. There were also, I'm sure, one or two reservations about what I might be able to do with the bat in any case. Whether they came to their decision for the right reasons or the wrong ones doesn't really matter, and although I was disappointed at the time, one look at the barrage they unleashed at Robin Smith when I tuned in to the TV back at home, went some way towards making me feel less sorry for myself.

CHAPTER THIRTEEN

Baron von Gower's low-flying circus

*T*HE new season was already under way when the England players returned, and after missing Hampshire's opening county game with Kent, I made 145 on my debut against Sussex at Southampton. It was a lovely way to start, and even better news followed when I was picked for the Texaco Trophy games against New Zealand. It was a welcome signal to me that the new blood, sweat and non-optional net regime still thought of me as something other than emergency injury cover. For my part, I gave a public affirmation of my willingness to knuckle down to anything that might be required of me over and above scoring runs, but after failing to score any runs in the one-dayers, I was tossed out for the Test series. I opened with Gooch both times, and Hadlee got me with the new ball both times. Thank you and good night. I thought it was slightly harsh to leave me out for the first Test, as I didn't exactly qualify as a first-time trialist, but I did get back in for the one-dayers against India, and this time kept my place for the Test matches as well.

I was not settled at Hampshire as Thorunn and I were still in rented accommodation and searching for somewhere suitable to put down the new roots, but the cricket side of it was proving as enjoyable and beneficial as I had hoped it would. I enjoyed the new faces and the change of scenery, but while I did not score the runs I would have liked for Hampshire that summer, there was nothing wrong with my timing when I did. The early century against Sussex helped me into the one-dayers against New Zealand, and shortly before the same selection process for India, I scored 44 not out and 126 not out against them at Southampton. This was not long after delivering my personal vote of confidence in the selectors – 'sod 'em' – following my omission from the New Zealand series. Luckily they did not hold that against me, as I privately feared they might, but it was actually meant to convey just how keenly I felt about still playing for England. The fact that I had also been named in the first Test squad, and was down to bat at No 3 instead of opening, also took some of the pressure off. I made 50 in the first one-day match at Headingley, although it was not a thing of great beauty by any means, and I was playing exceptionally well in the second game at Trent Bridge when I was out in circumstances that were incredibly dozy even by my high standards.

I had, I think, hit six boundaries in that 25, but just when I might have given the impression that I was playing the Indians in my sleep, it took on a more literal connotation. I turned down Mike Atherton's invitation for a single, stood and watched the wicketkeeper take the throw at his end, and then stood and watched the keeper throw the ball at the bowler's stumps. All of this would have been in order had I not been standing outside my crease, and by the time I twigged that something embarrassing might be about to happen, it had. In the first Test at Lord's I was almost as disappointed as I can ever remember, because I was well aware that the new regime were looking for signs that I could graft, and I had put my head down to score 40 in about two and a half hours when I was given out caught off bat and pad. Sometimes these things are close, but on this occasion I was not within six inches of the ball. Still, what with Gooch scoring 333, it all rather got lost in the wash. Old Trafford was another disappointment, a careless slash to gully followed by a drag on via inside edge and right boot, and I had missed out enough in a series when runs were coming out of other people's bootlaces, for speculation to grow that I needed a big innings at the Oval to make the tour party to Australia. I tended to go along with that, if only for the fact that no-one else, certainly not the skipper, had told me any different. I had enjoyed my previous winter with the biro and the microphone, but this time I had a burning desire to go as a player rather than a journalist.

It was another belting pitch – they all seemed to be in that long, hot summer – and my cause was not advanced by India taking up most of the first two days in scoring 600, and me getting out for eight

Nice innocent photo: D.I.G. and I.T.B. relax on a yacht off St Vincent in 1986. Unfortunately England at that moment were on their way to defeat against the Windward Islands, so this was deemed 'not a good thing'.

By 1990 I was allowed to relax – I was only in the Caribbean as a broadcaster and journalist. Allan Lamb is one of my closest friends in the game, so who better to fill me in on the latest news and tactics than he?

This apparently immaculate position belies the fact that I am only slightly better than a novice on the Cresta Run. The cartoon below attests that driving on lakes was not such a good idea either. Losing the hired car in the lake in St Moritz meant it was a very expensive long weekend, even more than usual in that part of the world!

'Could you speak up Mr Gower. I can't hear a word you're saying!'

GOWER AND MORRIS ARE INNOCENT---OK

Talking of expensive moments, the £1000 fine levied by the TCCB on both John Morris and I after we had buzzed the ground at Carrara while Smith and Lamb were batting to set up England's victory over Queensland meant that our fifteen-minute joyride probably cost us more than Lord's paid for our return tickets for the tour!

At least the white water rafting, in New Zealand, was on an official day off (sorry, *the* official day off). It was cheaper – and more fun.

Skiing is another favourite relaxation. The fact that fiancée Thorunn and I are pictured with Ali Ross, who definitely can ski, does not mean that we will be entering the next winter Olympics.

Celebrating our engagement in traditional fashion, November 1991.

The other great passion of my life – wildlife and its conservation. One of my favourite beasts is the leopard and I snapped this female at one of my favourite safari venues. Londolozi, in the eastern Transvaal.

on the third. I never really settled, and when I was horribly adjacent to the lively seamer Atul Wassan, it must have looked a curious dismissal to those not close to it. I got everything behind the ball except my bat, which was at least another bat's width away from making contact. People must have thought that I was in urgent need of an eye test, but I had managed to get the bat caught behind the pad as it came down, and it was knocked totally out of alignment. We went into the rest day needing another 114 from our last three wickets to avoid the follow-on, and I had dinner on the Sunday night with friends near Lord's. Myself and Thorunn, Robin and Leonie Askwith, Eric and Tanya Idle, and Gary and Michelle Lineker. It was a very convivial evening, which was mostly spent in taking the piss out of me, and, if the intention was to relax the slightly fretting left-hander before a potentially crucial innings, it certainly worked. The highlight of the evening came when Eric and Tanya's baby somehow found its way onto my lap, and someone said, 'Mind it doesn't shit on you.' To which Eric replied, 'Why not? Everyone else has.' It was perhaps over-stating the case a little, but I think we were all aware – I certainly was – that the selectorial blade was once again hovering dangerous close to my neck.

From a purely selfish point of view, I was grateful to the Indians for wrapping up our innings on Monday morning and enforcing the follow-on, as it meant one last chance for me to either cement, or blow, my winter passage to Australia. However, I spent most of the day waiting to go in while Gooch and Atherton put on 176 for the first wicket, and we always felt we had it in us to draw the match on a very good pitch. For one thing, the ball was not swinging as it had in our first innings, and although the opposition's efforts to make it wobble around did not preclude some surreptitious scuffing-up on one side of the ball, this was quickly sniffed out by the former Fraud Squad officer, now Test match umpire, Nigel Plews. It perhaps won't surprise many people to know that I spent most of the day asleep with my pads on in a corner of the dressing room, although the more voluble crowd noises did have the effect of half waking me. However, this was simply a mechanism to get over a fairly serious attack of nerves by my standards, and when the crowd noise indicated the fall of Gooch rather than another boundary, I had a quick splash under the cold tap before setting off for the middle.

Middle, in that final passage of play, turned out to be the appropriate word. I middled absolutely everything, and the thought of going in to bat had turned out to be – not for the first time – far worse than actually getting out there and taking guard. I've talked before about things clicking into place straight away, feeling in top fettle both mentally and physically, and this was a classic example. From my very first ball, I felt as though I was 150 not out, and it was a great disappointment to have to come off. I was well aware that it is entirely possible for your touch, for no apparent reason, to disappear overnight, although on this occasion it did not. The bowling was relatively undemanding, but contrary to the popular theory that my idea of pressure is mislaying the corkscrew, I was as tight as piano wire that morning. When I reached three figures I initially attempted to match the captain's deadpan expression on these occasions, but failed, and the general feeling about an innings of 157 not out was that it had not only saved the match for England, but also a seat on the plane to Australia for its scorer. I drank in the applause when I walked off, and thought to myself that this is the sort of thing that keeps you going. I enjoy all the sports I play, not because I am consistently good at them – I'm not – but because I have my moments. There are moments playing tennis when I feel like Edberg, and there are moments playing golf (a lot fewer of them, I'm bound to say) when I feel like Ballesteros. Cricket, for me, has only ever been an extension of that – enjoying the moments when they come – and the only real difference is that I've always been that bit better at cricket than tennis, golf and skiing. I enjoy these moments so much, that they are invariably followed by an urge to go out and practise eight hours a day so that they will come along more often. This urge, I have to say, disappears almost as quickly as it arrives.

It goes without saying that I enjoyed that final evening after the century, and it was made all the more pleasurable by the knowledge that Thorunn and Robin and Leonie Askwith had been in the crowd. When I raised my bat for the century, and again for the 150, the thought of people close to me being there added a certain amount of poignancy, and a great deal of satisfaction. I was still, however, slightly irked by the feeling that I had needed those runs for something other than purely cricketing reasons; that I was a misfit in the current system who was constantly required to prove his commitment for England. This feeling was reinforced by a conversation I had with Dilip Vengsarkar after the innings. Down the years, Dilip, for all his consistency as a batsman, had been at odds with the Indian selectors and Indian politics, which is virtually one and the same thing, and he said to me, 'Well played, I suppose this means you'll have to go to Australia now.' The suggestion was that I did not really want to go, because I would not fit into the system.

There were elements of truth in my feeling uncomfortable with the way the team was now being run, but in broad terms I was willing to fit in with almost anything to carry on playing Test cricket. I certainly felt under pressure when the tour party gathered at Lilleshall for fitness training, partly because I had not managed to drag myself out onto the roads five times a day, and would not quite be up to the sort of gruelling routines I knew they had in mind, and partly because I felt that the hierarchy would be fascinated to see how I performed there. I didn't do too badly, without quite looking the picture of happiness throughout it all, and the gentleman appointed to put us through our paces did manage to get a certain amount of vomit from me on the football field. I blew up at him more than once, although this again could have been perceived wrongly in that I have always needed a certain amount of anger to drive me on through hard physical exercise. Fortunately, given the imminence of our departure for Australia, it was only two or three days worth, and protest though I did at times, I was well aware of the value of getting together in this way before a tour. After all, I had been the one who first suggested it after the Caribbean disaster of 1985-86.

The mission down under did not get off to the best of starts, either in terms of performance or team morale. You can defend the work ethic in terms of what you put in, you tend to get out, and Graham is the best example I have played with who would leave nothing to chance, either physically or technically. It does not suit everyone, however, and there was a lot of early niggling about the way we were preparing. Days off appeared to be out of the question, and a non-playing day tended to follow a regimented pattern; down to the training ground, a longish session of physical fitness training, followed by nets, middle practice, and back to the hotel sometime in mid-afternoon.

Okay, this was not hard work in the sense of eight hours at the office, or a shift at the coal face, but it was the establishment of a basic routine, with all the implications of that word. Routine is a word that implies a certain ennui, a hint of boredom, and a lack of initiative and imagination. Painting by numbers, if you like. You accept that there are things you must do to get yourself into a position to be fully prepared for a hard game of cricket, but there is a fine line between a dedicated approach and contentment, and overkill and resentment. We had the situation in which people like Devon were getting bawled out by Micky. The bowlers were complaining that they had run too far and were knackered before they came to bowl, and when they did come to bowl, they were driven too hard. No tour is niggle-free from the outset, but there was an undercurrent about this one in that I felt we were being required not to enjoy ourselves under any circumstances.

Graham was very unhappy with our early performance against Western Australia, with every justification, but I groaned a little when I saw him quoted as saying, 'We have the talent, but we must work a lot harder at making it gel on the field.' Gooch's whole philosophy was based around the blood, sweat and tears ethic, but he must also have known that there are times when you need to put your feet up. Australia had had a winter (our summer) off, whereas we had been playing virtually non-stop since leaving for the West Indies ten months earlier. To be tired before you have started is hardly ideal preparation, and in my view we were not making the situation any better by the way we were going about things. There was a further dip in morale when we moved on to Adelaide for the match against South Australia. The finger injury that Graham had picked up in a practice game had become infected, and he was now in hospital with blood poisoning. He was in a private room with a portable TV, but watching our game against SA may have led to a serious downturn in his condition. We followed on against what was reckoned to be the weakest state side (barring Tasmania, possibly) and eventually lost by six wickets.

Despite a draw against Tasmania in Hobart, we left for Brisbane and the first Test being roundly written off. 'Atrocious Poms Face

Ashes Whitewash' was the headline in one of Australia's more sober Sunday newspapers, and although one of the local pundits got a bit confused with his metaphors when he referred to England's top three batsmen as having 'all the never-say-die qualities of a kamikaze pilot' – I think I know what he meant – we had certainly not clicked with the bat. The situation had become even gloomier with the news that the captain would certainly miss the first Test, and possibly the second in Melbourne as well. All in all, we went to Brisbane firmly installed as second favourites. Those of us who had been on Gatt's tour four years earlier were slightly less worried, in that we had played like total idiots before the series, and then, in a ship that appeared to have all the buoyancy of a leaking bath tub, we ran up the Jolly Roger and slaughtered them.

We had genuine worries, and needed to work on them, but if we had remained a bit calmer, things might have turned out better. As it was, the atmosphere filtering through from the top was one of mild panic. There was a lot of technical bullshit flying about, and Devon was getting horribly harassed by Micky. Devon appeared to have sorted most of his problems out in Hobart, but while most of us were thinking 'Thank God for that', Micky remained firmly on his back. Gladstone Small, who felt happy with his bowling, was constantly being badgered about extra nets, and whether he felt he should be doing this, that or the other; what he really wanted was to be left alone. Whatever I might have felt at this stage, I was definitely keeping it to myself. I wasn't going to be seen to rock the boat, and I got on with whatever I was asked to do. Australia is not the ideal tour to bond a team together if things are not going well on the field and the training ground, in that the side always fragments after dark. If your only option in the evening is to meet in the team room, as in Pakistan, then that's what you do. If you can go to any one of hundreds of different restaurants, bars and clubs, then it's entirely different. With all these options available, then the natural splits in a touring side become more exaggerated. You have the management, the senior players, the young bloods, and people like myself and Lamby who could probably be described as senior young bloods. So, we all go off like the Red Arrows, and meet up again for the business at hand the next morning.

Where the build-up was going wrong was the management's

attitude of telling everyone what to do. The more you relieve people of individual responsibility, the more master-slave the relationship becomes and the more resentment creeps in. The thing was being run like a puppet show. No-one expects to be handed a questionnaire to fill in every morning. What would you like to do today? How do you want your eggs done? What time would you like a net, sir? I'm not saying that at all. There has to be a basic team discipline, and indeed conformity. But each touring side develops an atmosphere. Get the emphasis right, and it will be a good one; get it wrong, and it won't.

I thought back to the contrast in the team meetings we had in Pakistan under Willis in 1983-84, when there was so much input from every member of the squad that we almost had to call a halt to prevent them from becoming counter-productive. In the home series against Australia in 1985, we called a team meeting after the pre-Test dinner at Edgbaston. Scarcely had I launched into my speech when I.T. Botham conveyed his opinion of my oratory with a fusillade of bread rolls directed at the captain's helmetless cranium. The meeting, not surprisingly, degenerated fairly rapidly, but schoolboyish though it might seem, it was symptomatic of the spirit and morale within the camp. The actual words on these occasions mean far less than the overall mood. The marked difference on this Australian tour was that once Gooch and Stewart had had their say, there was precious little reaction (either light-hearted or otherwise) from the players themselves.

We did not go into the Brisbane Test, minus Gooch, as a beaten side, but we were a long way from being a happy one, and we were stuffed out of sight in three days. There is a theory in sport that you get the luck you deserve, which probably made it inevitable that we would lose a highly important toss. With Queensland tinder-dry and teetering on the edge of a barbecue ban, an electrical storm had juiced up the Gabba the day before the Test, and on the morning of the game it was a steamy, turkish-bath sort of atmosphere even by Brisbane's tropical standards. None the less, Lamby and myself appeared to have got through the worst of it at 117 for 2 by mid-afternoon, when he sliced Greg Matthews carelessly to backward point, I was caught behind for 61 slashing equally carelessly at Bruce Reid, and the wheels came tumbling off. All out 194.

One of the more subtle banners at the Gabba (colonial perception of our personal hygiene not being over-complimentary) was, 'Hide The Ashes Under A Bar Of Soap', and when the game ended in a ten-wicket defeat, there was no argument that the Pommie towel (dry or otherwise) had seldom been thrown in quite so thoroughly. What made it all the more galling was the scale of our fightback on the second day. Fraser, Small and Lewis bowled so well that we actually took a first innings lead, and although we lost three wickets ourselves that evening, mine among them, there was the great psychological boost of seeing Border drop Lamb in the slips just before the close. However, Lamby was leg before to Alderman in the first over next morning, and we fell apart even more spectacularly than we had in the first innings. All out 114. Having top scored in the first innings with 61, I did so again in the second with nothing better than 27. I would have needed a fair amount of good fortune to escape, and when two good early appeals against the Australians were turned down, it seemed we were fresh out of that too. Given their reprieves, Marsh and Taylor grew as confident as we became deflated, and they finished us off comfortably.

Appropriately enough for a team apparently still to wake up, the next chunk of the itinerary involved spending a good deal of time in pyjamas. The World Series Cup, a one-day competition between England, Australia, and New Zealand was upon us, and the one bonus of this meant around a month's breathing space (and in Gooch's case, healing space) before the second Test. However, no sooner had we flown from Brisbane to Adelaide for the first of two practice games before our first one-dayer against New Zealand, than the press got their teeth into what they regarded as a poor show off the field, as well as on it. This concerned a trip to a Queensland casino by two England players – Lamb and myself – during the course of that first Test. Ever since the New Zealand tour of 1983-84, the ground rules of cricket reporting had changed significantly, in that everything a player, or a team does runs the risk of being scrutinized. Rule one is, that if you are winning, you might conceivably get away with it. Rule two is, that if you are losing, you definitely won't. Any morsel, any minor titbit that comes up is fair game for the media. Before the Test, Tony Greig, a resident in Australia since the days of World Series Cricket and close friend of

Kerry Packer, told me in somewhat vague terms that Packer was keen to take Lamby and myself out on the town for an evening, and I was equally keen to take him up on the offer. People like Packer are not over-common and I had never met him before. So I thought that he was bound to be an interesting man to talk to. Greigy then set it up for the second evening of the Test, a car was sent down from the Gold Coast to meet us, and we spent the first part of the evening having dinner in the casino.

Packer, as I had suspected he might be, turned out to be a fascinating dinner companion. He's a very forceful man, as you would expect, and delivers his opinions in a way that suggests there can be no counterargument. He firmly believes that the one-day international will take over from Test cricket as the entertainment of the future, which in many parts of the world is already coming true, and has little truck with those (like myself) who believe that the five-day game is, (a) more important, and (b) should be protected at all costs. I got the firm impression that he has always been annoyed by people suspecting his motives in cricket, and one of the points he brought out was the coloured clothing issue introduced into his World Series Cricket circus in the late seventies. Most people, I imagine, would suspect that it was a marketing gimmick, something to add to the hype and razzmatazz that Australians are so fond of. In fact, and I was quite proud of myself for knowing the answer when he asked me if I was aware of the reason, it was purely because the white ball employed for night cricket used to get lost in the players' clothing. We flitted through all sorts of topics, which mostly involved him talking and us listening, and he generally deported himself as one would expect of a tycoon.

After dinner, we all headed off to the members' club of the casino in which we were dining. With time getting on, Lamby and myself ought probably to have thanked him for the evening and left. He certainly gave us the option, but partly because he was clearly enjoying himself (he was winning at the time) and partly because he was killing time until the Rugby League international between Great Britain and Australia came on the TV at 2 a.m., we told him that we were happy to stay a bit longer. I certainly was, as I did not have to bat at eleven o'clock the next morning and was clutching a glass of rather expensive brandy. Lamby, on the other hand, had stuck

198

rigidly to the coffee after dinner, and was beginning to cast the occasional glance at his watch when we decided, around midnight, that we really did have to get away. However, Greigy drove us back to Brisbane at high speed, and we flopped into bed at about one o'clock in the morning. Okay, it wasn't eleven in the evening, but neither was it three, and in the league table of nights of shame for England cricketers, it was barely a runner.

Unfortunately, the local newspaper in Brisbane had discovered our visit and chose to make it an issue. The story was not very big, and I remember chuckling at one of the lines used by the reporter. 'They were not seen drinking.' Bloody hell, I thought, things have come to a pretty pass. 'England Cricketers In Non-Drinking Shock-Horror.' The English press naturally got hold of it, and as Lamby had the misfortune to get out early the following morning, they made an even bigger issue out of it. At some stage of every Australian tour I have ever been on, the management have felt obliged at some stage to say something stern about after-dark activities, and this one was no exception. On this occasion they chose, quite properly, not to wield any of the bigger sticks at their disposal, but who knows what bearing it had when they came to pick a vice-captain for the following summer? Coincidence or not, Lamby had lost the job.

He had now lost three consecutive Tests as emergency captain, and it was clearly a difficult time for him. He is an instinctive player, the same adjective applies to his captaincy, and, it has to be said, his off-duty demeanour. Everyone knows that Lamby has a greater capacity than most to enjoy himself in his spare time (he also has the capacity to absorb that and play bloody well) and it was a touch ironic that he had taken over as captain on a tour where the ethic was 'don't enjoy yourself or else'. The rules were 'play hard, practise hard, and go to bed early'. If things go wrong, human nature demands that your lifestyle is placed under the microscope. Graham would set this paragon-like example, whereas the players were well aware that Lamby was flawed. They enjoyed him for what he was, and appreciated the fact that he was a fine player, but they knew that he liked a good time, and enjoyed a drink, and under the set-up at that time, it left him vulnerable. With human nature being what it is, there was scope for saying, 'Well, if the skipper can go out and have a skinful, why not us?' It was also hard for Allan because Graham had established himself so firmly in the job, and, not to put too fine a point on it, was a difficult act to follow. On top of that, we collapsed twice in Brisbane, and when you are captaining a batting side, there is not much you can do. You are basically relying on individuals putting in a performance.

What was so disappointing about Brisbane was our failure, or apparent failure, to get fired up after that second day. The way we bowled and caught our catches, we must have looked like the best side in the world, but somehow we failed to carry it over to the next day. We had two good lbw shouts early in their second innings which, had they gone our way, would have caused a flutter in their dressing room, and while I'm not saying we would necessarily have bowled them out, it would have made for a far better atmosphere in our own camp had we at least made them sweat for their victory. In much the same way as had been the case in '89 in England, the whole psychology of the series was settled in that fourth innings.

We were, oddly enough, awarded the next day off after losing the Test, but Stewart was not in such a benevolent mood when we were beaten by New Zealand in our opening World Series match and ordered us in for nets. The fact that this delayed our visit to the Mount Hurtle vineyard, as guests of the main man and an old friend of ours, Geoff Merrill, was only a minor irritation. For once, I sympathized with Stewart's decision, in that we had been little short of hopeless. I was also aware that my own stock may not have risen with the manager – out, fourth ball of the match, for six, a total achieved with one smite off the second ball. Things, however, did not improve much. I cracked my thumb playing in the one-day game against a Prime Minister's XI in Canberra, which kept me out of action for the next fortnight, Lamby did a hamstring running back to the team hotel in Ballarat during the last game before the second Test, and Chris Lewis's back was playing him up sufficiently for Phillip DeFreitas to be flown in as emergency cover. Meantime, on the field, we continued to provide light relief for an Australian public grumbling about their economic recession. The one uplifting note concerned Robin Smith, whose planned trip home for the birth of his first child had been cancelled amidst all the crisis talk, but whose mood picked up appreciably when the news came through that his son had been safely delivered.

A corresponding dip in morale was then suffered by Mike Atherton, who found himself dropped for the next one-dayer in Perth without anyone having spoken to him. Stewart made the speech to the press on his behalf, and it was a mini-classic. 'He is not on the best of terms with himself batting wise, and we wanted, on the tempo we are looking for in this particular game, for him not to force things outside his natural game.' It was real answers-on-a-postcard-please stuff, but I think it meant, 'He's been dropped for slow scoring.' Gooch's finger injury had now improved sufficiently for him to play in an up-country one-dayer against a Don Bradman XI in Bowral, and while it was reassuring to see him back in the saddle, it also meant that he had his first close-quarter look for some time at the wretched state we were in. At the schoolboy home of the Don, we were minced by a team barely out of short trousers, chaperoned by their forty-five-year-old captain, Doug Walters. This was embarrassing enough for the presentation ceremonies to be delayed while Micky read the riot act behind locked dressing room doors. His basic message, predictably, was 'more hard work'. By the time we got to Ballarat, we had been in Australia for sixty-two days, of which precisely three had concerned the prime reason for our being there, namely the Ashes. We deserved the flak we were getting, but the team is not always helped by the people who draw up this sort of itinerary. For the game against Victoria it had been decided that I should drop down to No 5 and Alec Stewart bat at No 3, with a clear hint that this was the way the selectors were thinking for the Test match. I was still not entirely happy with my injury, and in any event the No 3 position had by now become associated with the sort of frenzied search unmatched since Cinderella mislaid a slipper.

We had a poor first day, with Dean Jones scoring one of two centuries, while Micky spent it under observation in a Melbourne hospital suffering from periodic numbness to the right leg. It was perhaps surprising that he had not been feeling numb all over, and even when we rallied through Lamby's brilliant century, the day still went horribly wrong for us. He decided to run the three or four miles back to the hotel that evening and managed to damage a calf muscle. It might have looked a daft thing to do, but it was literally one of those things that you just don't consider can possibly happen until it does. He came off a kerb awkwardly, and twang, he was out of the Test. He was our one batsman in prime form, and we would be without him in Melbourne. It put a bit of a dampener on our preparations to say the least. I had played pretty well in helping to save the game with a half-century in the second innings, but here again the picture was anything but rosy. Having got over the finger, I was now suffering from a bruised and painful right wrist, barely up to raising a glass of Bollinger over the Christmas lunch. The morning (Boxing Day) of the Melbourne Test began with Small, Lamb and Lewis all unfit, and Graham asking me whether I was fit enough to play. Raising a quorum was clearly going to be a triumph in this game, never mind raising the thought that we could actually come back and win the series.

As far as I was concerned I was no better than fifty-fifty, and I was more or less talked into playing. I was not, I'm afraid, very helpful when Graham asked me. I said something like, 'Yes, I can play, but...' The inference being don't blame me if I don't get a run. However, just to prove what a perverse game this can be sometimes, I then went out and scored 100 runs. I was indeed at No 5, although Lamby's injury allowed 'Ned' Larkins in at No 3 with Alec batting one place below me, and Ned's half-century allowed me to walk out – pumped up on pain killers – with the comparatively comforting sight of 100 up on the board with three wickets down. Again, despite the wrist, I felt good from the outset, and in company with Alec, we posted a good first-day total. Even then the Aussies introduced a note of sarcasm, as we woke up next morning to the headline in the *Melbourne Age*: 'A Dull Day At The Cricket: England Fails To Collapse.' It was nice to think, though, that we might have drawn some of the cockiness out of them. The mood in the series thus far had been nothing like as bitter as in 1989, when they had been less confident of success, and correspondingly more aggressive. This time, when they clearly expected to win, they had more of a superior air than a nasty one, and it felt good to have taken some of the wind from their sails. This good feeling was not, however, to last for long. I was out immediately after my century, but it was more of an unlucky dismissal than any lapse in concentration after reaching a landmark. I got one high on the bat against Bruce Reid, which no other bowler on either side would have got near, but Bruce possesses something closer to tentacles than arms and he snaked one out to take an improbable caught and bowled.

We were not entirely happy with our first innings total of 352, but, as they did in Brisbane, Australia again collapsed – from 224 for 3 – to give us a first innings lead of 48. This time, at 103 for 1, we were not going to give it away again, surely? However, there then followed one of the most spectacular collapses in Ashes history. Our last nine wickets went down for forty-seven and the last six for three. It was almost beyond belief, and although we had them two down for about ten on the third evening, they did not lose another wicket in scoring the 197 they needed on the fourth day. Boon and Marsh played exceptionally well, and the only sniff we got was when Boon got a hard snick into Jack Russell's gloves cutting at Tufnell and was given not out by Peter McConnell. Tuffers, who had bowled for most of the day without any success, did not take it at all well. He was caught out by the TV cameras after stalking out to his fielding position near the boundary, when it did not require a degree in lip reading to work out that of the two words he employed to appraise spectators of his opinion of Australians, one of them was 'cheats'. He did not, in my hearing anyway, say anything directly to McConnell, apart from, 'How many balls left, please?' It was not an inquiry lodged in a particularly friendly manner, but McConnell's reaction was astounding. Accompanied by a not inconsiderable number of expletives, McConnell, who I think had a fair idea he had got the decision badly wrong, told him to get back to his mark and bowl, and not to be quite so irritating. Tufnell then complained that he had only asked a civil question and all in all it was not a very wholesome exchange. McConnell has a reputation for possessing a short fuse, and on this occasion I would have to say that umpire was more at fault than player.

There can be a lot of pressure in a Test match, on both umpires and players, and in some respects it is a surprise that altercations don't happen more often. Had it been one of their bowlers it would have been a bloody sight worse because Australians give their own umpires unbelievable stick. Someone like Alderman would have gone demented, whereas at least Tuffers confined himself to muttering and kicking a few lumps out of the turf. If you catch an Australian umpire on a quiet day he will tell you that he doesn't really enjoy it, not even the state matches, because of the abuse he comes in for from the players. Quite apart from anything else, I don't think it does anything for their umpiring standards, very good though one or two of them are. I don't know why they get so little respect, but it is entirely different from the way English cricketers carry on. Perhaps it is because our umpires are, generally speaking, so good. Most players around the world regard English umpires as the best, and one logical explanation of that is that most of them have played the game at first-class level, and are therefore familiar with what goes on and know exactly what to look for. They also, given our domestic programme, get more practice than they do elsewhere.

No matter what country you play in, or at what level, the stereotype of any umpire is a bloke whose standard uniform is dark glasses, white stick and a dog. Pakistan is generally held to be the chief breeding ground for the more advanced form of incompetent, although on the one tour I made there (sorry, Gatt) I didn't find their umpires too bad at all. There is no doubt at all that their job has become far more difficult. Once upon a time, when players mostly walked, all they had to do was be able to work out an lbw, and count to six. Nowadays, it is not so much a question of being able to count the marbles in your pocket, as hang onto the ones in your head. One-day matches have not helped, what with over-rates, calculations, and the like. Something seems to change every winter to make their job still harder. One quality that all the best umpires have, however, and which I don't think is perhaps that widely appreciated, is the ability to get on with players. If you can establish a dialogue with the combatants, it makes for much better understanding all round. Someone like David Shepherd, for example, is so easy to get on with that there is rarely any bad feeling on the field, and while I won't go so far as to say that it's a pleasure when he gives you out, you are far more likely to forgive him a mistake than some po-faced, humourless individual who never says a word apart from 'out', 'not out', or 'over'.

Pakistani umpires may have got our backs up over the years, but when you come up against people you have little in common with, it is harder to build a relationship and iron out potential misunderstandings. Umpires all over the world will complain, justifiably, that there is no longer a reciprocal arrangement with players, whereby everyone sets out to make everyone else's job easier. So players cheat. They don't walk any more, and appeal for catches they know full well are not out. This, unfortunately, is partially true. Most players, however, are not rabidly dishonest. I've done a lot of fielding at silly point, and if I think there is a chance that the batsman might have got a bat-pad, then I'll appeal. Similarly, I will also shout 'catch it!' if the ball is going to another fielder. That's an instinctive thing that someone started somewhere along the line, and has become a habit. It is when the dividing line is crossed between asking the umpire to make a decision and attempting to bully him into one that the problems arise. If, every time a ball comes off a pad, everyone within fifty yards shouts and screams, then that is not very helpful to the umpire. This, in turn, has led to counter measures from the batsman – pointedly staring at his inside edge for lbw appeals, and rubbing his shirtsleeve when the fielders go up for a catch off the glove. Someone is trying to con somebody, and unfortunately for the umpire, in Test cricket certainly, it is often a case of dog-eat-dog. Someone like Willis, for example, captaining England against Pakistan, would make a point of saying to us, 'Now look, these are unsavoury characters, perfectly nice off the field, but out to cheat you on it, and I don't want my batsmen walking.'

Like many other batsmen, I tend to walk when it suits me, and stay there when it doesn't. I have always walked more readily in county cricket than Test cricket, which is nothing unique to me, and I recall getting away on one occasion in the 1982 series against Pakistan. I nicked one off Abdul Qadir and was caught behind by Wasim Bari, and nonchalantly carried on prodding down an imaginary divot and remarking my guard. The finger stayed down and I got away with it. I copped some horrible language from Bari, but I didn't feel overwhelmed with guilt. It was ironic getting called all sorts of unmentionable things by someone like him, who never thought twice about appealing when the ball had missed your bat by a yard. There are other kinds of kidology that do not result in the umpire intervening, such as, 'This bloke can't play, skip, let's bring in another slip …' and the old chestnut from the bowler, 'I'll send you down a piano, see if you can play that.' There are all sorts of psychological ploys to unsettle a batsman. Phil Edmonds would crouch at short leg chuntering away between deliveries, which was deemed slightly unsporting. The only time something like that has ever bugged me was when Viv Richards became unpleasantly abusive at silly point during the final Test in Antigua in 1986. I actually brought the umpire in on that one, but by and large it's never been a problem.

The Chappell brothers and Rod Marsh could be pretty abusive when they wanted, but it was all very much angled towards unsettling the batsman, while someone like Lenny Pascoe was genuinely off his rocker. He really did flip at times. Rodney Hogg could be as fierce with the verbals as he was with the ball, but he was a lovely bloke off the field. Merv Hughes was another opponent who was fierce on the field and gentle off it, and to a certain extent all of these people set out to fill a role. Fast bowlers are supposed to be mean, so they glower, bristle and let you have bouncers. It's mostly image. Some batsmen, of course, deliberately set out to wind up the more volatile bowlers, but I have never subscribed to this approach, particularly with the ones who are slightly quicker than average. If a bloke is going to bowl at my head, I don't want to be the one who's talked him into it. Keep mum, that's my motto.

Umpires like to talk as well, or some do. There was one in India, P.D. Reporter, who was impossible to shut up, and he would even address everyone by their nicknames. I remember he gave me out lbw at Delhi, a decision that defied every law of geometry, but because we had a good relationship I was able to sit down and have a chat about it. Another Indian, Ramaswamy, umpired the last two Tests on my tour to India in 1984-85, and did so as well as any umpire in the world. Officials, like players, are going to have off days, and require a run of games in order to be judged fairly.

I think that umpires in county cricket resent, to a certain extent, the system by which a captain is responsible for marking them from 0 to 5, and upon which Lord's largely base their end-of-season 'league table' for making Test panel selections. Perhaps that should be done away with, particularly as it can result in unfair markings due to personality clashes. Before the late David Evans became a Test umpire, he was convinced – although I had no evidence at all to back him up – that the then Leicestershire captain Ray Illingworth awarded him a nought before he even tossed up. Some of our players, equally unfairly no doubt, then thought that Evans, thinking he was down for a bad mark anyway, did not, shall we say, lean towards Leicestershire when appeals were made. I still feel, though, that many of the problems (and there are relatively few in county cricket) can be overcome by dialogue. I made the point quite forcibly at the annual captain's meeting, when I was in charge at Leicestershire, that captains and umpires should be encouraged more to talk about the marks that were given and the reasons behind them. If there are decisions that need talking about, captains should not be afraid of talking them over with the official concerned. It does not always work because human nature often takes over and you end up with a stand-off. However, socializing between player and umpire (perhaps not so much in Test cricket, where the opposition might suspect partiality) is important in county cricket, not least because umpiring can be a lonely job. They are on the road far more often than we are, and with only the one colleague, who may for some reason disappear in a different direction at close of play, it is nice if they have some familiar company in which to unwind. It doesn't matter which relationship you are talking about in the game, whether it be player/umpire or chairman of selectors/gateman: the friendlier it is, the easier it is for people to do their respective jobs.

It's fair to say that Gooch and Tufnell did not have much of a social relationship in Australia (they tended to keep different hours and Goochie is not a great one for the disco) and following the umpiring spat at Melbourne, there was another outbreak of hostility – this time between player and captain – in the third Test at Sydney. Ironically, Tufnell was to have Boon given out caught behind off him in this game, when the ball comfortably turned past the outside edge, and Tuffers doubtless advanced his cricketing education by realizing that sometimes it's your day, and sometimes it isn't. In cricketing terms he was very green, and he would often lose confidence with his bowling. On these occasions he tended to blame Graham for not giving him the right field, and Graham would end up telling him to show more fight and character – a bit more bottle. Knowing that he would not see too much of him after dark, Graham also spent a lot of time during matches and practices trying to find some common ground and what made Tuffers tick. Phil's temperament was such that he threw the odd tantrum, and there's no doubt at all that it got up Graham's nose.

Eddie Hemmings was actually in more hot water than Tufnell at Sydney, hoofing the ball away when he had an appeal turned down and later getting fined for it. However, Tufnell made further inroads into the captain's nostrils when he too had an appeal turned down and decided to let off steam with a burst of sarcasm at the umpire, Tony Crafter. Gooch moved in with a suitably headmasterly comment. When he captured his maiden Test wicket, Tufnell pointedly refused Gooch's proferred handshake. Gooch was understandably put out, despite the allowances he would have made for Tufnell's rawness. Tuffers is an entertaining character, but there is an awful lot of bluff to him. He came across as streetwise, but in reality he was not. He was nothing like as cocksure as he would have people believe. He needed more nurturing, but in the all stick and no carrot atmosphere of that tour, he became a somewhat bewildered and lost soul. He came to me at the end of the match with a plaintive, 'What am I doing wrong, Lubo?' and it was clear that he was totally confused by the whole business of Test match cricket. Above all, he had become the butt for every spectator in Australia. His fielding was not exactly reminiscent of Randall in his heyday, but he was far better than he came across. His confidence, though, was shot. I was able to counsel him on improving his attitude and appearance, a scenario that would probably have made Micky's hair drop out, and told him that international cricket did not offer the opportunity of a leisurely learning course. You had to learn to swim pretty quickly, otherwise you sank.

Complex characters require special handling as I often found out with a far more experienced spinner, Phil Edmonds. Philippe, by and large, was very easy to captain, but he also threw the odd tantrum and on rare occasions would hand me the ball and decline to bowl. At times like this I would just let him simmer somewhere in the field, employ someone else for two or three overs, then wander over and ask him whether he was ready for another crack. Invariably, he was. It's annoying for a captain when the bowler most suited tactically to the situation is either not bowling well, or doesn't want to bowl, but you've got to work out how to get round it. Ranting and raving doesn't help a jot.

That third Test eventually showed what a fine prospect Tufnell was when he took five second innings wickets and might have had a hat-trick had I clung on to a ball that flew very fast into the close off-side cordon from Dean Jones. It might have been given bat-pad, we'll never know, but it was one of those that either stick or do not. This one just got away from me. We came away from Sydney with morale improved, even though we did not get the victory we badly needed. Australia made 500 in their first innings, but we came back so well that Gooch was even able to declare. We were a few runs adrift, but it gave us an enormous lift and it almost led to us winning the match.

I batted as well as I could ever remember in that match, particularly after resuming on 33 not out overnight. Mike Atherton was on 94, and by the time he had moved on to 96, I was 79. He beat me to the century in the end, but the sound of the ball pinging off the middle of the bat was almost as sweet as the sound of the Australians bickering away as though they were 2-0 down instead of 2-0 up. If it had not been for a remarkable innings from Carl Rackemann we would probably have won. He went almost an hour and a quarter without scoring, and eventually held us up for the best part of two hours on the final day before Devon came back on to bowl and cleaned him up straight away. It had been a difficult one for Gooch, in that Devon was not 100 per cent, and with the time-runs equation so important, we felt that if he came on and got clattered we would lose what slim chance we had. With hindsight, it was a mistake as we were left with the impossible target of 255 from 28 overs. We still had a go at it, and when I opened with Gooch we made 84 from 12 overs and could barely make out a single fielder without the aid of binoculars. It was too much of course, but within two days the lads were busy packing the mosquito nets and fly repellant for a trip to Albury rather than the anti-glare cream and coloured gear for the World Series Cup finals.

Thanks largely to the fact that we had come unstuck twice against New Zealand, we needed to beat Australia in the final qualifying match at the MCG to go through, and did well enough in restricting them to 222 from their 50 overs. I felt in great nick opening the innings with Gooch, making 26 at almost a run a ball until I was given out lbw to one from Alderman that I felt at the time would have missed leg stump by some margin. The TV replays did nothing to shake that conviction. We then had a spectacular mid-innings collapse, and although Fraser and Martin Bicknell dragged us back into it with some educated slogging, Tuffers failed to hit the four required off the last ball of the game. So, while Australia and New Zealand assembled for the three-match final, we now faced a trip to Albury-Wodonga for a game against New South Wales that had been arranged in case we failed to qualify. It did not go down terribly well. We had come to Australia to play cricket, of course we had, but this match had all the connotations of punishment for being a naughty boy. Most of us felt that a combination of practice and a few days relaxation in Melbourne would have done far more to lift morale, and never can an England team have assembled to meet the Sheffield Shield champions with greater reluctance. The one member of the management team who argued for more time off was Lamb, but he got little change from Micky, and again this might have told against him when they sat down to discuss the vice-captaincy. Lamby was no great admirer of the manager and his way of dealing with people, as for instance, just before the Texaco series against the West Indies in 1991.

Graham took Lamby to one side before the game at Lord's and told him he had lost the job, whereupon he bumped into Stewart who promptly denied it. Lamby exploded and said: 'Look, the captain tells me I'm sacked, and you tell me I'm not. Someone's lying here.' Well, it wasn't Gooch, but the messy way the thing was handled led to Lamb and Gooch having a fairly public spat on the balcony after the game.

The Albury game highlighted once again the question of balance, the balance between hard work and relaxation that you need on every long tour. Players spend a lot of time emotionally wound up for matches, and with modern day travelling and playing schedules being what they are, there is precious little chance to unwind. Here we had an opportunity, but partly because it went against the management grain, and partly, I am certain, because they were worried about press reaction to the award of a four-day holiday after being bombed out of the World Series Cup, it was passed up. The only two people who were excused attendance were Gooch and myself, and while I was very grateful to get away to Sydney, Alice Springs and Ayers Rock, I was also well aware of the undercurrent of discontent that it caused among some of the other players.

The Stewart-Gooch argument was that you must keep practising in order to get better, but if you keep hammering away at it you are actually driving people into the ground and making matters worse. Jankers games rarely do anyone any good because the whole psychology of the match is wrong. I felt at the time that we would have been far better served as a unit to say, 'We've lost this one-day thing, and we have not been playing very well. However, we are still in with a chance of levelling the Test series, go away and do what you want for the next four days.' I did not say anything because my relationship with authority was not terribly good and it would have been counterproductive. Had they been going to give us a break, and I'd piped up asking for one, they would probably have done the opposite. Graham and myself had played a lot of cricket together down the years, and had always got on fairly well, but by now we had drifted apart in terms of what we thought was best for the side, and I felt more and more like a square peg in a round hole. I could not pretend that I was enjoying the regimentation, and this made Graham increasingly impatient with individual things such as my fielding practice and, on a more general level, what he perceived to be an uncaring attitude. He had various moans at me throughout the tour and finally blew up in New Zealand right at the end before the one-day international in Christchurch. As we set out on a lap of the ground, another David Gower – a namesake who I had met out there before – turned up inquiring about the possiblity of a drink and a night out, and after asking him to hang on for me, I jogged across for a chat in between our twenty-minute run and the fielding practice that had been convened.

I tried to take no more than the time needed to take a card and promise to phone the man later, but it was too much for Graham and he made his displeasure patently obvious. I thought this entirely unnecessary and blew my own fuse in return. I think it is safe to say that the pressure of touring was getting to us!

I thought I might have made half a point in favour of my own views on having time off in the aftermath of the Albury game which, incidentally, we lost sufficiently early on the final day for Stewart to arrange even more jankers in the form of a practice match between our own players. I had not gone to Albury because my wrist had been playing up again. Laurie Brown, the physio, had already ruled out any chance of me playing in the game, and I convinced the management that there was little point in my pitching up just to watch cricket for four days. So, I had my break, and for those players who did not take part in the Albury match, a special training session was arranged two days before the following game against Queensland in Cararra. I can say, in all honesty, that the enthusiasm and effort put into that session stood out like a sore thumb. I certainly felt refreshed, and I actually quite enjoyed it. I should also say that the two people who looked and acted the freshest at that session were the two who had had time off, namely myself and Graham.

On Bob Willis's tour several years earlier, when we had again failed to qualify for the one-day finals, the gap left in the itinerary had indeed been given over to recreation, and while I admit that the rewards and pressures in international cricket had grown considerably in the intervening years, I could still not see the requirement for a different approach. It is impossible to maintain a peak of fitness day in and day out without some form of release. The occasional late night and a lie-in, or a trip out on a yacht, is far more beneficial than the constant cracking of the whip, and I personally believe that the results on this tour go a long way towards proving it.

Carrara, of course, is where my tour took off – although the fact that this take-off involved a Tiger Moth aeroplane did not ultimately do my prospects for career advancement a great deal of good. It was an interesting venue, a stretch of kiss-me-quick-hat plastic paradise on Queensland's Gold Coast 50 miles north of Brisbane, built, as I had discovered during dinner with Packer, around gambling, and almost as artificial as Las Vegas. There were all the usual holiday diversions, and judging by the size of the crowds at the Brisbane Bears Aussie Rules Football Stadium, a visit from the England cricket team ranked well down the list. What was soon to bother the England management was not so much the poor attendance from spectators as the absence of some of the players from the dressing room. Among the aforementioned recreational pursuits were aeroplane rides and, shortly after lunch on the third day, attention from the game was briefly diverted by a low-level visit from a couple of Tiger Moths.

Ordinarily, this would have passed off as nothing more than an occupational hazard of playing cricket in a place modelled somewhere between Miami and Mablethorpe, except that the two intrepid aviators (complete with leather helmet and goggles) turned out to be D.I. Gower and J.E. Morris. As it turned out, there was holy hell to pay. The background to all this began with the game, and the fact that we were well aware of these planes regularly flying across the ground – albeit at a greater height than the two ultimately in question. We were also aware that the airport was just across the road from the ground, although the plan to take to the skies was an impromptu one rather than anything pre-planned. There was certainly nothing sinister in the fact that Morris, who made a century, and myself, both got out within a few minutes of one another on the third morning. During lunch, however, a little lamp came on in my head – a flicker of mischievousness. I mentioned the possibility to Lamby, who was batting with Robin Smith at the time, and it was unfortunate for John (as things turned out) that he overheard our conversation. He, doubtless feeling buoyant after his hundred, asked to come, and probably thought that any escapade being talked over between senior player and vice-captain could not have been too far over the top. I did think of asking Graham for permission to visit the airfield, but I knew he would have been unhappy with us flying, and as that was the entire point of the exercise, I decided that it was best not to mention it at all.

The idea, by now, had become irresistible, and after jotting down the phone number of the ground (to which we would be so close that we could have been back in time to field whatever happened), off we went. We had to wait a while for a flight, but after checking that Allan and Robin were still batting, we each hopped into a plane and took to the air. I had already talked my pilot into a spot of low-level flying, and we duly dipped down between the floodlight pylons and waggled the wings – in salute, as we later discovered, to the century that Robin had just completed. Lamby had told him of the lunch-time conversation, and the only two people on the ground to know who was in the cockpit, playfully pretended to shoot us down with their bats. Unbeknown to us, the pilot had alerted the local newspaper before taking off, and one of the British cameramen, Adrian Murrell, thought he spotted something familiar through a long lens while we were in the air. So, when we landed, there was something of a reception committee. Flashbulbs duly went off, and the cat, as they say, was out of the bag. We had not intended to make a publicity stunt out of it, and what rankled later was Peter Lush, the tour manager, complaining that we had sought to do so. We still thought it was best not to give too much away, so when we bumped into Goochie back at the ground, and he asked somewhat suspiciously, 'That wasn't you up there, by any chance?' I put on my best choirboy face and said something like 'Who, me? Heavens, no.'

Events, however, quickly overtook us. By this time the entire press corps had cottoned on, and it did not help our cause when they brought the matter to the attention of the management at the close of play press conference. Lush's face, by all accounts, was a picture when he found out. By this time, though, we were back at the airport posing for pictures, which did nothing to decrease the tour manager's apoplexy. It was a mistake to have gone back as it only added fuel to Lush's suspicions that we were courting publicity. But we already knew that the game was up, and we were merely helping out a good mate in the photographic corps, Graham Morris. He had been blissfully taking pictures of the cricket when we landed, and therefore missed out on the shots that he knew his employers would want. You can well imagine it. 'Hang the picture of Lamb's caught behind, what about Gower in his Biggles' gear?'

When Morris (Graham, that is) got back to the hotel, he was ambushed by a steaming Lush in the lobby who demanded to know what had been going on, and when Morris, J. (whom I shall now refer to by his nickname of 'Animal' to differentiate) puffed in shortly afterwards he was pounced on by this human volcano. Lush, by all accounts, was determined to hold an immediate inquiry, but was then thwarted again by the news that one of the protagonists (me) had gone out to dinner. The minus points, as you can guess, were beginning to mount up. I was having dinner with David Frith, the editor of *Wisden Cricket Monthly*, who had also been at the airport when we landed, and when the phone rang it was Animal. 'I think,' he said, with great perspicacity, 'that we're in a bit of trouble.' I told him not to worry, he told me that Lush wanted to see me immediately, and I told him that I was not about to abandon my dinner for an evening of Lush blowing hot air in my direction. I had still not appreciated the weight of the management's displeasure, although the discovery of three notes from Lush under my door when I eventually got back gave me a clue that something more than minor retribution might be at hand. The first one read, 'Come and see me when you get back,' the second, 'Come and see me when you get back,' and the third, 'Come and see me at 8.15 in the morning.' I could see the mounting fury in the handwriting. I duly arrived, on time, in the manager's suite to be met by the Big Four, Lush, Stewart, Gooch, and Lamb. Micky started by complaining that he had had to get up early for his breakfast, Lush said he was very unhappy with me, Stewart wanted to know why I had done it, Graham said he was very disappointed, and Lamby was turned to the wall trying hard not to wet himself.

I tried to be suitably contrite, and gave them the old mountaineer's motto: 'I did it because it was there', that sort of thing. I realized they had two choices, and told them so. 'You can either be heavy about it, or you can treat it as a harmless prank.' No prizes for guessing which one I recommended. I owned up to an error in judgement, but tried to impress upon them that the game was going well, Animal had played well and morale for once was very good. In other words, don't spoil it now with anything heavy-handed. However, they soon got on to general attitude. How long did I want to going on playing? Was I enjoying it? Graham, in fact, said, 'I don't think you enjoy playing this game very much, Lubo,' which got me a bit het-up. I was honest with him, and replied, 'If you mean I don't enjoy every single day of it, you're right. I know you don't think much of my fielding practice, and I'll own up to less than 100 per cent enthusiasm. I've got problems with my shoulder, and my hand, and there are times when they give me a lot of pain.' 'Well why haven't you said anything about it?' 'Because I don't want to be labelled a moaner.' 'Well what about your attitude? These players look up to you.' 'Please don't tell me that someone like Atherton, who is an intelligent man, is going to be unduly affected by what I do. We get on well. He knows what makes me tick and what doesn't.' And so it went on. It was, in many ways, real heart-to-heart stuff.

I think, like most average cricket watchers who did not know me, that they were all under the impression that I had always found the game easy, and perhaps felt that this explained why I did not (or appeared not to) treat the game as a matter of life and death. In fact, it had been many years since I thought the game easy. I found it bloody hard, in fact, physically and mentally, and whatever I did that was perceived to be against the system was only my own way of keeping myself as fresh and alert as possible. I hate to use the old cliché about being misunderstood, but in this area, I think I have been.

The meeting ended with a 'we'll let you know' message as to any disciplinary action, and after winning the match against Queensland, we then flew to Adelaide to prepare for the fourth Test. Lush gravely informed the press that he would 'deal with the matter in the appropriate manner', in a tone that suggested he believed that it lay somewhere close to Faisalabad on the tour upset scale. I got the impression that it was going to be something more than having my pilot's license endorsed. I was still a bit on edge, and when I had a TV camera lens poked at me at Adelaide, I contented myself with a brusque, 'I had a good time, John had a good time, end of story.' End of story, however, it was not. Not long after, Animal and I were once again summoned to the headmaster's study where Lush read out the statement he was about to issue to the press. 'Immature, ill-judged, and ill-timed. Fined £1000.' I had him take out a couple of words, told him he had been guilty of a huge over-reaction, and left. I was not impressed.

So, a £27 aeroplane ride had now been subject to a £1000 management-fuelled surcharge – the maximum permissible under our contracts. It was a bloody sight more, I can tell you, than the fines levied on Hemmings, Alec Stewart or Tufnell for showing dissent in a Test match, and it seemed to me that it was typical of this regime. In their terms, the equivalent of flicking ink pellets at the teacher was a far more heinous crime than setting fire to the chemistry lab. Lush, I recalled, had sat in adjudication on Chris Broad when he refused to leave the field after being given out in a Test match, and did not fine him a penny. He also complained to the press that the Tiger Moth flight had 'detracted from a solid performance', as if this were in any way relevant. So now we knew. We had paid the penalty for hogging the newspaper headlines during a match in which England were doing well – which on this particular tour was about as unlucky as you could get. Lush asked me not to comment on the punishment, which was bloody rich. I told the press that I thought £1000 for twenty minutes in the air was scandalous in the days of deregulation, but behind the apparent sang-froid, I was boiling. I was well on the way to my target of 500 runs in the series, but there was no way I was able to play the next Test match in the right frame of mind. It has been said, and I tend to believe it, that the stroke I got out to in the first innings at Adelaide more or less finished me with Gooch, but there was never a moment in that match in which I felt comfortable batting. I am not blaming that dismissal over the aeroplane business, but it did not have an uplifting effect on my spirits.

I also got the impression that Lush's decision had not endeared him to everyone at Lord's. I had spoken to my agent, Jon Holmes, who told me that he had formed the impression from a conversation with Mike Turner (who was on the TCCB's executive committee) that an appeal against the fine would be looked upon favourably. Animal did not want to get involved, but I asked Lush whether an appeal was possible, and he, very politely and affably, said that he would look into it. Oddly enough, for the rest of the tour Lush couldn't have been nicer. Anything I wanted – extra tickets, you name it – and he bent over backwards. Eventually he told me, however, that under the terms of the contract, there was no right of appeal for a fine – only if you are sent home. It struck me that it would have been a bit too late for an appeal once you had been sent home, but I later discovered how close I had come to being dealt with in almost that way. I discovered from Lamby, who had obviously been part of the disciplinary committee, that they had seriously considered suspending us for the rest of the tour. Apparently, it was only because we were doing so badly on the field, and they thought they might need us, that steered them away from that course. Obviously, our relative assessments of the severity of the incident were even more at odds than I had imagined.

Adelaide, with its Royal Ascot type atmosphere, is more of a social event than a competitive game of cricket, with a pitch that dare not misbehave for fear of impinging on five days of cucumber sandwiches, ladies' hat parades, and the occasional excursion out of the marquee for a glimpse of the third new ball scuttling across the boundary rope. Yet, on day one, we had Australia 125 for 5 until

Mark Waugh's maiden Test century helped them to reach almost 400, and on the flattest wicket in Australia we were then bowled out for 229. Gooch and Smith made half-centuries, but it was the same old collapse, this time from 137 for 2. Gooch's finger was causing concern again, Fraser's hip injury was beginning to look serious, Martin Bicknell was out of the tour with a rib tear and Phil Newport was on his way out from the A tour to join us as cover for, well, almost everyone. The next low-level pilot to visit the England team, it seemed, was less likely to be D.I. Gower than the Flying Doctor.

There were those, I know, who felt that I might be next requiring medical attention when Gooch got back to the dressing room after the stroke I got out to during that collapse, a pick-up shot off McDermott that floated straight down Hughes's throat at backward square leg. They had set the man there for the shot, I went for it, and what made it worse was the fact that it was the last ball of the morning session. There is not much I want to say in my defence, other than I felt out of sorts from the moment I went out to bat. I could not time the ball, was having trouble picking up the right line, and was basically just trying to get through to lunch. I wasn't playing for lunch in the accepted sense of the term, otherwise I would have been blocking, but it is often the case that an interval can suddenly help you click things back into place. It can sometimes work the other way, of course, but this time I needed the break to gather my thoughts. McDermott had already tempted me once in that over with a leg stump delivery that I miss-hit in the air, but safely, and I was as exasperated as Graham must have been when I fell for the second one. He had not spoken to me before that last over (Graham rarely says anything while you are batting with him other than 'keep going' or 'battle it out'), neither did he say anything to me when he followed me back into the dressing room. He didn't have to. You are always aware when you have done something wrong, and don't really need anyone to tell you. Neither did I need anyone to tell me that Graham was upset, but someone did anyway. Lamby had tried to fight my corner with the standard Gower speech: 'You know what Lubo's like, you have to take the rough with the smooth.' But this time, according to Lamby, the skipper was not really wearing it. Again, it is hard to explain something that you cannot really put your finger on yourself, but what I will say is that I felt more comfortable at the crease when I was scoring 0 in the second innings in Melbourne than I did in Adelaide. When the slating arrived, it was worse than I had expected. It was a rare bad day for me in the series, and yet I was made to feel that I had not scored a run for years.

The match itself was drawn, although, as at Sydney, we gave the opposition quite a fright chasing an improbable target. We were left to make 453 on the final day, were 203 for 0 by the mid-afternoon drinks session, and the irony for me after the first innings was that they ended up bowling two feet wide of the leg stump when I came in. This time, I couldn't possibly reach the ball, and I actually volunteered to retire hurt when we came in for tea. Eventually, I was given out lbw to a ball from Hughes that would have missed off stump by six inches, which just about put the tin lid on it.

We had lost the series, and had one final Test match – at Perth – in which to convey to the Australian public that we were not complete duffers. We failed, losing in four days by nine wickets. It was hard to believe that we could collapse yet again, but sure enough, 191 for 2 became 244 all out. I went in No 5, and was left stranded on 28 not out, which should give you some idea of how swiftly the wheels flew off. After that, I thought that I would have to be spotted piloting a low-flying pig for us to get out of this one, and we were duly bowled out again for 182. For some time now, Graham had been starting to steam, and he finally came to the boil at the Perth press conference. He talked about players' careers being on the line, people having to look at themselves honestly and decide whether they had given their best, weeding people out the following summer, and, once again, attitude. I had the feeling that somewhere in that little lot, there was an unspoken reference to me.

CHAPTER FOURTEEN

Grounded

A LOT of the players were upset that the captain should have spoken out as fiercely as Gooch did at the end of the tour to Australia in 1990-91, whatever the pressure. For my part, I looked back over the previous three months or so and considered that I had had a reasonable series. I had not been very far short of the 500-run target I had set myself. I was disappointed about the last two games, and would have liked to have passed Boycott's record of runs for England. I wanted 67 at Perth and made 33. I was also aware that Gooch was referring to matters over and above pure statistics, but in my own mind I knew I had battled hard throughout the five Test matches. I had not agreed with the way the tour had been run in many ways – there had certainly been a poor spirit right the way through – but although I had spoken out against management policy once or twice, I had also done my best to fit in.

One example of this were the two attempts I made on the tour to get the team involved in something I passionately believe has a big future in professional cricket – sports psychology. Neither was acted upon, which made a brief conversation I had with Ted Dexter early the following summer all the more galling. We had gathered at Lord's for a pre-season get-together, involving the England touring squads, the forty or so 'hopefuls' for the season, Dexter, Stewart, Lush, Lush's successor Bob Bennett, and Colin Tomlins, our physical fitness coordinator at Lilleshall. We convened for what turned out to be an interesting dinner after a training session at the ground, and after Ted and Micky's post-mortems into Australia (Ted was suitably obtuse, while Micky managed to trace all our problems back to the pre-war days), Graham and Bob Bennett both made impressive speeches. Graham, who had been surprised at being asked to speak at such an informal meeting, said that anyone wanting to play under him had to give the familiar 110 per cent, but generally put across the commitment message in an honest and heartfelt way. Bob simply added that everyone would do well to remember that the game should be enjoyed, and that alongside the obvious need to play it hard, the traditional spirit and camaraderie of the game should not be forgotten either. Between the two of them, I thought, they had summed up the ideal approach to cricket.

During the dinner, Ted made the announcement that the Reverend Andrew Wingfield-Digby had been appointed as England's pastoral caretaker, to offer our players spiritual assistance and a voice to counsel away from the immediate cricketing side of things. As the West Indies were that summer's visitors, it seemed appropriate enough to call in the director of 'Christians In Sport' for a series in which we (apparently) hadn't a prayer, but as I happened to be sitting next to Ted, I took the opportunity to ask him why we had not gone for more terrestrial assistance to go along with the divine variety: namely, a sports psychologist. 'Well,' he replied, 'we haven't been able to find one we trusted.' This irritated me somewhat, as I had twice during the Australian tour (through an expatriate friend of mine, Nick Duncan) orchestrated offers from two of the best sports psychologists in Australia. One was based in Sydney, and came highly recommended, as was another guy from Perth, who had been heavily involved with Western Australia's champion basketball team that year.

I had long thought that there was great potential for sports psychology in professional cricket. The people involved would not be concerned with issues such as team selection, they have no particular axes to grind about who is playing for England or who isn't, they are genuinely neutral, and by definition they are there to help both the team as a unit and the individuals within that team. There are players around the country who already benefit from individual advisers, and while results at Grace Road during our own two-year association with a psychologist did not seem to be a great advertisement, Leicestershire had employed him only as a pre-season motivator, and on both occasions the positive early-season effects disappeared when we were left to our own devices.

I see a lot of potential value in this sort of assistance, especially when you consider how many of the world's top sportsmen rely upon it. Cricket, on the other hand, has buried its head in the sand, and to relegate psychology below spiritual advice on the list of priorities made little sense to me. Nice man though Wingfield-Digby is, and reasonable Minor Counties' standard cricketer that he was, it is not the most natural reaction in a dressing room to seek out the help of God when things are not going too well. It strikes me that a sports psychologist is better qualified to handle a cricketer's problems than the chairman of 'Christians In Sport', whatever the relative merits of both professions.

However, when I made what I considered to be a highly constructive proposal in Australia, Micky and Graham threw out the offers of help and decided to stick by their own basic system. That was their decision, which was fair enough, but it did not quite square with the management's overall assessment about my relative lack of input and commitment on that trip. All these matters needed to be discussed properly, and eventually in Wellington Graham and I found an empty restaurant. He paid for the food, I did the wine – and both were excellent. But I cannot say that we settled our professional differences, even if we were doing better in trying to remain friends. It was the standard argument from him, about people looking up to me and how he wanted to see more evidence of my enthusiasm and evidence of my commitment to playing for England.

I told him that people, himself included, had seen me play for the past fifteen years, they knew what I was like. By and large I got on with people, did my best to help others, and all in all did not see myself in the problematical light that he did. I had never tried to undermine him as captain, and the biggest question I had for him was this. If I was so lacking in commitment, how did I go out and score two centuries? Where did the four hundred and odd runs come from? Was that pure luck? I did not really get an answer, merely, 'Ah, but you don't look as though you're enjoying it.' In the end, we had to agree to disagree. He told me that I had to provide evidence of commitment next summer, and that the only evidence he would accept was scoring runs. This was good news, as I had previously been under the misapprehension that eight hours fielding practice a day was more important than scoring runs, although why scoring runs the following summer was to be acceptable as evidence, while scoring runs on that tour was not, I could not quite fathom. It had been an unsatisfactory discussion for me, and my overriding feeling was that my good points appeared to have got lost amidst some fairly trivial bad points. Still, go and get runs for Hampshire was the message, and go and get runs for Hampshire was what I intended to do. It did not, unfortunately, work out that way.

The first thing I had to come to terms with, having enjoyed the atmosphere of Test match cricket in Australia – which is always something special – was how to get over my traditional ambivalence for the start of an English season. My hand and shoulder were beginning to protest at the very average temperatures encountered in April and May, and we were once again scheduled for a ridiculously early start. I did not score many runs early on, and even with Gooch's words still ringing in my ears, and the extra motivation of a still relatively new county, I cannot pretend that my appetite for domestic cricket had not gradually diminished over the years. I still enjoyed the way of life, but the freshness had gone, and I had certainly become more weary of the duller aspects of the game, like dragging yourself to different parts of the country three times a week. Hove to Old Trafford on a Friday night does lose its appeal after a while, especially when the M25 is proceeding like a West Indian over-rate. The previous summer, I had gone from Leeds on the Wednesday to the Oval on the Friday for one-dayers against New Zealand, and I was due back at Leeds for Hampshire's game against Yorkshire on the Saturday morning. So Robin Smith and I had stayed at my house in Leicester on the Friday night just to break it up a bit.

There are times, during those early season B & H zonal games and county matches, that I find it amazing to see any bums – thermal-lined no doubt – on seats at all. I've often wondered why they don't set fire to the stand to keep warm, then at least the players could pretend it was a Test match in India. At this time of year, the players need a bit of choke to get out of the garage as well as the car, and it is not a feeling entirely peculiar to me.

Not many of our winter batsmen were drunk with runs by the

time the selectors sat down to pick their Texaco Trophy squad, although I was experiencing one of the worst troughs of form of my career. I was finding it a hard game to play, and the nadir came at Headingley in our final B & H group match against Yorkshire. We had already qualified for the knockout stages, but needed to win to clinch a home match, and got rolled over for 50. It gave me a fairly shameful double in that having been a member of the Leicestershire side that held the previous lowest B & H total – against Minor Counties would you believe – I had now managed to get below it with Hampshire. From there we went to Northampton for a Sunday League match, and I was invited round to the Lambs along with the Smith brothers on the Saturday night. I was nursing a heavy cold which, despite several glasses of Lamby's red wine that night, left me in such a poor physical and mental state that I ended up sitting out the game. Things were not good!

We were at Hove when the selectors met to choose the one-day squad, and Gooch phoned to give me the unsurprising news that I was not in it. I said, 'Fair enough, I haven't got the runs you wanted, but can you tell me what the feeling is with the Test matches?' He was slightly evasive, muttering something about keeping me in mind, but then added, 'I'm afraid you won't get much support from the other two.' Meaning Micky and Ted, of course. So that was not exactly an over-encouraging message. Again we went through the same sort of conversation as before, and again I had to say, 'I'm sorry to keep bringing this up, but what do Test hundreds count for?' He didn't really answer that, in effect confirming that the problem remained the England hierachy's attitude to my perceived attitude.

When you are in the sort of rut I found myself in at the beginning of the 1991 season, it is very easy to feel sorry for yourself, and in my case it was not helped by the media, who were also asking the 'is this the end?' question. Meantime, Mark Nicholas was beginning to feel the heat from various Hampshire factions – members, committee, local press – over me, and more than one strong hint was dropped in his direction along the lines of, 'Isn't it about time Gower was despatched to the Second XI?' Tony Middleton and Julian Wood were scoring runs in the second team, and I was holding back young players. Mark did speak to me, making me aware of this undercurrent of discontent, and it did act as a jolt. Happily, Mark was of the opinion that second-team cricket would not necessarily do me any good, and, without uprooting any trees, I did manage to improve my form over the next few weeks.

In the past, I used to work on the principle that things would come right soon enough, and invariably they did. On this occasion, though, I felt so out of sorts that I did decide to engage the hard work ethic. I had extra nets, employed the bowling machine, had long sessions with the coach Peter Sainsbury, and even engaged the help of John Smith, father of Chris and Robin. If I was failing in the middle, it was not for want of preparation. A minor turning point came at Bath, which, as a spa town, is supposed to have certain therapeutic qualities, and on a low, slow pitch far from ideal for fluent strokeplay, I grafted a long time for 60-odd. Having got that far, I was actually quite desperate to turn it into a century, but I got myself caught at silly point poking at a ball from David Graveney and I was almost as deflated as I would have been getting out for single figures.

One unfortunate sideline to this prolonged struggle was that, having drifted apart from one good friend in Gooch, my relationship with another, Nicholas, began to come under increasing strain. I had become a little niggly and testy, which did not make the skipper's job any easier, but I certainly got the impression from Mark that I was letting him down badly. There were no specific instances when we actually fell out, but the atmosphere became increasingly cool. People were on his back, spectators included, and there were one or two incidents involving the crowd. I could sense a certain tension around the members' pavilion, and while some people were radiating sympathy, others were becoming increasingly hot and bothered about my performances. We were playing Minor Counties at Trowbridge in the usual B & H zonal-round weather (we actually sent out to the local camping shop for handwarmers) when I got some (unfair) stick for what some yokel in the beer tent decided was a piece of indifferent fielding. The loud response was, 'What the (expletive deleted) do you want me to do? Dive twenty yards?' The occupants did not appear to be great fans of mine, as they had also had a side-bet that day that I wouldn't get double figures. Unfortunately, they collected. It did not help either that the *Daily Telegraph* reporter was looking for a line at round about the same time as Gerald Ratner, of jewellery shop fame, had described all his stuff as 'crap'. A brief résumé of my innings in the *Telegraph* report ended with '– Ratners'. My thoughts at this stage of the season were not hugely positive. In fact, I went so far as to wonder whether this parody of a left-handed batsman was receiving a huge hint from on high to find some kind of alternative employment. Something that he might be halfway good at. The Tests were now under way without me, and I seriously considered whether retirement might not be an attractive option. I had been following the West Indies series, of course, with particular interest in those picked ahead of me. It is a very human reaction to want to compare the results of your replacements against your own possible performance, although there is no guarantee that I would have done any better or worse than the likes of Hick or Ramprakash.

Wanting to be in the team is a natural emotion, and here was the guy keeping me out who wasn't scoring runs. Maybe, I thought, people will realize that Test cricket isn't quite so easy after all. Cricket can be a selfish game, and it makes me chuckle when I read comments from centre forwards in a soccer team such as, 'I don't care whether I score or not, as long as the team keeps winning.' It's got to be bullshit. He would have been thinking, 'If I don't score soon, I'm out on my ear,' which is what Hick must have been telling himself after every failure. He had come in under a lot of pressure, of course, and I also had a genuine sympathy for him. However, I could have handled being out of the side far better if they had picked me for the opening Test and given me the opportunity to either do well or fail. If I had failed and been kicked out, even after one match, I would have said, 'Fair enough.'

Another factor against me was that I had lost an ally close to the selectors with Lamby losing the vice-captaincy, although he was still close enough to the hierarchy to be able to confirm, as I had suspected, that my stock was pretty low. It was probably not improved in mid-season when Worcestershire came to Portsmouth for a match, involving Hick, Gower, and Botham, attended by Stewart. Ian had an ordinary sort of game, Hick did just the right thing by scoring a big hundred in the second innings, and I did just the wrong thing by chucking a hundred away. I was in the 70s and playing well, when Hick came on to bowl his off spin, and, with the field well back, I promptly holed out to extra cover. I had decided that I would prefer to entertain both myself and the crowd by taking him apart rather than proceeding quietly to three figures, but when it failed, I knew that I had lost the gamble to impress the team manager. To be honest, that probably summed up why I was no longer playing Test cricket.

Fortunately, the motivation to keep going that summer was provided by Hampshire's progress in the NatWest Trophy. They had never reached the final of the 60-over competition in its 29-year history, but we played so well that we actually arrived at Lord's for the loss of only six wickets in four matches. It reminded me of Leicestershire winning the 1985 Benson and Hedges final after equally emphatic progress. I captained them that day at Lord's, and, by a quirk of fate, I was destined to captain Hampshire on this occasion. Surrey were our opponents in the final, and the Lord's fixture computer had arranged that they were also to be our opponents in a four-day county match at the Oval immediately before the game. We lost it, but this was far less of an imposition than losing our skipper with a broken knuckle. Waqar Younis, who was having a sensational season with Surrey, took his usual hatful of wickets in the game, including mine twice, but also inflicted physical damage. He first thudded one into Kevan James's box, and then produced a horrid delivery to Nicholas that Mark only kept out of his visor at the expense of his knuckles.

There is always this nagging feeling before a big game that something is going to go wrong for someone. It's a bit like going skiing. If you allow yourself to think you are going to break a leg, you probably will. However, the fact that it was Mark was especially cruel. He is a very emotional character, and had dreamt of playing in the showpiece one-day match ever since, as a boy, his father had taken him to see his first Gillette final. Mark knew almost at once that he would not be fit to play, and there then followed a period of speculation as to who would captain the side on the Saturday. Chris Smith had been the senior professional and had taken over earlier in the season when Mark had once been absent, but the fact that he was now in Perth, West Australia, rather ruled him out. Thus it seemed to be, at least in the media's eyes, a straight choice between myself and Paul Terry.

Paul had been Mark's vice-captain for some years, an apparently natural partnership, as the pair had in effect grown up together in cricketing terms ever since they joined up at Hampshire on their first day together. However, that partnership was dissolved just before my arrival at the club, ostensibly allowing Paul to concentrate on his batting at the top of the Hampshire order, where he can be a prolific performer. He is certainly the best fielder in the club in any position and probably the best natural games player we have.

However, he had only just resigned his commission when Mark found himself stricken with malaria at the start of that 1990 season, and Paul was back leading the side. Furthermore, I had only deputized once for Mark, leading the side one Sunday in that same season, and had even turned down the chance to do so again a few weeks before the final. On that occasion, Tim Tremlett had suggested to Mark, bowed down by a heavy season and the pressures of his benefit, that he might take a Sunday off to recharge his batteries before a difficult run in to the final. I gave Mark an honest if blunt 'no' to his proposition. I had not been playing on Sundays for several weeks, had no real desire to do so (further symptoms of my decline that season), and said it would be completely hypocritical to feign the enthusiasm required to captain the side on such a day.

In terms of enthusiasm, one cannot fault Mark himself in his devotion to the job as Hampshire captain. He loves it and all that goes with it, not least the kudos of success (who doesn't?). He has been accused of being somewhat haughty and Jardinesque in his approach, and would be the first to admit that it is no easy task keeping a county side entirely happy throughout one's reign as captain – I would have to admit entirely the same thing myself!

Indeed Mark has adjusted his style in dealing with his players in an attempt to improve any problems in his relations with them as often as has seemed necessary. He can rightly say that he has presided over one of the happier dressing rooms on the county circuit, though naturally much of that reflects on the characters of the players involved. Certainly this was one of the major attractions of playing for Hampshire that Mark had highlighted when he had originally sensed my desire to change clubs.

One of the thoughts behind my decision to leave Leicestershire had been to see if playing elsewhere might make a substantial difference to the process of getting out onto the field and enjoying the game. Bearing in mind that a lot of one's success is due to self-motivation, a mere geographical move in itself was never going to make that much of a difference to this part of the game. You can expect a different atmosphere in the dressing room, with a host of new faces and a different set of in-jokes, that will perhaps refresh the mind and its willingness to help you play near your best. You live in hope of an ideal dressing room where there are no niggles, character clashes or problems of form and ambition.

There were, of course, a number of old friends. People like Robin and Chris Smith I knew from England tours, and of course Paul Terry had also played under me for England. Malcolm Marshall was a long-time opponent both at Test and county level, a man I much respected and liked. Without going through the entire team, Hampshire were, overall, a sound and professional bunch, who got on with the business of playing cricket and enjoying it. They were not without success either, just checking the number of trophies that had been won in recent years.

Another factor was that Mark does not believe in the over-regimentation of a county side, and Hampshire players were given plenty of leeway to assume responsibility for their preperation, albeit governed by a basic set of rules and requirements, which is a system that allows a free and relaxed atmosphere to prevail. It was that atmosphere that allowed both the club and the players to show so much understanding and give me plenty of support when my batting at the start of that 1991 season bore so little resemblance to the sort of thing they had in mind when they had signed me on. Its safe to say that I was very happy with my move south, both with the cricket we were playing and the atmosphere in which it was played.

So it was against this background that the club had to decide upon a man to captain the side at Lord's. I did not necessarily expect it, but in fact the decision was made within an hour of the finish of the game at the Oval, and the job was mine. Someone in the media speculated that Hampshire had made me captain in order to guarantee my full attention on the day, and I later found out that there had been some jocular speculation in the press box at Chelmsford – where most of the cricket correspondents had been gathered to watch Essex closing in on the championship – as to the dialogue surrounding my appointment. Nicholas: 'How do you fancy leading the side on Saturday?' Gower: 'I'd love to. Who are we playing?' I suppose it comes with the laid-back reputation, but in truth, I was as keyed up as I had been for any Test match. A century would go a long way towards winning over one or two Hampshire detractors, and who knows? It might, just might, squeeze me a place on the winter tour. I was nervous, and well aware that there were only two possibilities in a game like this. Glory or disaster. However, I enjoyed this sort of stage and, I have to confess, needed it. The incentives were there, the adrenalin was pumping and the first tricky decision was over the toss. It was not one of those NatWest September wickets where you win the toss and win the game by sticking the opposition in. It was one of those pitches where the side batting first could have put the opposition out of the game.

As we had won all our matches en route to Lord's batting second we opted to chase again. We got one thing right in picking Jon Ayling, who had a more than testing game in the championship match at the Oval, but he not only bowled exceptionally well, but also hit us to victory when Robin Smith's unlucky run out put us under pressure right at the end. Tony Middleton, who played instead of Kippy, scored 78, and everything worked out right for us on the day. Not everything worked out right for me, in that Waqar got me again, but personal ambition had long since gone in the heat of battle. There were the usual dressing room scenes at the end, in that you are suddenly surrounded by all sorts of people you have never seen before in your life. There were friends and relatives of course, and even Micky Stewart popped in for a brief 'Well done'.

So where did I go from here? That final at Lord's, the wonderful setting and of course the successful outcome to the match summed up everything I had missed by not being involved in England's international summer at any stage. The tour party for the winter was certainly not going to include my name after the events, or rather the absence of events through my own county season, so fresh plans would have to be made. This kind of disappointment can be horribly pervasive and I spent much of my time after the season had ended brooding over matters and their repercussions, even ruing that missed opportunity in Australia to have passed G. Boycott's record.

Not everything was gloom and doom, however, and the first thing on the horizon was the fund-raising safari to Zimbabwe, Zambia, Botswana and South Africa that Thorunn and I were to host on behalf of the SAVE charity in Australia. As I said earlier, safari is one of my great passions in life, and being able to go to Africa and to enjoy the magic of the bush, as well as trying to do something to preserve part of that land's heritage (in particular the rhino, the emblem for our trip), meant that the problems of cricket and career receded a long way into the background. It was a fabulous safari accompanied by some very good people, and it obviously left me in an excellent mood, as, just towards the end of it, on Thorunn's birthday, I asked her to marry me and after thinking about it for the statutory twenty seconds, she accepted. Perhaps I was growing up after all!

As for what to do next, it took a phone call to Tony Greig in Sydney, some negotiations, and my next media job was organized. Channel 9's cricket coverage is much admired worldwide, so there was plenty to look forward to in Australia. There was the World Cup, and there was the added bonus of more journalistic work, this time writing for the *Daily Telegraph*. In the meantime, I had agreed to join an embryonic PR company, Head PR, which specializes in PR for legal firms. The wheel had turned full circle and I was back to the law again!

Twelve months on from the unhappy experience of the Australian tour and all had changed for England. The side grew in confidence following their success against the West Indies in the summer of 1991, and no observer could be anything other than impressed by their cricket and their collective will to win. There were one or two differences of approach, I am told, even to the extent that a little extra time off was allowed into the system. I know Ian Botham's style and personality will have been in marked contrast to the general ethic, but the good news seemed to be that England were finely tuning their game, balancing out the need for good, solid hard work against the need to keep the spirit fresh. There is absolutely no reason why Gooch and Stewart should not take credit for that, along with the players who supported them so well and contributed their all to the side's successes. I would begrudge them nothing in the way of praise and plaudits.

I enjoyed watching them on the occasions that Channel 9 were covering their games. But also I enjoyed the different atmosphere in the commentary box, even if I missed the adrenalin shots that go with playing. 'Time spent on reconnaissance is seldom wasted,' and as such those six weeks in Australia gave me the feeling that, given a little time and more experience, here was something I could turn my hand to in the future and apply those same principles of fun, style and excellence with which we started.

CHAPTER FIFTEEN

You must be ★★★★ing joking

*A*s the years of a cricket career roll by, I must admit that the attractions of pre-season training as a means toward pure enjoyment do somewhat diminish. At Leicestershire I had hardly built up a formidable reputation as one of the world's great trainers, but had survived the demands of all of our appointed slavedrivers through whatever natural fitness I could muster, if not with the greatest enthusiasm.

There was even a famous occasion at the start of one of our fitness campaigns, when as captain of the county I took pity on the players one very cold April morning and decreed that we might just drive to the Polytechnic gym, our designated place of torture, and perhaps leave that two and a half mile run down Leicester's incredibly scenic canal towpath until a more appealing day. I then popped into Mike Turner's office for a very quick meeting before slipping behind the wheel of the Quattro to join the rest of the players, only to realise that they had all opted to take the towpath route. I was cutting a relatively solitary figure when I arrived by car.

Such an approach was definitely not what was required at the beginning of the 1992 season if I was to start the summer in the right physical and mental shape. Even though I had done my stuff on the odd hotel treadmill or exercise bike while covering the World Cup for Channel Nine in Australia, there was still more than a token effort required both for my own benefit and that of my Hampshire colleagues.

At least I was happy to be back in harness actually looking forward to the season, remembering only too well the traps I had fallen into

233

just twelve months previously. I was keen to take the right steps to avoid any repetition of those mistakes. Yes, I had nets.

There was one minor early season drama, when the management decided after one very uninspiring early performance in a scratch match amongst the Hampshire playing staff, that it was time to have a stern word or two with their senior professional. Overall, though, I was very happy with my preparation and the build-up to the season, and it seemed to show in the early games.

I began to banish from my mind some of the fears that come from taking time off from the first-class game, such as the basic worry of whether you will actually remember how to play the game after six months enforced inactivity. However, after some time spent at the crease, my confidence with a bat in hand re-emerged.

The first good signs were spotted with a hundred in the Benson and Hedges Cup against Allan Lamb's Northampton side, which helped us clinch that rain-affected match and start us on the right track to winning the trophy. A few weeks later it was at Basingstoke that Yorkshire became the victims of my first first-class century since the Australian tour two winter's ago.

While all this was going on, I had to keep an interested eye on the thoughts and actions of the England selectors and Graham Gooch in particular. With the relative success of the England side on the winter tour, for me to entertain any serious thoughts of making a comeback I needed to maintain my own form at a high level and, unfortunately for them, one of the current incumbents had to suffer a run of bad luck or poor form, for a space to become available.

As to those in power, it was hardly encouraging when Graham himself went into print with the publication and serialisation of his new book on captaincy with some very forthright criticisms of one D.I. Gower that emanated in essence from the same tour of Australia. When the England captain is quoted as saying he feels more comfortable with you not in his side, it tends to suggest that reconvincing him of your talent and potential worth to the side is not going to be easy!

The fact that cricket is a team game is always useful in keeping personal ambitions under some sort of control. Whatever your own feelings might be there is always the team's welfare to keep in mind, even if when the international season starts there is a part of you thinking how good it would be to take the field with the likes of Lamb and Botham, showing the cricket world that the old dogs can still muster enough life to be of service to their country. I know that sounds a little like Kitchener and 'Your country needs you' but it never does any harm to add a touch of passion to your ambition. And you did not even know I had it in me!

Ironically the 'revelations' of Graham's book seemed to work far more in my favour than in his. The reaction of press and public alike tended more towards the feeling that those criticisms had been badly timed and generally misplaced, although of course their source lay somewhere in the distant past. This allowed me to keep my head high, because, although Graham can certainly be one to stick to a theory once he has been through the effort of hatching it, I felt there would always be enough residual respect that, if I could put together enough good performances, I would be able to convince him and his co-selectors to give me that break.

It was thus a case of mixed feelings when Pakistan clinched the Lord's Test after a highly charged final day's play. One's county colleagues tend to be slightly parochial but very supportive and optimistic at times such as this, and the gist of their comments seemed to be that one or two heads must be about to roll in the England camp, so good luck at Manchester. I am certainly not one to start counting unhatched chickens at a time like this and in any case Wimbledon and the tennis were due, so why not take advantage of the odd day off and pop up to south west London?

Some years previously, while on yet another tour of Australia, I had received a call from ex-Wimbledon referee Fred Hoyles, asking if there was any chance of tickets to the Melbourne Test, a request which I had been happy to satisfy. Ever since, Fred has kindly checked every year to see if I am free for an early day at Wimbledon. This I am normally very happy to take up, and if Fred fancies a day at cricket again, this is seldom a problem. In fact the only slightly unfair aspect of the whole deal is that, whereas Fred as a Wimbledon member is able to entertain us over lunch, I struggle to offer him the same courtesy in the middle of a NatWest quarter final!

On this particular visit to the All England Club, Thorunn and I also ran into John Feaver of the LTA, who out of sympathy or just plain good natured hospitality uttered the dangerous words, 'What are you doing on finals' day?' Now I was aware that the next England side was being picked in the interim, and that if the gods of cricket were about to smile on me there was a rest day at Manchester (actually as a direct result of the conflict in the sporting calendar). This could be an offer too good to miss! I was also aware of the likelihood that all would come to nought if the selectors stuck by their current side, and that it would be the dreaded Sunday League after all.

Therefore when the news turned out to be good, one of my first tasks was to book a couple of seats on the plane from Manchester to get down to London and the tennis, before phoning Feaver to confirm our availability, and then beginning some mental preparations for the return to the fold. Lest anyone at this stage should get the wrong impression as to whether the cricket or the tennis were more important, please believe me that all I am trying to demonstrate is a capacity not to let a good opportunity escape at the same time as being able to focus on the main event. And, furthermore, I did also take the precaution of checking with the management if my plans were acceptable to them. After all, these would be scheduled flights this time in something more suitable than a Tiger Moth.

Arriving at Manchester for the usual preamble to the Test, uppermost in my mind was the need to erase any hints of mistrust between Graham Gooch and myself that might be lingering on from early season extracts from his book. Bearing in mind the nature of England warm-ups nowadays, 'preamble' is probably the wrong word, and we had all been through the running, stretching and fielding practice before Graham had a chance of a quiet word. As we were both preparing for a turn in the nets, he was able to say, in effect, 'What is gone is gone. Let's get on with our jobs and good luck.'

This was all either of us required to get back on the right track together. Graham certainly did not want to make a long speech about it and I did not want to listen to one. Basically both of us knew the expectations that Graham has of the players he selects for his sides and of me in particular. We had already discussed all that in the restaurant in New Zealand, and as far as I was concerned the ball was now in my court (staying on the Wimbledon theme) to prove Graham right in his decision to pick me.

To continue another theme, that of military conflict, England expected, Graham Gooch expected, and the public seemed to be hoping, as was I, that things would go well. I suppose the only man slightly confused at this stage might have been Geoff Boycott, who would have to reconcile his patriotism against the threat to his proudly held scoring record. In actual fact he had a job to do describing the game for the BBC, and I had mine to try and help England towards the target of winning a Test match and squaring the series.

Peter Marron, the Old Trafford groundsman, had done a super job in producing a good true wicket for the game; not as quick and bouncy necessarily as some of the strips he has produced for county matches there, but nevertheless quicker and bouncier than anything the two sides had encountered so far in the series. Whoever won the toss was definitely going to bat and would be disappointed not to make a big score – a pity it was not going to be us. Graham had given me back the same position in the batting order that I last occupied in Australia. So whether we batted or fielded the chances were that I would have a little time to settle back into the atmosphere.

As it turned out, it also meant that I was not needed at the crease on the Saturday evening, when Javed Miandad's declaration, some murky light and typically hostile bowling from Wasim and Waqar all added up to a torrid session for the immediate top order. On the other hand, the fact that we had reached the rest day and I was still pondering my own potential fortunes meant I was not quite as relaxed as I might have been hopping onto the Heathrow shuttle on Sunday morning.

I tend to be fatalistic at times, another ploy to help take the pressure out of life in general, so it did not take me too long to become absorbed in what was one of the best Wimbledon finals for many a year, five sets of very high class tennis between Andre Agassi and Goran Ivanisevic that kept the attention of the entire Centre Court audience throughout the afternoon. Even Thorunn became so wrapped up in the match that thoughts of slipping out of the arena briefly to find a cooling ice cream completely evaporated until the contest was over.

Fortunately the ice cream had not, and I found the whole day highly inspirational. I left Wimbledon believing that if the two protagonists on that day could produce such glorious tennis for our entertainment, then the least I could do would be to try and offer similar fare to the crowd at Old Trafford; and when Monday morning also brought bright blue skies to replace the sombre conditions of Saturday evening, I really did think that this was going to be my day, as long as Graham and Robin Smith did not decide to hog the crease!

For once Robin did not. On the way to the wicket I have to admit to feeling as nervous as I ever have been in that situation, but also as pumped up as I had felt for some time. Probably an ideal combination when having to face the likes of Wasim, Waqar and the rest of the Pakistani bowling attack with England still having a stiff task to avoid the follow-on. And in the back of my mind there was the thought that if things went well, there was a little record that could be broken too.

I enjoyed the bouncer that greeted me from Aqib Javed, who had been a lot friendlier as a colleague at Hampshire, mainly because I like to get the first 'headhunter' out of the way early, but also because it proved to me that everything seemed to in good working order on the day. I had seen it and reacted in just the way an England batsman should, so if I was nervous at least it did not appear to be having a detrimental effect on my batting. It is amazing the confidence one can gain from the simple act of ducking under a bouncer!

What I enjoyed even more was the act of charity from Salim Malik in dropping me off the same bowler when I had reached 16 and decided to try and force one off the back foot, only to find that the ball had bounced a little more than expected. At least I picked the right man to nick it to, as Salim was having one of those spells at slip that meant he might as well have stood there blindfold with his hands coated in Teflon for all the likelihood there was of him catching it. Let me assure you he was trying and even though he was standing well back the ball did seem to reach him very quickly. Just prior to that incident I had been chatting to him at mid-on and he had literally said that if I was going to nick the ball I could do worse than do so in his direction as he was not backing himself to catch much that day at slip!

I tell the story in no way attempting to indict Salim for being unprofessional or uncommitted to his fielding, for we all have days like that at any level of cricket when we just have the feeling that it is not going to be our day. In any case, he has proven many a time by his batting what a talented player he really is. The fact is that in amongst the burning competition of international cricket, there are those of us who can still find time for a little wry, possibly self-deprecating humour, without detracting from our performance one bit. While I am on the subject, I should say that despite all the controversy that was to follow over the next few weeks, I found it very easy to get on with most of the touring Pakistanis, even if not all my colleagues shared that ability. Part of the enjoyment of the game of cricket as a whole is the spirit in which the game can be played at any level.

The missed chance was all I needed to convince me that the gods were smiling, and as the runs flowed quickly it was not long before I was facing Aqib again, knowing that one decent shot would take me past Geoff Boycott's landmark. That moment will linger in my mind for ever, and the amount of space I have devoted to it proves that it was certainly not just some casual little milestone I was passing. After all it had taken me fifteen years to get there, so to pay it scant attention hardly seems fair, especially as at the time, satisfying though it all was, there was still the job of saving the follow-on. In fact it also occurred to me that it would be the perfect return to celebrate by scoring a hundred as well, something that any batsman sets his sights on at the start of an innings.

One more thought did very briefly cross my mind, wondering what G. Boycott might be forcing himself to say on the television. Apparently I need not have worried as he was allegedly nowhere near a microphone at the relevant moment.

I did not get that hundred. My critics would not have been surprised to see me edging what was actually quite a quick delivery from Wasim Akram to the keeper soon after lunch. Even my agent Jon Holmes made some typically dry comment about lunch coming at the wrong time again, but at least he had the consolation that one of his charges had passed a significant milestone, after the disappointment of seeing Gary Lineker unable to get past Bobby Charlton's tally of goals for England in the European Championships. Gary, of course, will not admit to losing too much sleep over that record in a wonderful career, and indeed he is one who is very good at moving on to the next chapter without the need to worry about what might have been. Still, he would have preferred to have at least equalled the record, however gracious he was in conceding that Charlton probably deserved the honour more.

If the Old Trafford Test will linger in my mind for the poignancy of the broken record, the following Test at Headingley turned out to be the better game of cricket and not just because England managed to win it. As ever the sides lined up at Headingley expecting a result, which is normally the one predictable element of the Headingley Test. As a venue Leeds has a knack of producing fascinating cricket, with the vagaries of the pitch, the weather, and the players' own performances all conspiring to make predictions there that much harder.

Once again the bowlers seemed to hold the balance of power, except when the Essex men, Malik for Pakistan and Gooch for England, were at the crease. Graham seems to appreciate the challenge that Headingley represents to batsmen, and was essentially instrumental in the winning of this contest, in the same way as, one year previously, he had been against the West Indies. The game itself went right down to the wire, with the two Ws, Akram and Younis, heavily involved and proving that, even on a wicket of no real pace and bounce, good fast bowlers can prosper by keeping the ball up to the bat. Those fast swinging yorkers had been the subject of many a team talk when discussing the problems of playing Pakistan, and it did not seem that they were suddenly going to forget how to bowl them now!

If the unplayability of those deliveries was somehow predictable, so was the fact that an umpiring decision might come under the microscope at some stage. At Old Trafford the Pakistanis had also been unplayable as far as poor Roy Palmer had been concerned, and during that last torrid session at Headingley, Graham Gooch was proven lucky to have been given in after an appeal for a run-out. Soon afterwards I survived another vociferous appeal, with the Pakistanis convinced that I had nicked a ball from Mushtaq Ahmed to the wicketkeeper. I knew full well that I had not nicked it, but it took me about ten minutes to convince anyone else. In fact, it was only when the next wicket fell that I had a gentle word with Moin Khan to put his mind at rest, not that it made any real difference.

However, to be able to see the game through to the end and oversee our victory gave me more satisfaction than any of my performances for some time. Apart from anything else, there is that little extra satisfaction from being able to suggest that experience does count for something, and that even the over-35s can contribute, though of course anyone who had watched Graham's first innings' hundred already knew that.

To all intents and purposes that was the end of my contribution to the summer's entertainment. The Pakistanis deservedly wrapped up the series at the Oval – no prizes for guessing who did most of the damage there – and England gained token revenge by cleaning up the one-day series. In the process an unholy and still to be resolved row was sparked off over suspicions that the visitors might have been treating the ball, in particular the one used at the Texaco Trophy match at Lord's, in such a fashion as to be gaining unfair advantage, in short, ball tampering.

It was my great mate, Allan Lamb, who blew the whistle, drawing the umpires' attention to the ball in question shortly before lunch. Obviously something was indeed amiss, because the ball had been changed during the interval, and the Pakistanis given something which Waqar then used to further devastating effect! The main problem was that a blanket of secrecy descended on the whole affair, and it seemed impossible to get an official explanation of events at Lord's on the fateful day, to the extent that the Pakistanis had left the country some time later with rumour and suspicion still rife.

Lamby then landed himself in hot water by revealing all to one of the tabloids, for which he was fined a hefty amount by the TCCB. He was then sued by by the former Pakistani bowler Sarfraz Nawaz for revealing that Sarfraz had tampered with the ball during his time at Northants, a case which ended when Sarfraz decided halfway through the hearing to drop the case. That was not the first time in matches involving England that Pakistan had been suspected of doing something to the ball. In the 1982 Test at Lord's, when Mudassar Nazar began swinging it all over the place, we had the ball sent away for forensic analysis. The report came back negative, although at that time in the evolution of ball tampering we were looking for substances applied to make the ball shine rather than, as subsequently became more prevalent, deliberately roughing up the

241

ball to obtain reverse swing. As far as reverse swing was concerned, it was well known within the game that Imran Khan had taught his team-mates at Sussex one or two tricks of the trade. However, it is one thing to do something to the ball, and quite another to have the skill to exploit it, and in that Pakistani series of 1992, there is no doubt that Wasim and Waqar would have bowled us out in any event. In the end, they were better bowlers than anything we had got, and if they did do things to the ball, it probably meant only that we got bowled out slightly quicker than we would have been anyway. I was never aware during my time as England captain of any of our bowlers getting involved in ball tampering, and if I had been, I would have issued only one instruction. 'I'd prefer it if you didn't do it, but if you do, don't get caught.' We had some trouble with Aqib Javed at Hampshire when he was caught one day and politely asked by the umpire to desist. Once back in the dressing room we told him that this was not the way we wanted to play the game, and while whatever he did for Pakistan was basically his and their business, he had to play the game properly when playing for us. We eventually lost all respect for Aqib at Hampshire, even before he had that public spat with umpire Roy Palmer at Old Trafford that summer. It happened when he played against Hampshire in the tourist match at Southampton, which was in fact the game immediately preceding the Old Trafford Test, and was sparked off by Aqib having an appeal for a catch turned down against Mark Nicholas. I was batting at the other end, and Aqib and the rest of the Pakistani team gave him quite one of the most spiteful, dreadful and abusive verbal batterings that I have ever had the misfortune to witness. Here was Aqib, who the previous summer had been a quiet likeable bloke, turning into a rabies case.

I always found with the Pakistanis that, on an individual basis, they were very nice people. And yet as a pack, they can be a complete shambles. It is a shame that for a very talented bunch of cricketers such problems continue to occur. Perhaps the most positive side of Imran's captaincy was that he did manage to unite and control them better than anyone in the role before or since. Latterly, the allegations against them turned from ball tampering into attempted bribery and corruption of opposing players, and their captain, Salim Malik, was not re-employed after being accused of offering cash to some of the Australians to lose a Test match. I don't know whether this had any substance or not, but I've never personally heard of bribes in Test cricket. Certainly no one has ever tried to bribe *me* to throw my wicket away – although it might have looked that way at times! However, no-one could have called my discipline or determination not to give my wicket away into question during the Headingley Test match against Pakistan in 1992, in which I battled for two hours to make 31 not out in the second innings to help England to square the series at 1–1. Following a more typical innings of 73 in the drawn game on my Test recall at Old Trafford, I was looking forward with guarded optimism to the announcement of England's party to tour India in the winter. However, following the not surprising decision to lift the ban on the South African rebel tourists, the field of possible aspirants had already increased, and the competition for places meant there were fewer of us in a position to take anything for granted. Especially as the projected tour itinerary, with just the three Tests and six one-day internationals, also gave rise to a number of possible theories as how best to construct the 16 man squad.

Ironically, the hardback edition of this book somehow made it to the bookstores ahead of the originally scheduled publication date, which also prompted our contracted tabloid newspaper to bring forward the serialisation of extracts from the book to the weekend immediately prior to the selectors' all important meeting. Having got this far in the book you will be in a position to judge whether or not some of the comments made herein might have affected the selectors' judgement. I actually do not think it made an awful lot of difference, as it seems that plans were already developing before those comments were published. I can, however, only guess at much of this, due to the lack of direct evidence.

As much as my recall in the summer brought me great satisfaction, the news that I was just as quickly redundant as an England cricketer left me seething with anger, not an emotion with which I am traditionally associated.

The selectors met and came to their decisions on the Friday, the night when I briefly saw Dexter and Stewart at the Cricket Writers' Dinner at the banquetting rooms of the Lord's Tavern. Already rumours were rife, and by Sunday one of the papers had run the story that I would not be touring India. Coincidentally and quite awkwardly I ran into Peter Hayter, who had written the story, at a rain-lashed and soon to be abandoned benefit match for Bobby Parks. Peter had to explain that he could not reveal his sources in the time-honoured tradition, but that they were unimpeachable!

At this stage, fully aware of the long standing traditional courtesy that the captain or manager will phone you in the event of impending bad news, I was banking on the fact that the lines had been nicely quiet to keep my hopes of employment on the subcontinent high. However, forty minutes before the scheduled announcement of the teams the phone rang and it was indeed the England captain, apparently on the car phone en route to the county ground at Derby. I do not suppose for one minute he had been looking forward to making the call, but I was in no mood to be fobbed off with vague excuses about age and the apparent surplus of batsmen over the age of 35. There were echoes of our conversation back in Wellington at the end of that Australasian tour of 1990-91, so that once again I found myself asking whether or not runs for England in Test matches actually counted for anything. I was livid and not about to let Graham off the hook, when the connection was broken, an aspect of mobile phones that so often proves dangerously frustrating. If only to prove that the disconnection was the phone's fault and not premeditated, Graham did phone back, but by the time we had said goodbye properly, I was still not a happy soul.

What actually hurt was that, despite my efforts to conform to the system and my successful return to the fold of international cricket, there were still suspicions in the minds of Graham and his fellow selectors as to the way I might conduct myself on tour and perhaps undermine the spirit thereof. I daresay that I will have the chance to discuss all this more amicably before the start of the next season, when, just for a change, it seems I will be starting off again in April with the task of having to prove to those that matter that they can pick me again. Pity – I would like to have done that in India.

It was not the ideal way to finish the season, and indeed Mark Nicholas spotted the fact that I might not be one hundred percent focused on Hampshire's last fixture of the season, and suggested that for me to miss that match might not be a complete disaster.

This left me free to concentrate on other matters, such as the build-up to a very significant date, September 18th, when I had a most important appointment at Winchester Cathedral, with our local rector, 130 invited guests, and the lady who was to become my wife. Only one thing remained before all that, which was to survive that traditional pagan rite, the stag night. Just to give you a clue as to the extent of the problem, need I say more than to reveal that the man in charge was one Ian Terrence Botham?

It was suggested at the time that this was akin to putting Dracula in charge of a bloodbank, and that I would do well to book a hospital bed to aid recovery in time to stagger up the aisle. But the man is one of my best mates in the game, so he wouldn't ruin the big day now, would he?

Officially, my best man was to be Christopher Cowdrey, and though we had toyed with simple ideas like a quiet night in London, Ian had been determined to get us down to Alderney, away from the possible attentions of any unwanted spectators, so that the chosen few could celebrate my demise from the ranks of bachelorhood in wholehearted fashion.

Rather than risk being fogged in on the island in the event of bad weather, Ian arranged for three private pilots to fly us down to Alderney, obviating the need to worry about scheduled flights and leaving us free to pick and choose our times of departure accordingly. We were met at Alderney International by our event coordinator and 'Mr Fixit', 'Mad Chris' Jones, but also by a reasonably large media contingent, who had discovered the plot and needed to take some pictures to justify their presence. At this stage I was quite relaxed about the situation, and we gave them a suitably posed photo opportunity. It was also an early excuse for the boys to pour some champagne over my head in the name of celebration. We then left Ian to relax while some of us attacked the golf course and steeled ourselves for the evening's festivities.

'Mad Chris' did us proud, as did everyone else who helped us along the way to physical ruin over the next twelve or so hours. We started at the cricket club, where we had some of the best oysters and prawns you will ever eat, with a little proper fizz to ease their passage down the throat. Then we transferred to the *First and Last* for dinner, with the doors firmly locked behind us by our hostess, Rita, so that we could be guaranteed the necessary privacy that this sort of event requires.

Not surprisingly, we left the venue some hours later in a pretty poor state, which is no reflection on the quality of the hospitality, but merely of the fact that 'Both' lost patience relatively early in the evening and decided that as well as eating my dinner, I should also wear substantial amounts of it. It is amazing, on reflection, how much summer pudding will lodge in one's ears.

Give the boys from the press their due, they were still on duty by the time we left, and were on hand to take a couple of very sharp snaps as the party piled out of the restaurant and into the waiting minibus. By this stage I had acquired a dark wig and a pair of sunglasses from my man from Dow's, Tim Stanley-Clarke, but as a disguise it left much to be desired. We lurched our way back to Ian's cottage to continue the party as best we could, but at this stage my stamina began to fade rapidly. Cowdrey, who had been pretending to look after me every now and again throughout the evening, now rather lost sight of his protective duties – and probably the ability to focus on anything else either. We both collapsed into the nearest available beds, but not before I had wandered outside to confront the lighthouse that is Ian's second-closest neighbour, and utter the only words I could think of at this demanding stage of the evening: 'Turn that bloody light out!' Hardly inspiring and completely ineffectual, I know, but it was the best I could do.

It would have been naive to think that we would get away with an early night, and we didn't, at least not as long as Both, Lamby and whoever else was still awake were popping in and out of the bedroom making sure we weren't missing anything. Come the morning, Ian appeared to be as strong as ever, while I continued to go downhill. At least our pilots had managed to pull themselves together, and the planes all left in due course and in complete control, to get us all back to the mainland in time to reassure the bride to-be that we would be joining her on the day.

While Thorunn went off to spend the night at Lainston House, the venue for the following day's reception, Chris, his wife Christel and I settled down for the evening over a Chinese takeaway, wrote most of our speeches, and collapsed.

The day itself was brilliant. Apart from the invited guests, there was a sizeable throng outside the Cathedral to add their support, and we had a ball. It was an international cast, with friends of mine from Australia, relatives of Thorunn's from Iceland, and as many friends and colleagues as I could muster from the cricketing world, with the odd exception! Nothing was going to intrude from that part of my life and spoil the day, and if there were any nerves they disappeared the moment I caught sight of the bride as she emerged through the screen at the bottom end of the Quire, looking absolutely resplendent and very beautiful. The altar got slightly more crowded than usual with Chris and I opposed by Thorunn, her uncle Pat, who gave her away, and her 'best lady', Carrie Zetter, so we all had to concentrate when it came to the exchange of rings just to remember who had which ring! I think we ended up with the right ones.

The weather held for us – a good omen I like to think – allowing the reception to take place largely al fresco, until the speeches, all naturally classics in their own right. Cowdrey began with the traditional run through the telegrams and faxes in alphabetical order: 'A, B, C, D, E, F, sorry, no Gs...' I told you we would not let cricketing matters affect the day.

I had thought that some of the great days of my career would take some beating, but whereas I might have passed a few landmarks on the cricket field over the years, none could rank as highly as this. Ian Botham had been saying how he had been waiting for this day for years – well, it was very much worth the wait.

The next day we flew to Kenya for the honeymoon: two weeks in the Aberdares, Mount Kenya Safari Club, and down to the Mara Safari Club, before finishing at the Norfolk Hotel. I have always loved the African bush, and had taken Thorunn out to that part of the world for the first time only the previous year, which was of course when I had originally proposed, so there was something very apposite about the choice of venue. We loved every moment of it.

Now at least the private side of my life was settled. That my future as a cricketer looked slightly more uncertain did not seem to matter. I had happily signed a fresh two-year contract with Hampshire, mutually and easily agreed despite the odd strange rumour that I had been demanding a five-year deal. After all the ups and downs of the last few seasons it was perfectly obvious that neither I nor the county were going to commit ourselves to anything more than this, which left me with another winter to fill in the meantime.

As it happened Channel Nine in Australia were happy enough to take me on again for the summer Down Under, and Sky appeared to need some assistance in India as well, so prospects for a busy few months were good; and there was always the next season to aim for, with the chance that I might be young enough again by then to play some decent cricket.

This was no time to dwell on life's misfortunes, but for optimism. Mr and Mrs Gower had much to look forward to.

CHAPTER SIXTEEN

Over and out

*A*h well, so much for optimism. Less than 12 months later, at the ripe old age of 36, it was all over. Part of me was sad, because I felt that I still had some decent cricket left in me, and part of me was relieved, because I could now wake up in the morning with a head uncluttered by thoughts about whether there was still any real point to what I was doing. I had missed out on a Test recall the following summer, and after being omitted for the 'new broom youth policy' tour to the West Indies, I suspected that there was more chance of colliding with a low-flying pig on my next Tiger Moth flight than winning back my Test match place. With that essential incentive now apparently having totally disappeared, it was time to call it a day and swap the helmet for the full-time journalist's hat. As one critic remarked, 'Gower can now spend his time raising a journalistic eyebrow whenever Gooch misses with an airy fairy waft outside the off stump.' Once I had made the decision, there was no question of brooding – simply to look forward to new challenges in a career for which I had already served a five-year apprenticeship. It could never replace the thrill of actually playing, but it was the next best thing.

A year earlier, however, my main ambition still revolved more around playing the game than reporting on it – as, apparently, was the case for a good many of my supporters. Even as I began packing my suitcase for a winter commentating for Channel Nine in Australia, and for Sky TV in India, a disaffected group of MCC members launched a protest campaign, calling for the England selectors to resign, and for me to be included in a re-vamped Indian tour party. Realistically, all they could hope to do was to blow Ted

Dexter and Co a loud public raspberry, and cause them maximum embarrassment, but it was still a source of considerable wonder to me that I could arouse this kind of feeling. Dennis Oliver, the dissident leader, was apparently inundated with letters of support, ranging from one lady refusing to do the teas for her village team any more, to people cancelling their holiday plans to watch the Test matches in India. Flattered though I was by all the support, it was hardly likely that Ted was suddenly going to turn around and say: 'Er, sorry, we've decided to pick Gower after all', and I decided that it was best if I kept a respectful distance from it all. Besides which, I was not the only issue in the MCC revolt, as Jack Russell's omission in favour of a bits and pieces wicketkeeper in Richard Blakey was also on their indictment sheet. What still bothered me most was the suspicion that there were other reasons than the selectors deciding to form their own branch of Age Concern, and the quote from them that they were 'worried about Gooch, Gatting and Gower all retiring at the same time.' Did the selectors have some ghastly apparition of the three of us shuffling down the aisle towards Fletcher's seat as the plane landed at Delhi and saying:'Sorry Fletch, but we've been having a chat during the flight and we think it's about time we called it a day'? The more I thought about it, the more I believed that a schoolboy attempting to explain not handing in his homework because it had been eaten by a Martian would be more plausible, but as I flew into Australia for the series against the West Indies, I forgot all about it. My only goal now was to do a good job for my winter employers, and to then score so many runs for Hampshire the following summer that not even England's selectors would be able to find a credible enough excuse to leave me out again.

As a venue for getting away from it all, Australia was highly therapeutic, and the work was as enjoyable as I had always found it. Australia's Channel Nine coverage used to come in for a good deal of mickey taking, what with Tony Greig's 'On your bike, Charlie!' when a batsman got out, the blubbling cartoon duck when someone was out for nought, and Bill Lawry bursting into hysterical hyperbole when someone brought off a diving slip catch. However, they are now, quite rightly, regarded as trailblazers in innovative coverage, and are so professional that to work for them is to automically improve your own disciplines. They do like their commentators to be boisterous and confrontational, but they also want the contrast offered by quieter characters such as myself. The BBC is generally less frenetic, and is more my sort of pace, but there is nothing like Channel Nine and Sky for getting the adrenalin pumping. They have also set the standards for the vastly improved camerawork we get today, and it could even be argued that the dirt in the pocket controversy that nearly ended Mike Atherton's captaincy in 1994 would not have happened several years earlier. Before Channel Nine came along, the BBC's coverage involved little more than focussing on batsman and bowler, and rarely if ever featured the kind of close-up shot of fielders that caught Atherton apparently doing something peculiar to the ball.

I saw a new cricketing superstar in the making when Brian Lara made 277 in Sydney, but it was an innings from another left hander which perked up this one into thinking that the end of the road might yet be a good few years away. Allan Border made a typically pugnatious century to help the Australians win the Test in Melbourne, proof that there was still some life in one old dog. He had been under pressure from various critics, to the effect that he had gone on too long, wasn't consistent any more, kept giving his wicket away, etc, etc. The basic message was 'retire, you silly old sod.' But watching him make that hundred at the MCG gave me just the encouragement I needed for the following summer, and I felt so sorry for him when Australia lost by one run in Adelaide when victory would have given them the series. I know he had not exactly been Mr Nice Guy when I was losing the home Ashes series, and the captaincy, in 1989, but that's how he was with everyone on the field (even his own players) and we had been good friends for many years. I also arranged for a Jeraboam of vintage Bollinger to be delivered to him when he broke the Test match run scoring record (which he achieved later that winter in New Zealand) before I flew off to Calcutta for the second leg of my working winter, as part of Sky's television team in India.

It was a somewhat hectic trip, spending half a night on a bench at Singapore Airport, discovering the usual bag missing at Calcutta Airport, before having to try to look as fresh as possible for the Test match the day after flying in. India was its customary chaotic self, and I had an early reminder of how cricketers are invested with a god-like status over there when waiting for a train from Calcutta to Jamshedphur in the company of fellow Sky commentators Geoff Boycott and Sunny Gavaskar. We were suddenly surrounded by about 5000 people, and the only escape was into the station master's hut, where we exchanged 5000 swarming fans for 5000 swarming mosquitoes. Whether the hut was more inviting than the platform was a close contest, which is more than could be said for the Test series. To describe England as hopeless would probably be undeserved flattery, and not even when I was at the sharp end of a couple of West Indian blackwashes have I witnessed an England side so thoroughly wiped out. If the selectors had received unfavourable reviews before the tour started, by this time they were the butt of every saloon bar joke in England, and it was perhaps not surprising that most people I met expected me to be feeling rather smug about it all. In practice, though, it does not really work that way. While England were batting against Kumble and the Indian spinners as though they'd had a longish session on some of the bootleg bathtub gin peddled around India's back alleys, one or two of my co-commentators not surprisingly found it hard to resist comments along the lines of 'maybe the top order would have benefitted from an experienced left-hander. What do you think, David?' I would offer back something equally tongue in cheek, and I was also aware that a series of batting disasters could hardly hurt my prospects of getting back into the side the following summer. However, when you know the players, you can't help but feel sorry for them, and my commentary voice would have had a sad inflection rather than a gleeful one. My duties did not require me to be constantly thrusting microphones under Gooch's moustache, which was probably just as well, and if there was one bloke there I felt less than sorry for, then it was the captain. It was a joyless tour, largely because Gooch was as miserable as sin all the way through it. He is not a great disguiser of moods, and never was this one more apparent. He was persuaded to tour against his better judgement, and his troops appeared to be dragged down with him. Also, my sympathies were absent for more personal reasons. Just about the last conversation we had before the squad was selected was along the lines of him saying to me 'see you on the plane', but having then decided to lop my head off, he had manifestly failed to explain his reasons for it. At least not in any coherent form. Basically, I was mostly concentrating on my job, and not allowing personal feelings to intrude. In all honesty, though, when it came to Gooch my feelings were more along the lines of 'well, there is a God after all.'

India was far more memorable for me for another reason in that Thorunn, who was there with me for the first two weeks, suddenly stopped taking her malaria tablets. 'Think about it', she said when I expressed my concern. And then the penny dropped. She was pregnant. Armed, therefore, with a new sense of responsibility, I decided for the flight home to take care of the seating arrangements for my co-commentators, whose subsequent experience means that this is a task they will only entrust me with again if they are bound and gagged. Boycott, as always, was travelling first class, while myself, Charles Colvile and Henry Blofeld were 'slumming it' in club class. Through my contact at Heathrow, I was issued with an upgrade to join Geoffrey, while the check-in clerk gave me unseated boarding passes for Charles and Henry while he made the necessary arrangements to secure them similar VIP treatment. Sadly, the clerk then forgot all about this, Henry and Charles disappeared off the passenger list altogether, and were subsequently told that they were not on the flight. In the end they were lucky when the airline bumped a couple of unfortunates off the flight to squeeze them into economy class, and whether or not they appreciated me sending them back a few glasses of complimentary champagne I don't really know. They are still speaking to me, anyway.

By the start of the first Test match against Australia at Old Trafford, I had not made enough runs to break into a top six reading Gooch, Atherton, Gatting, Hick, Smith and Stewart, but on the first day of the series, I scored what appeared to be a timely 150 at Trent Bridge. However, on the last day of that county match, I damaged a rib diving for a slip catch off Shaun Udal, and although it did not seem too serious at first, it put me out of action for almost a month. So, even though England made wholesale changes after defeat in the opening two Tests (Hick and Gatting gone, Lathwell and Hussain in, and Gooch down the order) I had been sitting around with no chance to impress. Finally, it was possibly one of those strange quirks of fate which finally decreed that I had played my last Test match. England had lost four of the first five Tests, Gooch and Dexter had both resigned, and I had just scored a century against Lancashire, in front of the new England captain Michael Atherton. On the morning of the final Test at The Oval, Graham Thorpe broke his thumb in the practice nets, and rumour had it that England's first thought was to send for another left hander, and that their first choice was me. Sadly, Hampshire's match that day was in Swansea, and they needed someone at The Oval faster than I could have got there. Middlesex, on the other hand, had a game just across the Thames, and so England sent for Mark Ramprakash instead. Had Hampshire been playing Middlesex at Lord's that day, instead of Northants, who knows? I might have been sent for. However, I was still hopeful of selection for the West Indies that winter, not to mention flabbergasted at the identity of the man pushing hardest for me to go on tour. Gooch, having once again declined to make himself available for a winter tour, burst into print saying that, in his absence, I would be his choice of senior pro to the West Indies. Talk about adding insult to injury.

It struck me as a touch ironic that Gooch should suddenly become a fan again the moment he lost his vote on selection, and, as it turned out, Atherton wasn't listening to him anyway. The squad was announced amidst much futuristic talk of new brooms, youth brigades, five-year plans, and a new way forward, and I think it was at that point that I finally realized it was all over. Even so, I made one final attempt to stall the decision by inviting Hampshire to allow me to report back late for the following summer, given that my winter contract with Sky would depend on being available to commentate on the final two Tests of the winter in Barbados and Antigua. Quite rightly, Hampshire decided this was a bit rich, and I got the answer I expected. The other factor was the *Sunday Express*, who had offered me a two year contract to become their cricket correspondent. Also, the BBC were also keen for me to work for them the following summer. All of a sudden, with an England place looking further away than at any time in my career, the decision became clear. I'd also learned enough about the newspaper business to know that the occasional exclusive keeps your employers happy, and here was one that I didn't have to work especially hard to get. Ergo 'GOWER QUITS' by David Gower duly hit the pages of the *Sunday Express*. I told my readers that the hardest decision for all athletes is knowing when to call it a day before someone else takes the decision for you. There was, inevitably, the lingering feeling of unfinished business, but at least I had gone out on a reasonably upbeat note by scoring three centuries for Hampshire towards the end of the season. My last game for Hampshire turned out to be a benefit match for Malcolm Marshall, and I made a few runs in that too. Someone suspected it might be my last exit, and took a photograph of me leaving the field, which the lads later signed and presented to me. All in all, the final decision was a positive one rather than a negative. I certainly wasn't about to walk dolefully into the sunset whistling 'My Way', regrets I've had a few, and all that stuff, because new challenges were on the horizon. Not least fatherhood.

The baby was due in October, and I'd cleared away any committments for a week either side of the scheduled date. However, a couple of weeks beforehand I'd returned from a lunch in London, and when I got back to Winchester Station I made a routine call home on the mobile. We were due to go to Windsor that night to see a play involving my old chum Robin Askwith, but when Thorunn answered the phone it soon became clear we weren't going to travel much further than Southampton Hospital's maternity ward. 'I think', she said 'my waters have broken.' Well *I* certainly wasn't qualified to make a judgement, but it was a fairly jittery 20 minute ride home in the car as all I could see in front of me were visions of saucepans of hot water, towels, and a stiff brandy. Anyway, by the time I got there the hospital had advised that Windsor Theatre perhaps wasn't a great plan under the circumstances, and Thorunn was admitted at six o'clock. At midnight, we are still 0 not out as it were, and I was packed off home to await further developments. Still nothing happened until around eight o'clock the following evening, and it was not until three minutes to nine the next morning that little Alexandra arrived. At that stage we had no name, so we temporarily settled on Sydney, which is where she was conceived. Had the calculations traced the conception back to Milton Keynes or Basingstoke we might have thought differently, but it wasn't too long before Syd became a slightly more feminine Alexandra Sylvia. Alexandra because we both liked the name, Sylvia after my mother. The next two weeks were entirely given over to her, and I did all the proud father stuff, in the course of which I surprised myself by only dropping her once. Got a bit casual again, probably. However, I am now in a position to sympathize with all those parents who have had a child suffering from colic, as we had two months of virtually non-stop crying and not much sleep. By the time England (and, in my new capacity as full-time journalist, myself) left for the Caribbean, I was more than a bit bleary-eyed, although needless to say no one thought I looked any different.

The tour itself was hard work, not least because the time difference made newspaper deadlines pretty hairy, although potentially even more hairy was the aquisition of a new 'roving' camera which allowed you to do interviews all around the ground. It produced some quite amusing incidents, one of which involved Charles Colvile being told to clamber up a tree overlooking the ground in Guyana and interview a bloke who was watching the game from one of the branches. Charles handed back to me in the commentary box by saying: 'This is the most exciting thing I've ever done in my life' to which I replied: 'Well viewers, you can tell how riveting life in the Colvile household must be.' As is usually the way of things when you indulge in a bit of leg pulling at someone else's expense, retribution was at hand. Later during the match, I was sent across the ground with the roving cameraman to interview Chris Lewis's sister and aunt who were sitting in the main stand in front of the old pavilion. 'Should be a piece of cake, Lubo' I was told. 'The cameraman has already been over there chatting to them, and they're funny, talkative, brilliant.' Anyhow, off we go on a live broadcast and … silence. Nothing. It was a nightmare. Lots of questions and no answers. It was only saved when Lewis, who was batting at the time, hooked a six onto the stand we were sitting in, which was the only time during the entire interview that either of them showed any animation whatsoever. Therefore, it was with some relief that I said: 'Well thanks ladies, and now back to Charles Colvile in the commentary position.' 'And our grateful thanks' Colvile chirruped 'to Jeremy Paxman, for that entertaining and incisive interview.'

The commentator noted for making Paxman seem shy and retiring by comparison was Geoffrey Boycott. Geoffrey knows what he's on about, and is rarely too modest to let everyone else have the benefit of his wisdom too. Geoff, more than the rest of us I think, relies on comparisons between himself and the person he is passing judgement upon, whereas Richie Benaud is brilliant at the even handed and objective comment. I doubt whether the words 'in my day' have ever left his lips. Boycs, on the other hand, has mellowed a lot since his playing days, when he was basically a troubled soul whose main goal in life was to promote himself and his achievements, and when most of his sentences, if not all, began with 'I'. He can still be a bit dogmatic, such as during England's last series against the West Indies when he kept banging on about the need for batsmen to 'get forward', 'get forward'. I felt it would have been helpful to the viewer to explain that not every batsman prodded routinely forward to West Indian fast bowlers by way of deeply ingrained natural instinct, possibly not even Geoffrey himself in his playing days. The bottom line with Geoffrey is that he is a bloody good man to talk cricket with, provided you can get him into an objective frame of mind.

The same is true of the man England appointed chairman of selectors during the 1994 West Indies tour, and, who became upon the sacking of team manager Keith Fletcher after the following tour to Australia, a kind of one man guru taking on both roles. Yorkshire cricket appears to spawn very knowledgable characters who are fiercely self-opinionated. Trueman, Close, Boycott and Illingworth are all out of the same mould, and it always struck me as extraordinary that any two of these four could ever get together and agree on whether or not it was a nice morning, let alone anything important. I remember Close once saying of Illingworth: 'The trouble with Illy is he always wants his own way.' I also remember Illingworth saying of Close: 'The trouble with Closey is he always wants his own way.'

It is also remarkable how this type of character seems to attract devoted acolytes. Ian Botham for example, possibly through his upbringing with Somerset, can't see anything past Closey, and has no time at all for Raymond. However, whether or not people believe Illy is the right man for the job, the great thing is that English cricket has always needed one man to take control. That man couldn't be Boycott, as he is basically too self centred a character, and although Illy has come in for a fair amount of criticism, some of it well deserved, he has a lot more plusses than any other candidate. Some of the criticism he's brought upon himself through the fact that, show

Illy a notebook or a microphone, and away he goes. For someone who should understand the media very well, Raymond is not very well disciplined in that area, and although, as a full-time journalist nowadays, it certainly makes my life a lot easier when the quotes are flowing, his outpourings are not always appreciated by the players. They certainly got upset in Australia when he was spouting off back in London, but I think what the players have got to realize is that the chairman of selectors/manager has got to be prepared to tell it as it is. There is no point in massaging players' egos for the sake of it, pat them on the back and say 'well, it's going awfully well' when you're 3–0 down in a Test series. You've got to get the players to understand what's going wrong, and what's required to put it right. In terms of talent, English cricket is not far off the mark, and a five per cent improvement would make a heck of a difference. So when Illy sounds off, players should not necessarily think he's trying to score points, or apportion blame elsewhere, but saying things that need saying. And if England is to regain its former position in world cricket, the response has to be more positive than simply whingeing about what the chairman might be saying. Now that Raymond has a place in the dressing room, Fletcher's old place as it happens, there should certainly be a more harmonious relationship.

As for Fletch, he has always been a very worthy and likeable man, but basically he did not have the kind of character required to drag England out of the mire. I think in the end he'd lost confidence in his ability to do the job, and that would have filtered through to the players. For instance, before the fourth Test in Adelaide, Fletch's team talk was along the lines of 'Well, you never know. We might even win it', which was not quite the positive up and at 'em attitude the boys were looking for. In the end, of course, England found just the spirit they needed to win the match on a memorable final day, and it was wonderful to watch. We've got to find that spirit more often, and also from a more constructive base. You can't talk yourself into the right mood and attitude unless there is some genuine substance underneath, and that's what English cricket has to find.

Fletch, in the end, got squeezed out between the captain and the chairman. The latter two, I believe, are the best men for the job, and one of the things they certainly have in common is a stubborn streak.

If you criticize Michael Atherton's captaincy, it will be three months before he might be prepared to admit you might have had a point. In Australia, he became quite indignant at the idea he might have been negative in the second Test in Melbourne, but in his end-of-tour speech he admitted to precisely that. You certainly need a strong character in charge, though, as you also need a strong chairman. From my experience, a captain can get so wound up in a series that his judgement can become clouded, and that's when a strong chairman must step in. Neither of them likes to admit to being wrong, and they will always have their fractious periods. Atherton, for instance, made public their disagreement over the squad selected for Australia, and although there was much talk about Illy getting his way in most areas after becoming chairman, I tend to believe Illy when he says that Athers mostly gets what he wants.

Athers is also, of course, extremely fortunate to still be in charge after the dirt in the pocket business at Lord's in the summer of 1994. I have never seen or heard of anyone carrying dirt in their pocket, and to say that he did not reveal this to the match referee because he was not asked specifically about dirt was both schoolboyish and suspicious. It was a bad misjudgement, and the furore that followed was a severe jolt to him. To get runs in the Headingley Test under all that media glare was a major effort, but to refer to the 'gutter press' in the press conference afterwards made me cringe when I heard him say it. It was the sort of mistake I might have made at the same point in the captaincy, but it's all part of the learning process. Captains need time to develop and mature. Look at Border. He started with a lot less than Athers. As for whether there was any cheating involved with the dirt, I have to go along with Richie Benaud's verdict. 'In the end' said Richie 'the only person who knows is Michael Atherton himself.'

All captains need the raw material to work with, and if Athers is very lucky, Darren Gough might turn out to be the hub around which England's Test match fortunes take a turn for the better. I played against him two or three times without finding him too testing an opponent, but watching him in Australia left me as impressed as everyone else. He has a completely uncomplicated attitude to the game, and has the right amount of bravado and self-confidence needed to succeed. Whether he can remain that way in years to come is something we'll find out. At the other end of the evolutionary scale, the Australian tour also saw the retirements, from Test cricket anyway, of Gooch and Gatting. They, of course, had the partial good fortune to go voluntarily and in harness, although both also ended as fairly sad, forlorn and worn-out figures. Thanks mostly to Gooch, I never had the chance to go out that way, so perhaps with hindsight I ought to thank him. It was undeniably disappointing at the time, though, not to be given the chance to tour India in 1992-93, and therefore get the chance to be in possession of a place for the Australian tour of England in the summer of 1993. That, to be honest, would have done me nicely, in that I always had a special fondness for an Ashes series, and had a particularly good record against Australia. I honestly don't think, given the chance, that I would have gone on too long, and become a doddery old embarrassment who didn't know when his time was up. Although the main reason for quitting was the realization that I had been pensioned off as a Test player, I have to be honest and say that the game had lost a certain amount of its wonder for me, and that mentally I was no longer able to give as much as I had for most of my career. I'm not saying the selectors did me a favour, but perhaps there was just a hint of the James Dean syndrome – gone before his time, and more popular because of it.

Above all, though, it is not about whether I could perhaps have squeezed in a few more Test matches, or gone out with an Ashes century, or any of that. It is the knowledge that people enjoyed watching me, and that most of them appear to have missed me when I was gone. That's what makes me look back and say, with complete honesty, that I wouldn't have changed a thing. Well, almost!

Gower – the career 1975-1993

TABULAR STATISTICS BY BILL FRINDALL

SUMMER 1975
Signs first contract for Leicestershire.
County championship debut against Lancashire at Blackpool.
Leicestershire win their first county championship and the Benson & Hedges Cup.

SUMMER 1976
Scores 86* against the touring West Indians.
Maiden century (102*) at Lord's against Middlesex.
Tours the West Indies with a Young England side.
Tours Canada with Derrick Robins' XI.

SUMMER 1977
Championship best for season (144*) against Hampshire.
Ian Botham's Test debut.
Leicestershire win John Player League; registers best Sunday score (135*) against
    Warwickshire.
Kerry Packer's World Series Cricket begins.

WINTER 1977-8
Derrick Robins' tour of the Far East.
Plays a season with Claremont-Cottesloe in Perth, Western Australia.

SUMMER 1978
One-day international debut against Pakistan at Old Trafford.
Scores first one-day international century (114*) against Pakistan at the Oval.
Test debut at Edgbaston against Pakistan, under the captaincy of Mike Brearley.
Averages 51 for the series against Pakistan.
First Test century (111) against New Zealand at the Oval.
Averages 57 for the series against New Zealand.
Scores 1000 runs in a season for the first time.
Ray Illingworth's last season as captain of Leicestershire.

WINTER 1978-79

England tour Australia, winning series 5-1, the first time an English team has won five Tests in any series.

Scores first overseas Test century (102) at Perth.

Heads the English averages with 42.00.

SUMMER 1979

World Cup in England: England lose to West Indies in the final.

Test series against India: scores 200* at Edgbaston.

Averages 72.25 for the series.

WINTER 1979-80

First post-Packer Test series against Australia. England lose 0-3 against a powerful Australian side.

Jubilee Test against India at Bombay.

SUMMER 1980

Ian Botham becomes captain of England.

Dropped after first Test against West Indies.

Lord's Centenary Test: recalled to the England side.

WINTER 1980-81

Tour to the West Indies.

Scores 154* in fifth Test at Sabina Park, but England defeated in the series.

Ken Barrington dies while tour manager.

SUMMER 1981

Brearley becomes captain again after the second Test against Australia at Lord's.

'Botham's Ashes'. His performances at Headingley, Edgbaston and Old Trafford play a major part in regaining the Ashes for England.

Dropped for final Test.

WINTER 1981-82

Tour of India and Sri Lanka under captaincy of Keith Fletcher.

England lose series against India 1-0.

Gooch leads rebel tour to South Africa.

SUMMER 1982

Appointed vice-captain under Bob Willis for the two series against India and Pakistan.

Captains England for the first time in the Lord's Test against Pakistan.

Allan Lamb makes his England debut.

WINTER 1982-83

Vice-captain on Willis's tour to Australia. England's most outstanding player in a series won by the Australians 2-1.

Scores three centuries in the World Series Cup competition, all against New Zealand, but England don't make the final.

Voted 'Player of the Summer' and wins a car which is subsequently sold and 'pooled'.

SUMMER 1983
World Cup in England; England losing semi-finalists. India defeat West Indies in the final.
Scores back-to-back centuries in series against New Zealand which England win 3-1.

WINTER 1983-84
Vice-captain on Willis's tour to New Zealand and Pakistan.
England lose series against New Zealand, amidst allegations in the press of various off-the-field activities.
After losing first Test against Pakistan, Willis returns home with mystery illness. Appointed captain in his place.
Scores two big hundreds in last two Tests – 152 at Faisalabad and 173* at Lahore – but England lose series.

SUMMER 1984
Appointed captain for series against the West Indies.
England lose all five Test matches.

WINTER 1984-85
Captain on tour of India and Sri Lanka: within hours of Engand's arrival Mrs Gandhi is assassinated.
England lose first Test but come back to win the series 2-1.

SUMMER 1985
England regain the Ashes, defeating Australia 3-1.
Scores two centuries and one double century in best ever series.
Leicestershire win the Benson & Hedges Cup defeating Essex in the final.

WINTER 1985-86
First trip to St Moritz and the Cresta Run.
Mother dies a week before England's tour to the West Indies.
England lose the series but comes top of the English averages with 37.00.
Tour noted for very harsh media coverage.

SUMMER 1986
After England lose first Test at Lord's against India, relieved of the captaincy by the selectors. Mike Gatting takes over.
India go on to win the series 2-0.
In the final Test against New Zealand at the Oval, scores 131 in a stand of 223 with Gatting. England, however, lose series. England have now played eleven Tests without a victory.
Loses captaincy of Leicestershire for a year; Peter Willey takes over.

WINTER 1986-87
Appointment of Micky Stewart as team manager after Ray Illingworth turns down the job.

England tour Australia and retain the Ashes. England also win the World Series Cup and the Perth Challenge Cup.

SUMMER 1987
Pakistan tour England and win series 1-0, beating England at Headingley.
Tops the Leicestershire averages with 56.00 in benefit year.

WINTER 1987-88
Decides to take a winter off from touring: misses the World Cup in India and Pakistan, the series against Pakistan and the Gatting-Shakoor Rana contretemps at Faisalabad, the series against New Zealand, and the Bicentenary Test in Sydney.
Takes time off on safari in Africa, skiing in Europe and at the Winter Olympics in Calgary, Canada.

SUMMER 1988
West Indies tour England.
Reappointed captain of Leicestershire.
Doesn't play in the one-day internationals but is recalled to the Test team.
After the first Test at Trent Bridge, Mike Gatting is sacked as captain of England. John Emburey takes charge for the next two, to be replaced by Chris Cowdrey for the fourth Test. Finally, in this summer of captains – but not English victories – Graham Gooch becomes captain for the final Test at the Oval.
100th Test match for England at Headingley; it also marks Robin Smith's Test debut.
Dropped for fifth Test after reaching 7000 Test runs at Headingley.

WINTER 1988-89
Winter tour cancelled after the Indians object to the presence of former South African rebel tourists in the English team.
Peter May retires as chairman of the selectors; Ted Dexter takes over.

SUMMER 1989
Reappointed England captain for the series against Australia.
Scores a double hundred for Leicestershire in the first match of the season against Glamorgan.
England lose first two Test matches, then draw at Edgbaston, but lose again at Old Trafford. Things not going too well.
Australia comfortably regain the Ashes. Sacked at the end of the series and Gooch reappointed to lead England in the Caribbean. Not selected for the tour.
Second rebel tour to South Africa announced under the captaincy of Mike Gatting.

WINTER 1989-90
Surgery on long-standing shoulder injury.
Resigns the captaincy of Leicestershire; Nigel Briers takes over.
Decision made to leave Leicestershire and join Hampshire.
Works for *The Times* and BBC Radio on the tour of the West Indies.

Called out of the press box to play for England against Barbados when injuries deplete the original squad.

England win first Test but lose series 2-1.

SUMMER 1990

Scores 145 on first-class debut for Hampshire against Sussex at Southampton.

Omitted for the Test series against New Zealand after playing in the one-day internationals, but regains place for the second series of the summer against India.

Gooch scores 333 in Lord's Test against India.

Score of 157* in the third Test saves the game for England and ensures a seat on the plane to Australia.

WINTER 1990-91

Fifth major tour of Australia.

England lose the first two Tests, then draw at Sydney. Scores hundreds at Melbourne and Sydney.

Tiger Moth incident at Carrara, Queensland. Maximum fines ensue.

England lose series 3-0.

SUMMER 1991

Left out of series against West Indies, which England draw 2-2.

Captains Hampshire to win the NatWest Trophy following an injury to Mark Nicholas prior to the match.

WINTER 1991-92

Another winter off. Takes a safari to Africa, helping to raise funds towards the preservation of the black rhino.

Engagement announced to Thorunn Nash.

More media work as a commentator for Channel 9 and journalist for the *Daily Telegraph* during the World Cup in Australia and New Zealand.

England lose in the World Cup final to Pakistan.

SUMMER 1992

Hampshire win Benson and Hedges Cup, beating Kent.

Recalled for Old Trafford Test, first Test since Perth, February 1991.

Becomes England's leading run scorer of all time, passing Geoff Boycott's record.

Not selected for England's tour of India and Sri Lanka.

Marries Thorunn Nash at Winchester Cathedral, 18th September.

WINTER 1992-93

Commentates for Channel 9 in Australia and for Sky TV in India.

Thorunn becomes pregnant.

SUMMER 1993

Not selected for home series against Australia.

Damages rib and is out of action for a month.

Not selected for England tour of West Indies.

Announces retirement from first-class cricket in November.

Summary of all First-Class Matches

Season	(Venue)	M	I	NO	HS	Runs	Avge
1975		3	5	-	32	65	13.00
1976		7	13	4	102*	323	35.88
1977		25	34	2	144*	745	23.28
1977-78	(SL)	2	2	-	59	76	38.00
1978		21	31	2	111	1098	37.86
1978-79	(A)	12	20	1	102	623	32.78
1979		17	27	4	200*	957	41.60
1979-80	(A/I)	9	15	2	98*	354	27.23
1980		24	36	1	138	1142	32.62
1981		19	33	4	156*	1418	48.89
1980-81	(WI)	8	14	1	187	726	55.84
1981-82	(I/SL)	13	18	3	94	755	50.33
1982		20	35	2	176*	1530	46.36
1982-83	(A)	10	19	1	114	821	45.61
1983		19	32	5	140	1253	46.40
1983-84	(NZ/P)	9	14	1	173*	746	57.38
1984		18	30	2	117*	999	35.67
1984-85	(SL/I)	11	15	1	86	482	34.42
1985		21	29	2	215	1477	54.70
1985-86	(WI)	8	16	-	90	447	27.93
1986		14	23	2	131	830	39.52
1986-87	(A)	9	16	2	136	508	36.28
1987		20	31	4	125	1197	44.33
1988		22	38	4	172	1317	38.73
1989		17	30	1	228	1102	38.00
1989-90	(WI)	1	1	-	4	4	4.00
1990		20	32	5	157*	1263	46.77
1990-91	(A)	10	19	1	123	578	32.11
1991		23	38	5	80*	1142	34.60
1992		20	33	7	155	1225	47.11
1993		16	28	1	153	1136	42.07
TOTALS		448	727	70	228	26339	40.08

100	50	Ct	St	O	R	W	Avge	BB	5w	10w
-	-	2	-	-						
1	1	4	-	-						
1	3	8	-	14	59	3	19.66	3-47	-	-
-	1	-	-	-						
2	5	6	-	1	2	-	-	-	-	-
1	3	7	-	-						
1	8	8	-	-						
-	3	6	-	-						
2	3	16	-	2	1	-	-	-	-	-
5	7	20								
2	2	4	-	-						
-	7	7	-	5	6	1	6.00	1-1	-	-
2	12	10	-	5	10	-	-	-	-	-
2	6	9	-	-						
5	5	18	-	9	102	-	-	-	-	-
2	4	7	-	-						
2	6	17	-	-						
-	4	10	-	3	13	-	-	-	-	-
6	3	10	-	2.1	16	-	-	-	-	-
-	3	4	-	-						
1	6	11	1	1	5	-	-	-	-	-
1	2	4	-	-						
2	6	5	-	1	9	-	-	-	-	-
2	5	16	-	-						
3	4	13	-	-						
-	-	-	-	-						
3	3	17	-	-						
2	3	3	-	-						
-	8	13	-	0.1	4	-	-	-	-	-
1	8	14	-	-						
4	5	11	-							
53	136	280	1	43.2	227	4	56.75	3-47	-	-

267

Test Match Summary

Season	V	M	I	NO	HS	Runs	Avge
1978	P	3	3	-	58	153	51.00
"	NZ	3	5	-	111	285	57.00
1978-9	in A	6	11	1	102	420	42.00
1979	I	4	5	1	200*	289	72.25
1979-80	in A	3	6	1	98*	152	30.40
"	in I	1	1	-	16	16	16.00
1980	WI	1	2	-	20	21	10.50
"	A	1	2	-	45	80	40.00
1980-81	in WI	4	8	1	154*	376	53.71
1981	A	5	10	-	89	250	25.00
1981-82	in I	6	9	1	85	375	46.87
"	in SL	1	2	1	89	131	131.00
1982	I	3	5	1	47	152	38.00
"	P	3	6	-	74	197	32.83
1982-83	in A	5	10	-	114	441	44.10
1983	NZ	4	8	1	112*	404	57.71
1983-84	in NZ	3	4	-	33	69	17.25
"	in P	3	5	1	173*	449	112.25
1984	WI	5	10	1	57*	171	19.00
"	SL	1	1	-	55	55	55.00
1984-85	in I	5	7	1	78	167	27.83
1985	A	6	9	-	215	732	81.33
1985-86	in WI	5	10	-	90	370	37.00
1986	I	2	4	-	49	101	25.25
"	NZ	3	5	-	131	293	58.60
1986-87	in A	5	8	1	136	404	57.71
1987	P	5	8	-	61	236	29.50
1988	WI	4	8	1	88*	211	30.14
1989	A	6	11	-	106	383	34.81
1990	I	3	6	2	157*	291	72.75
1990-91	in A	5	10	1	123	407	45.22
1992	P	3	5	2	73	150	50.00
	A	42	77	4	215	3269	44.78
	WI	19	38	3	154*	1149	32.82
	NZ	13	22	1	131	1051	50.04
	I	24	37	6	200*	1391	44.87
	P	17	27	3	173*	1185	49.37
	SL	2	3	1	89	186	93.00
Home		65	113	9	215	4454	42.82
Overseas		52	91	9	173*	3777	46.06
TOTALS		117	204	18	215	8231	44.25

100	50	Ct	St	O	R	W	Avge	BB	5w	10w
-	2	-		-						
1	1	-		-						
1	1	4		-						
1	1	2		-						
-	1	3		-						
-	-	-		-						
-	-	1		-						
-	-	-		-						
1	1	2		-						
-	1	3		-						
-	4	1		2	2	1	2.00	1-1		
-	1	4		-						
-	-	2		-						
-	2	2		-						
1	3	4		-						
2	1	6		-						
-	-	2		-						
2	2	3		-						
-	1	3		-						
-	1	1		-						
-	1	6		3	13	-	-	-		
3	1	6		-						
-	3	3		-						
-	-	2		-						
1	2	3		1	5	-	-	-		
1	2	1		-						
-	2	2		-						
-	1	2		-						
1	2	4		-						
1	-	-		-						
2	1	1		-						
-	1	1		-						
9	12	26		-						
1	6	11		-						
4	4	11		1	5	-	-	-		
2	6	13		-						
2	9	8		-						
-	2	5		-						
10	19	40		1	5	-	-	-		
8	20	34		5	15	1	15.00	1-1		
18	39	74		6	20	1	20.00	1-1		

County Championship Summary

Season	M	I	NO	HS	Runs	Avge
1975	3	5	-	32	65	13.00
1976	6	11	2	102*	212	23.55
1977	21	29	2	144*	589	21.81
1978	9	15	1	61	347	24.78
1979	10	18	3	98	515	34.33
1980	19	29	1	138	929	33.17
1981	13	21	3	156*	1009	56.05
1982	9	16	-	111	716	44.75
1983	13	21	4	140	702	41.29
1984	9	13	1	117*	660	55.00
1985	12	17	2	128	575	38.33
1986	9	14	2	83	436	36.33
1987	12	19	4	125	840	56.00
1988	17	29	3	172	1080	41.53
1989	9	17	1	228	664	41.50
LEICS	171	274	29	228	9339	38.11
1990	14	21	1	145	684	34.20
1991	22	37	5	80*	1132	35.37
1992	16	26	5	155	1005	47.85
1993	15	26	0	153	1105	42.50
HANTS	67	110	11	155	3926	39.65
TOTALS	238	384	40	228	13265	38.56

Championship Hundreds (27)

For Leicestershire

102*	Middlesex	Lord's	1976
144*	Hampshire	Leicester	1977
100	Derbyshire	Burton upon Trent	1980
138	Hampshire	Southampton	1980
109	Hampshire	Leicester	1981
115	Kent	Tunbridge Wells	1981
156*	Essex	Leicester	1981
117*	Northamptonshire	Leicester	1981
111	Somerset	Taunton	1982
108*	Glamorgan	Hinckley	1983
140	Sussex	Hove	1983
103	Worcestershire	Worcester	1984
117*	Warwickshire	Birmingham	1984

100	50	Ct	St	O	R	W	Avge	BB	5w	10w
-	-	2	-	-						
1	-	4	-	-						
1	2	6	-	14	59	3	19.66	3-47		
-	1	4	-	-						
-	5	4	-	-						
2	2	13	-	1	1	-	-	-	-	-
4	5	17	-	-						
1	7	4	-	5	10	-	-	-	-	-
2	4	12	-	9	102	-	-	-	-	-
2	4	4	-	-						
2	2	1	-	2.1	16	-	-	-	-	-
-	4	6	1	-						
2	4	2	-	-						
2	4	14	-	-						
2	2	7	-	-						
21	46	100	1	31.1	188	3	62.66	3-47	-	-
1	2	14	-	-						
-	8	13	-	0.1	4	-	-	-	-	
1	6	13	-	-						
4	5	11	-	-						
6	21	51	-	0.1	4	-	-	-	-	-
27	67	151	1	31.2	192	3	64.00	3-47	-	-

100*	Glamorgan	Leicester	1985
128	Sussex	Hove	1985
105*	Gloucestershire	Cheltenham	1987
125	Derbyshire	Derby	1987
146	Nottinghamshire	Leicester	1988
172	Essex	Chelmsford	1988
228	Glamorgan	Leicester	1989
109	Essex	Leicester	1989

For Hampshire

145	Sussex	Southampton	1990
155	Yorkshire	Basingstoke	1992
153	Nottinghamshire	Trent Bridge	1993
117	Lancashire	Southampton	1993
113	Sussex	Portsmouth	1993
134	Essex	Chelmsford	1993

First-Class Career Summary by Team and Venue

	M	I	NO	HS	Runs	Avge
ENGLAND	117	204	18	215	8231	44.25
ENGLAND XI	48	76	4	187	2267	31.48
YOUNG ENGLAND	1	2	-	108	145	72.50
MCC	10	15	1	108	610	43.57
LEICESTERSHIRE	196	307	33	228	10685	38.99
HAMPSHIRE	73	120	14	155	4325	40.80
D.H.ROBINS' XI	3	3	-	59	76	25.33
UK/HOME	346	558	57	228	20219	40.35
AUSTRALIA	49	88	7	136	2868	35:40
INDIA	22	30	3	94	1018	37.70
NEW ZEALAND	6	9	-	84	297	33.00
PAKISTAN	3	5	1	173 *	449	112.25
SRI LANKA	5	6	1	89	311	62.20
WEST INDIES	17	31	1	187	1177	39.29
OVERSEAS	102	169	13	187	6120	39.23
CAREER	448	727	70	228	26339	40.08

Non-Test Match or County Championship Hundreds

For ENGLAND XI (2)

| 187 | President's Young WI XI | Pointe-à-Pierre | 1980-81 |
| 100 | Queensland | Brisbane | 1982-83 |

For YOUNG ENGLAND (1)

| 108 | New Zealanders | Leicester | 1978 |

For MCC (1)

| 108 | Middlesex | Lord's | 1981 |

For LEICESTERSHIRE (3)

176*	Pakistanis	Leicester	1982
124	Cambridge University	Cambridge	1983
135	Australians	Leicester	1985

For HAMPSHIRE (1)

| 126* | Indians | Southampton | 1990 |

100	50	Ct	St	O	R	W	Avge	BB
18	39	74	-	6	20	1	20.00	1-1
2	17	27	-	3	4	-	-	-
1	-	-	-	1	2	-	-	-
1	5	8	-	-				
24	51	117	1	33.1	197	3	65.66	3-47
7	23	54	-	0.1	4	-	-	-
-	1	-	-	-				
43	98	219	1	35.2	208	3	69.33	3-47
6	17	29	-	-				
-	9	11	-	8	19	1	19.00	1-1
-	2	4	-	-				
2	2	3	-	-				
-	3	6	-	-				
2	5	8	-	-				
10	38	61	-	8	19	1	19.00	1-1
53	136	280	1	43.2	227	4	56.75	3-47

273

Test Match Analysis
BATTING AND FIELDING

Series	Opponents	T	Venue	Result	Batting 1st			Batting 2nd			Ct
					No	R	HO	No	R	HO	
1978	Pakistan	1	Birmingham	W-I &57	4	58	c	-	-	-	-
		2	Lords	W-I & 120	4	56	b	-	-	-	-
		3	Leeds	D	4	39	lbw	-	-	-	-
1978	New Zealand	1	Oval	W-7w	4	111	ro	4	11	c	-
		2	Nottingham	W-I & 119	4	46	c	-	-	-	-
		3	Lord's	W-7w	4	71	c	4	46	c	-
1978-79	Australia	1	Brisbane	W-7w	6	44	c	5	48	*	-
		2	Perth	W-166	5	102	b	5	12	c	-
		3	Melbourne	L-103	5	29	lbw	5	49	lbw	1
		4	Sydney	W-93	5	7	c	5	34	c	-
		5	Adelaide	W-205	5	9	lbw	5	21	lbw	2
		6	Sydney	W-9w	5	65	c	-	-	-	1
1979	India	1	Birmingham	W-I&83	5	200	*	-	-	-	-
		2	Lord's	D	4	82	b	-	-	-	1
		3	Leeds	D	4	0	lbw	-	-	-	-
		4	Oval	D	4	0	lbw	4	7	c	1
1979-80	Australia	1	Perth	L-138	4	17	c	4	23	c	1
		2	Sydney	L-6w	6	3	b	7	98	*	1
		3	Melbourne	L-8w	4	0	lbw	4	11	b	1
1979-80	India		Bombay	W-10w	4	16	lbw	-	-	-	-
1980	West Indies	1	Nottingham	L-2w	5	20	c	5	1	lbw	1
1980	Australia		Lord's	D	4	45	b	4	35	b	-
1980-81	West Indies	1	Port-of-Spain	L-I & 79	4	48	lbw	4	27	c	1
		3	Bridgetown	L-298	4	17	c	4	54	b	-
		4	St John's	D	4	32	c	4	22	c	1
		5	Kingston	D	4	22	b	4	154	*	-
1981	Australia	1	Nottingham	L-4w	4	26	c	4	28	c	1
		2	Lord's	D	4	27	c	4	89	c	1
		3	Leeds	W-18	4	24	c	4	9	c	-
		4	Birmingham	W-29	3	0	c	3	23	c	-
		5	Manchester	W-103	4	23	c	4	1	c	1
1981-82	India	1	Bombay	L-138	4	5	ro	4	20	lbw	-
		2	Bangalore	D	4	82	lbw	4	34	*	-
		3	Delhi	D	4	0	lbw	-	-	-	-
		4	Calcutta	D	4	11	c	4	74	ro	-
		5	Madras	D	4	64	lbw	-	-	-	-
		6	Kanpur	D	4	85	lbw	-	-	-	1
1981-82	Sri-Lanka		Colombo SO	W-7w	4	89	c	4	42	*	-
1982	India	1	Lord's	W-7w	4	37	c	5	14	*	1
		2	Manchester	D	4	9	c	-	-	-	-
		3	Oval	D	4	47	c	4	45	c	1

Series	Opponents	T	Venue	Result	Batting 1st			Batting 2nd			Ct
					No	R	HO	No	R	HO	
1982	Pakistan	1	Birmingham	W-113	4	74	c	4	13	c	1
		†2	Lord's	L-10w	4	29	c	4	0	c	-
		3	Leeds	W-3w	5	74	c	5	7	c	1
1982-83	Australia	1	Perth	D	3	72	c	3	28	lbw	-
		2	Brisbane	L-7w	3	18	c	3	34	c	-
		3	Adelaide	L-8w	3	60	c	3	114	b	2
		4	Melbourne	W-3	4	18	c	4	3	c	-
		5	Sydney	D	3	70	c	4	24	c	2
1983	New Zealand	1	Oval	W-189	3	11	b	3	25	c	2
		2	Leeds	L-5w	3	9	c	3	112	*	1
		3	Lord's	W-127	3	108	lbw	3	34	c	1
		4	Nottingham	W-165	3	72	b	3	33	c	2
1983-84	New Zealand	1	Wellington	D	3	33	c	-	-	-	2
		2	Christchurch	L-1 & 132	3	2	lbw	3	8	c	-
		3	Auckland	D	3	26	b	-	-	-	-
1983-84	Pakistan	1	Karachi	L-3w	3	58	lbw	3	57	c	-
		†2	Faisalabad	D	5	152	st	-	-	-	-
		†3	Lahore	D	3	9	c	4	173	*	3
1984	West Indies	†1	Birmingham	L-1 & 180	4	10	c	4	12	c	1
		†2	Lord's	L-9w	3	3	lbw	3	21	c	-
		†3	Leeds	L-8w	4	2	lbw	4	43	c	1
		†4	Manchester	L-1 &64	4	4	c	4	57	*	-
		†5	Oval	L-172	5	12	c	4	7	lbw	1
1984	Sri Lanka	†	Lord's	D	4	55	c	-	-	-	1
1984-85	India	†1	Bombay	L-8w	4	13	b	4	2	c	2
		†2	Delhi	W-8w	5	5	lbw	-	-	-	1
		†3	Calcutta	D	3	19	c	-	-	-	1
		†4	Madras	W-9w	7	18	b	-	-	-	1
		†5	Kanpur	D	5	78	lbw	1	32	*	1
1985	Australia	†1	Leeds	W-5w	3	17	c	3	5	c	1
		†2	Lord's	L-4w	3	86	c	5	22	c	-
		†3	Nottingham	D	3	166	c	3	17	c	-
		†4	Manchester	D	3	47	c	-	-	-	1
		†5	Birmingham	W-1 & 118	3	215	c	-	-	-	3
		†6	Oval	W-1 & 94	3	157	c	-	-	-	1
1985-86	West Indies	†1	Kingston	L-10w	3	16	lbw	3	9	c	-
		†2	Port-of-Spain	L-7w	3	66	lbw	3	47	b	1
		†3	Bridgetown	L-1 & 30	3	66	c	3	23	c	1
		†4	Port-of-Spain	L-10w	3	10	c	3	22	lbw	-
		†5	St John's	L-240	4	90	c	5	21	c	1
1986	India	†1	Lord's	L-5w	3	18	c	3	8	lbw	-
		3	Birmingham	D	4	49	lbw	4	26	c	2
1986	New Zealand	1	Lord's	D	4	62	c	4	3	b	3
		2	Nottingham	L-8w	4	71	lbw	5	26	c	-

Series	Opponents	T	Venue	Result	Batting 1st			Batting 2nd			Ct
					No	R	HO	No	R	HO	
1986	New Zealand	3	Oval	D	3	131	b	-	-	-	-
1986-87	Australia	1	Brisbane	W-7w	5	51	c	5	15	*	-
		2	Perth	D	5	136	c	5	48	c	-
		3	Adelaide	D	5	38	lbw	-	-	-	-
		4	Melbourne	W-1 &14	5	7	c	-	-	-	1
		5	Sydney	L-55	5	72	c	3	37	c	-
1987	Pakistan	1	Manchester	D	6	22	c	-	-	-	-
		2	Lord's	D	4	8	c	-	-	-	-
		3	Leeds	L-1 &18	4	10	b	4	55	b	1
		4	Birmingham	D	4	61	c	3	18	b	-
		5	Oval	D	4	28	b	4	34	c	1
1988	West Indies	1	Nottingham	D	4	18	c	4	88	*	-
		2	Lord's	L-134	4	46	c	4	1	c	1
		3	Manchester	L-1 & 156	4	9	c	4	34	c	-
		4	Leeds	L-10w	4	13	c	4	2	c	1
1989	Australia	†1	Leeds	L-210	5	26	c	5	34	c	-
		†2	Lord's	L-6w	5	57	b	5	106	c	-
		†3	Birmingham	D	3	8	lbw	-	-	-	-
		†4	Manchester	L-9w	5	35	lbw	5	15	c	1
		†5	Nottingham	L-1 &180	5	11	c	1	5	b	2
		†6	Oval	D	5	79	c	5	7	c	1
1990	India	1	Lord's	W-247	3	40	c	3	32	*	-
		2	Manchester	D	3	38	c	3	16	b	-
		3	Oval	D	4	8	lbw	3	157	*	-
1990-91	Australia	1	Brisbane	L-10w	3	61	c	3	27	b	-
		2	Melbourne	L-8w	5	100	c	5	0	c	-
		3	Sydney	D	5	123	c	2	36	c	1
		4	Adelaide	D	5	11	c	4	16	lbw	-
		5	Perth	L-9w	5	28	*	5	5	c	-
1992	Pakistan	3	Manchester	D	5	73	c	-	-	-	1
		4	Leeds	W-6w	5	18	*	4	31	*	-
		5	Oval	L-10w	5	27	b	5	1	b	-

BOWLING

Series	Opponents	T	Venue	Bowling 1st				Bowling 2nd			
				O	M	R	W	O	M	R	W
1981-82	India	5	Madras					1	-	1	-
		6	Kanpur	1	-	1	1				
1984-85	India	†3	Calcutta	3	-	13	-				
1986	New Zealand	1	Lord's					1	-	1	-
		2	Nottingham					-	-	4	-

* not out   † captain

Tours

Australia 1978-79, 1979-80, 1982-83, 1986-87, 1990-91.
West Indies 1980-81, 1985-86c, 1989-90 (part).
New Zealand 1983-84.
India 1979-80, 1981-82, 1984-85c.
Pakistan 1983-84.
Sri Lanka 1977-78 (D.H.Robins' XI), 1981-82, 1984-85c.
(c = captain)

Career Notes

TEST MATCHES
Batting Milestones

Series	v	T	Venue	Runs	Matches	Innings
1979	I	1	Birmingham	1000	13	20
1981	A	4	Birmingham	2000	30	51
1982-83	A	2	Brisbane	3000	46	78
1983	P	2	Faisalabad	4000	58	100
1985	A	4	Manchester	5000	74	127
1986	NZ	2	Nottingham	6000	85	147
1988	WI	4	Leeds	7000	100	172
1990-91	A	3	Sydney	8000	112	195

Notable Feats

1978 (v Pakistan at Birmingham): hit first ball in Test cricket (from Liaquat Ali) for four.

1981-82 (v India at Kanpur): took the wicket of Kapil Dev with his seventh ball in Test cricket.

1983-84 (v Pakistan at Faisalabad): first England captain to score a Test hundred since A. W. Greig in 1976-77. Shared record England v Pakistan 7th-wicket partnership of 167 with V. J. Marks.

1985 (v Australia at Nottingham): his 166 is the highest score by an England captain at Trent Bridge.

1985 (v Australia at Birmingham): his 215 is the highest score against Australia at Edgbaston and the second-highest by an England captain against Australia anywhere. Shared 2nd-wicket partnership of 331 with R. T. Robinson.

1985 (v Australia at the Oval): completed 2000 runs against Australia and shared 2nd-wicket partnership of 351 with G. A. Gooch – England's second-highest for any wicket against Australia.

1986-87 (v Australia at Perth): his partnership of 207 with C. J. Richards is an England 6th-wicket record in Australia.

1988 (v West Indies at Leeds): became the fifth (and then youngest) to appear in 100 Test matches.

1990 (v India at Lord's): became the first to appear in 17 Tests at Lord's and overtook G. Boycott's record Test aggregate of 1189 runs for that ground (surpassed on same day by G. A. Gooch).

1990-91 (v Australia at Melbourne): extended his world record number of consecutive Test innings without a duck to 119.

1992 (v Pakistan at Manchester): exceeded G. Boycott's record England Test aggregate of 8114 runs when his first innings score reached 34.

Notes

1986 (v New Zealand at Nottingham): became the first England bowler to be no-balled for throwing in a Test in England.

1989 (v Australia at Lord's): became the first captain of any national Test team to preside over eight successive defeats.

FIRST-CLASS MATCHES

Career Highlights

1975	Made first-class debut in Championship-winning team.
1977	Awarded Leicestershire 1st XI cap.
1978	Cricket Writers' Club's 'Young Cricketer of the Year'.
1979	One of Wisden's five Cricketers of the Year (1978).
1981	Shared with J.C. Balderstone in Leicestershire record 2nd-wicket partnership of 289 (unbroken) against Essex at Leicester.
1984-86)	Captain of Leicestershire.
1988-89)	" " "
1990	Awarded Hampshire 1st XI cap.
1992	Awarded OBE in Birthday Honours for services to cricket.
1993	Exceeded 1000 runs in a season for the 13th time.

Limited-Overs Internationals
Career Record

Batting and Fielding

M	I	NO	HS	Runs	Avge	100	50	Ct
114	111	8	158	3170	30.77	7	12	44

Bowling

O	M	R	W
0.5	0	14	0

Sunday Hundreds (5)
For Leicestershire (5)

135*	Warwickshire	Leicester	28.8.77
100	Derbyshire	Leicester	9.5.82
115	Surrey	Oval	30.5.82
107	Warwickshire	Leicester	4.7.82
114*	Warwickshire	Leicester	21.7.82

Benson & Hedges Hundreds (2)
For Leicestershire (1)

114*	Derbyshire	Derby	22.5.80

For Hampshire (1)

118*	Northamptonshire	Southampton	1.5.92

Gillette Cup/NatWest Trophy Hundreds (5)
For Leicestershire (5)

117*	Hertfordshire	Leicester	29.6.77
138*	Gloucestershire	Leicester	20.7.83
156	Derbyshire	Leicester	18.7.84
121*	Ireland	Leicester	25.6.86
101*	Shropshire	Telford	28.6.89

Sunday Matches

	M	I	NO	HS	Runs	Avge	100	50	Ct
For Leics	139	138	21	135*	4249	33.45	5	26	55
For Hants	43	41	3	66*	985	25.92	-	6	12
TOTALS	182	179	24	135*	5234	33.76	5	32	67

No bowling

Benson & Hedges Cup

	M	I	NO	HS	Runs	Avge	100	50	Ct
For Leics	52	52	6	114*	1220	26.52	1	2	22
For Hants	18	18	4	118*	511	36.50	1	1	8
TOTALS	70	70	10	118*	1731	28.85	2	3	30

No bowling

Gillette Cup/NatWest Trophy

	M	I	NO	HS	Runs	Avge	100	50	Ct
For Leics	33	32	5	156	1504	55.70	5	6	9
For Hants	13	10	1	86	260	28.88	-	2	4
TOTALS	46	42	6	156	1764	49.00	5	8	13

Bowling

	Overs	Runs	W
Leics	2.3	16	-
Hants	-		
TOTALS	2.3	16	-

Limited-overs international hundreds (7)

				Match
114*	Pakistan	Oval	26.5.78	2
101*	Australia	Melbourne	4.2.79	7
122	New Zealand	Melbourne	13.1.83	40
158	New Zealand	Brisbane	15.1.83	41
109	New Zealand	Adelaide	29.1.83	46
130	Sri Lanka	Taunton	11.6.83	53
102	Australia	Lord's	3.6.85	77

Index